THE GOOD LAWYER

The Good Lawyer explores the ethical and professional challenges that confront people who work in the law – or are considering it – and offers principled and pragmatic advice about how to overcome such challenges. It shows you how to develop personal judgment when you may be pulled one way by rules, another way by decided cases and yet another way by conventional 'role morality'.

Going beyond typical treatments of lawyers' ethical pitfalls, this book takes a holistic approach that begins with your innate humanity. It urges you to examine your motives for seeking a career in law, to foster a deep understanding of what it means to be 'good', and to draw on your virtue and judgment when difficult choices arise, rather than relying on compliance with rules or codes.

The Good Lawyer analyses four important areas of legal ethics – truth and deception, professional secrets, conflicts of interest, and professional competence – and explains the choices that are available when determining a course of moral action. It links theory to practice, and includes many examples, diagrams and source documents to illustrate ethical concepts, scenarios and decision making.

Written by an expert on legal ethics, *The Good Lawyer* encourages you to develop a sense of social and moral responsibility as the foundation of better legal practice, and is an invaluable reference for students considering a law degree, or a career in law, and for new lawyers seeking more insight into the moral dimensions of their profession.

Adrian Evans is Professor of Law at Monash University. He has taught, practised law and consulted in clinical legal education and legal ethics for over three decades.

THE GOOD LAWYER

Adrian Evans

CAMBRIDGE
UNIVERSITY PRESS

University Printing House, Cambridge CB2 8BS, United Kingdom

One Liberty Plaza, 20th Floor, New York, NY 10006, USA

477 Williamstown Road, Port Melbourne, VIC 3207, Australia

314-321, 3rd Floor, Plot 3, Splendor Forum, Jasola District Centre, New Delhi - 110025, India

79 Anson Road, #06-04/06, Singapore 079906

Cambridge University Press is part of the University of Cambridge.

It furthers the University's mission by disseminating knowledge in the pursuit of education, learning and research at the highest international levels of excellence.

www.cambridge.org
Information on this title: www.cambridge.org/9781107423435

© Cambridge University Press 2014

This publication is in copyright. Subject to statutory exception and to the provisions of relevant collective licensing agreements, no reproduction of any part may take place without the written permission of Cambridge University Press.

First published 2014

Cover designed by Studio Pounce
Typeset by Integra Software Services Pvt. Ltd

A Cataloguing-in-Publication entry is available from the catalogue of the National Library of Australia at www.nla.gov.au

ISBN 978-1-107-42343-5 Paperback

Reproduction and communication for educational purposes
The Australian *Copyright Act 1968* (the Act) allows a maximum of one chapter or 10% of the pages of this work, whichever is the greater, to be reproduced and/or communicated by any educational institution for its educational purposes provided that the educational institution (or the body that administers it) has given a remuneration notice to Copyright Agency Limited (CAL) under the Act.

For details of the CAL licence for educational institutions contact:

Copyright Agency Limited
Level 15, 233 Castlereagh Street
Sydney NSW 2000
Telephone: (02) 9394 7600
Facsimile: (02) 9394 7601
E-mail: info@copyright.com.au

Reproduction and communication for other purposes
Except as permitted under the Act (for example a fair dealing for the purposes of study, research, criticism or review) no part of this publication may be reproduced, stored in a retrieval system, communicated or transmitted in any form or by any means without prior written permission. All inquiries should be made to the publisher at the address above.

Cambridge University Press has no responsibility for the persistence or accuracy of URLs for external or third-party internet websites referred to in this publication, and does not guarantee that any content on such websites is, or will remain, accurate or appropriate.

To Maria, Angus, Dan, James and Hugh

CONTENTS

List of figures and diagrams	*page* x
List of tables	xi
Preface	xiii
Acknowledgements	xv

1	**Good legal education**	**1**
	1.1 Introduction: Forget money	1
	1.2 Types of law degrees	3
	1.3 Being good requires more than expertise	3
	1.4 Coverage of this book	5
	1.5 Identifying a good law school	11
	1.6 Questions to ask your preferred law school	14
	1.7 Choosing electives	15
	1.8 Essentials in the process of law study	16
	1.9 Managing your mental health	17
	1.10 A 'structural' connection between legal education and student health: Rationality but not emotion	18
	1.11 After you graduate: Practical legal training (PLT)	21
	1.12 Seeking admission to legal practice	22
2	**The law practice landscape: choosing to be a 'good' lawyer in a good law firm**	**32**
	2.1 The connection between good lawyering and good legal communities	32
	2.2 Common themes in major examples of poor lawyering	33
	2.3 Failures of lawyers' regulation, not just of lawyers' character	36
	2.4 The ethical environment in different areas of law and types of legal practice	38
	2.5 Questions new lawyers can ask law firms when assessing their worth	45
	2.6 Inside the ideal commercial law firm	47
	2.7 The regulation of not-so-good lawyering	52
	2.8 *Uniform Conduct Rules* (UCR)	53

vii

viii   Contents

3   Values, ethics and virtue in lawyering   62
   3.1 Inside the law: First do no harm?   62
   3.2 Do we have a choice about our behaviour?   64
   3.3 The legal limit: Why 'law' and 'rules' are not enough
      to produce good lawyering   65
   3.4 Determining a priority between law and ethics   68
   3.5 General morality: The three major systems of ethical thought   70
   3.6 Understanding general morality through the distinctions
      between the ethics of duty and virtue ethics   73
   3.7 Conclusion: Strengthening our self-respect   80

4   Connecting character to lawyers' roles   85
   4.1 Introduction: Character-laden law   85
   4.2 Strengthening underlying character   86
   4.3 Connecting with your own sense of general morality   86
   4.4 Being and remaining 'positive' about life as a lawyer   87
   4.5 Why is role morality (zealous advocacy, the dominant
      legal ethic) so important for lawyers?   89
   4.6 Central criticisms of role morality   91
   4.7 Virtue and character as a more stable foundation for modern legal
      ethics   95
   4.8 Identifying virtues   97
   4.9 Can virtue ethics stand up to criticism?   98
   4.10 Role morality versus the rest: Connecting character and
      attitudes to positive and preferred lawyer 'types'   102
   4.11 Challenging morality: Large law firms as a special case?   104
   4.12 Conclusion   107

5   Truth and deception   114
   5.1 Introduction: Tools for analysis   114
   5.2 Key issues in truth and deception: Active and passive deceit   119
   5.3 Hiding embarrassing documents   120
   5.4 Hiding the true purpose of a legal action   122
   5.5 Criminal lawyers who 'know too much'   125
   5.6 Evading tax   128
   5.7 Conclusion: The possible consequences if caught 'lying'   130

6   Professional secrets   134
   6.1 Introduction: The shrinking world of secrets   134
   6.2 Professional secrecy remains important: Confidentiality and client
      privilege   138
      6.2.1 Confidentiality   139
      6.2.2 Client privilege   142
   6.3 Keeping quiet – murder   144
   6.4 Keeping quiet – corruption   146
   6.5 Hit-run-hide   148
   6.6 Conclusion   150

Contents   ix

7   Conflicts of loyalty and interest   155
   7.1 Introduction: What is a conflict of interest and why are conflicts so
       difficult?   155
   7.2 An overview of lawyer–client conflicts   160
   7.3 Client–client (concurrent) conflict   162
   7.4 Acting against former clients – successive conflicts   169
   7.5 Conclusion   175

8   The morality of competence   178
   8.1 Introduction: Competence requires morality   178
   8.2 Commercialism and competent legal practice   179
   8.3 Contract, tort and the advocates' exit clause   181
   8.4 Financial competency   184
   8.5 Billing and bribery: Challenges to competency   188
   8.6 Staying competent   192
      8.6.1 Continuing Professional Development (CPD)   192
      8.6.2 Artificial Intelligence   194
      8.6.3 Specialist accreditation   195
      8.6.4 Risk management   196
   8.7 Conclusion: Moral competency and competent morality   197

9   Practical wisdom for lawyers   200
   9.1 Introduction: A far greater authority   200
   9.2 Strengthening the general morality of legal profession discipline
      structures   203
   9.3 Practical wisdom in regulation   207
   9.4 Conclusion: Maintaining physical and moral resilience inside legal
      workplaces   209

Appendix A: Self-assessment of legal ethical preferences   213
Appendix B: Safety nets for lawyers   218
   B1 Professional Indemnity Insurance – the 'back-up'
      for practitioner negligence   218
   B2 Professional standards schemes   219
   B3 Fidelity compensation   220
Index   224

FIGURES AND DIAGRAMS

1.1	What makes a law school good?	*page* 14
1.2	Disclosure during admission	26
2.1	Arguably legal	48
2.2	Life balance	51
2.3	Moral illegitimacy and conduct rules	54
4.1	Close encounters of three kinds	104
5.1	The formal hierarchy of lawyers' duties	115
6.1	Confidentiality distinguished from privilege	139
7.1	Types of lawyer–client conflict	160
7.2	Communicating wisely about costs	162
7.3	Realities of information barriers	167
7.4	Successive conflict connected to *McCabe*	174
8.1	Competence and morality	193
9.1	Framework of Australian lawyers' regulation	205
B1	Funding the fidelity compensation system	221

TABLES

1.1	Disclosure requirements for admission to practice	*page* 25
2.1	Themes in poor lawyering	33
2.2	Ethical challenges and opportunities faced by different types of legal practice	38
3.1	General morality	70
3.2	Distinctions for lawyers between the ethics of duty and virtue ethics	74
4.1	Key virtues of good lawyers	88
4.2	Guidance available from different ethical frameworks and conduct rules	101
5.1	The apparent distinction between active and passive deceit	117
5.2	Producing or destroying documents	120
5.3	Duty not to abuse process	122
5.4	On knowing too much – acting for apparently 'guilty' clients	125
5.5	How much tax avoidance is morally acceptable?	128
6.1	Keeping the past in the past – the Lake Pleasant bodies	144
6.2	Privilege as a cover up for corruption and bribery – AWB in Iraq	146
6.3	Leaving the scene – Eugene McGee	149
7.1	Costing your clients too much – Keddies Lawyers	163
7.2	Differences between 'commercial' and prohibited conflicts of interest	165
7.3	The instability of concurrent, opposed clients – Allens and Big Pharma	170
8.1	Advocates' immunity – a separation of law and morality?	182

8.2	Trust accounting basics	186
8.3	Pinching a lot of trust money – Magarey Farlam	187
B1	The funding of legal aid when governments are uninterested – should we keep clients in the dark?	221

PREFACE

There is a significant double standard facing law students and new Australian lawyers.

What the profession generally provides – and wants to provide, no matter what law societies say – is an ongoing winnowing process for new graduates. Firms assert that they provide interesting work and a rewarding career, but the economic model of many depends still on stretching and moulding new lawyers to the point where those least able to cope leave within a few years. This is not peculiar to law and is indeed no different from the wider market economy, but contemporary law graduates' personal characteristics and expectations leave them particularly unprepared.

Today's graduates are used to feeling anxious at law school, but are articulate, optimistic and overly expectant of power. In their first work-place, they are often confused by a lack of gender equality and disappointed as the months go by when things do not change much. Today's new lawyers become adept at comparing their lack of life–work balance to that of their non-lawyer friends and are often disillusioned by repetitive work with little opportunity to 'make a difference'. Their relief from no longer 'being broke' fades. So departure seems like their only option.

Law societies see this reality gap quite clearly, yet are relatively powerless to change the attitudes of managing partners in the largest firms. These lawyers quietly communicate their acceptance of an 'eat what you kill' approach and are generally content with the model. To generalise, with profits per partner the reference point – per month or per quarter – and global boards of directors in control, there is little immediate incentive for such lawyers to take a longer term approach. As they see it, both increasing cost pressures and continuing economic uncertainty require them to in effect exploit new graduates so that only the strongest – that is, those who generate the most fees – survive and remain in the profession. Short of the true calamities of the sort that blighted everyone in the 20th century, there is no prospect of a major medium-term upset in these priorities.

But smaller firms, though still large, can have more time for wider and deeper values. Some of these grasp the advantages of nurturing their new lawyers' wider and deeper motives, and their sense of developing professional responsibility. These firms know that their longer term reputations – and their financial futures – depend on their employing exactly this sort of lawyer.

As legal educators, we will do best to develop this mature sort of law graduate rather than the commercially effective but often, it seems, morally shallow individual. The graduates we want to create will be as knowledgeable as any and more skilled in a practice-ready sense than most; but they will also be aware of and be developing their values and virtues. They will identify with their emotional intelligence and interpersonal sensitivity and they will have jobs because they will be willing to work where others will not – for example, in smaller firms and in regional and rural areas.

The general premise is that society does not necessarily need more lawyers, but it does need and will pay a premium for better lawyers. Good lawyers. This book tries to generate an enthusiasm for good lawyering in Year 11–12 students, in law students, in practical legal training students, in new lawyers and in law teachers. *The Good Lawyer* researches the way in which general morality can align good legal education with good legal practice, so that from cradle to grave, good and not-so-good lawyers are strengthened.

Adrian Evans
February 2014

ACKNOWLEDGEMENTS

David Luban's edited 1983 collection (*The Good Lawyer: Lawyers' Roles and Lawyers' Ethics*, Rowman & Allanheld, Totowa, NJ) is the primary inspiration for this work.

Christopher Peterson and Martin Seligman's *Character Strengths and Virtues: A Handbook and Classification* (Oxford University Press, New York, 2004) has also been influential. Table 3.2 is derived with permission from the work of Stan Van Hooft (specifically Table 1, in *Understanding Virtue Ethics*, Acumen Publishing, Chesham, Buckinghamshire, 2006), which in turn was influenced by my colleague Justin Oakley's earlier general classifications (see Justin Oakley, 'Varieties of Virtue Ethics' (1996) *IX Ratio* (New Series) 128) of the distinctions between virtue ethics and both consequential and Kantian approaches to ethical problem solving.

The self-assessment tool published in Appendix A has been previously published in the appendix to Christine Parker and Adrian Evans, *Inside Lawyers' Ethics* (2nd edn, Cambridge University Press, Melbourne, 2014), and is fully discussed in Adrian Evans and Helen Forgasz 'Framing Lawyers' Choices: Factor Analysis of a Psychological Scale to Self-Assess Lawyers' Ethical Preferences' ((2013) 16(1) *Legal Ethics* 134).

Considerable thanks are due to my clinical and legal ethics colleagues at Monash University law school and to my clients over the years, all of whom have reinforced the need for ways and means to think about legal ethics problems in a coherent way, since many of the ethical dramas facing new lawyers do not present themselves with any real clarity.

Chapter 1

GOOD LEGAL EDUCATION

1.1 Introduction: Forget money

There are a range of reasons for choosing to study law. Some students are just unsure what to do and some are really interested in the idea of law as a concept and do not intend to become lawyers, but many are in the middle somewhere – they are attracted to the possibility of courtroom excitement and have a desire to 'make a difference'. Advocacy in courts, in negotiation, mediation and in numerous lawyers' offices has a marvellous potential to change the law and improve the lives of others. Assuming you have a choice, how will you decide which law school will be best for you?

All law schools must cover a specific set of subjects[1] which will develop a base level of legal knowledge and some skills. Many will prepare you for the broad range of lawyers' roles. Some do it better than others. If you can comfortably make a decision about which law school to go to on your own, then go ahead. But some parents and families also want to get involved with choosing law schools and while they (of course) want a rewarding and secure career for you, they are sometimes thinking about big incomes too. When that happens, identifying preferences for a particular law school can get more complicated. The important thing is to know what your own motives are for aiming at a particular law school and law degree. Large incomes are available in some types of legal practice, but not as commonly as you may think. A

2 The Good Lawyer

small number of lawyers make a great deal of money, but most do not. If you think your priority is to make a lot of money quickly from business and you don't really mind how, then this book will not assist you greatly. However, if you like reading, problem solving, negotiating, arguing, working independently and as a team; if you want to be a lawyer and make a reasonable income that is less likely to disappear when the economy turns down; if you want to contribute to society and do justice, but not at the cost of your self-respect or your friends and relationships, then keep reading.

Law students and new lawyers will also find much to engage them in this book, because the primary focus is on the moral (ethical[2]) challenges of legal practice. There are many publications and short courses which address the technical knowledge and skills of lawyering, but fewer in the area of ethics and morality. Morality remains uncomfortable for many people, including many lawyers, and represents a professional risk that is often left lying around until a problem appears. The main problem areas are in truthfulness and lying, in keeping and divulging secrets, and in conflicts of interest, though these do not exhaust the list.

Australia has a considerable number of lawyers relative to total population and more are immigrating every day. But there are too few of us in regional and rural areas and in key justice occupations, and probably too many in banking and finance. The competition among us for legal work is fierce, particularly in commercial and corporate areas. Sometimes, that competition causes problems. Even though many lawyers are vaguely aware of ethical danger, corners are cut, bills overloaded, reputations are damaged and justice suffers. As a consequence, the wider community is wary of us and wary of our priorities, even if everyone wants to know and trust their own lawyer. So while Australia overall probably has enough lawyers, what our communities actually need is *better* lawyers. This book aims to make you a better person and, I hope, a better lawyer. 'Better' does not mean clever or more highly skilled – although that is necessary and should go without saying; it means more socially and morally responsible. That is, a 'good' lawyer. This focus on the *good lawyer* should guide you in a decision to study law and help you to decide what type of law practice to aim for and how to be ethical in whatever field you subsequently choose.

1.2 Types of law degrees

You may think you want to be a lawyer, but don't really know what is involved in studying law or the 'lawyering' that comes afterwards. You may decide not to practise law at a later date or might think, correctly, that knowledge of law will be useful in some other occupation. Ethical lawyering capacity will be very valuable in a range of occupations, particularly finance, accounting, auditing, estate planning, taxation, sustainable development, management and banking. So it does not matter whether you are a senior secondary student who wants to go straight to law school at the age of 17, 18 or 19, or a mature-age graduate with qualifications in another discipline.

What degree options are available? The LLB (Bachelor of Laws)[3] in Australia is classified at Level 7 by the Australian Qualifications Framework (AQF).[4] The LLB is usually chosen by students who want to study law as soon as they finish secondary education.[5] An alternative route for graduates who have a bachelor's degree in another discipline is the Juris Doctor (JD) degree, which will be taught at the higher Masters standard (AQF Level 9), as from 2015. JD courses are usually more expensive than LLB degrees,[6] but both lead to a right to seek admission as a legal practitioner, after completion of various practical legal training (PLT), undertaken at the end of either degree.[7] The problem, however, is that neither offers an easy or automatic way to work out whether it will provide you with a good legal education, as defined above.

1.3 Being good requires more than expertise

If your ambition is to be a good lawyer and to find the right law degree for this, then knowing what good *is* seems important. Over 30 years ago, US legal ethicist David Luban edited a book entitled *The Good Lawyer: Lawyers' Roles and Lawyers' Ethics*.[8] Luban's objective was to set out, for that era and culture, what good lawyering was and all the reasons why good lawyering makes more sense than any other approach. Luban defined a good lawyer as a moral (ethical) person, not just someone who knows the law well. His radical – and some said his heretical[9] – prescription was to turn legal ethics on its head by suggesting a move away from dependence on sets of rules about what to do or not do in difficult or dodgy situations, or simply prioritising their client no matter what, and look carefully at the idea of goodness. He and his co-authors proposed a difficult question: *who* is the good lawyer? Luban and his colleagues hoped the ground would shift under legal ethics to such an extent that *who* we are as lawyers, rather than *what* we do, would be the first concern. Luban's approach followed *virtue ethics*, derived from Aristotle in the pre-Christian era,[10] which asserts that goodness depends on character and that good character is shown by the virtues we display in our behaviour. His argument, simply stated, was and is that we lawyers cannot get away from wider moral obligations that impact on the rest of society and claim that we are permitted (almost automatically) to lie and cheat, providing we do it within rules.

You may think that Luban's recipe for goodness is a bit weak or soft or idealistic, and certainly his conception is very remote and detached from the 'cut and thrust' image of the trial lawyer portrayed in the media, particularly television or novels. You would be right, and this reality tends to show that Luban was not overly successful in his quest.[11] But the impact of this book was still considerable. Interest in who we are as lawyers – and not just in what we do and what rules apply to us – has never disappeared.

As Joseph Tomain indicated when he reviewed Luban's book:

> *The Good Lawyer* is about being a lawyer, and its thesis is astonishingly simple. Being a lawyer is not unconnected with being a person ... Further, being a good person does not preclude you from being a good lawyer – if anything, lawyers should be "more moral" ... These assertions are not astonishing because of their simplicity but rather because of the heresies they contain and because of their complexity. They are heretical because they are contrary to over 100 years of orthodoxy in the thought, writing, and institutionalization of professional ethics.[12]

Despite the thousands of Australian lawyers who struggle conscientiously with ethics, there have been both major and minor moral disasters in the 30 years since Luban's book was published. Notorious cases and headlines have demonstrated a lack of interest in who we are as lawyers and a too-common readiness by our fellow lawyers to argue that 'no rules were broken', or that the rules were ambiguous. Some of the more notable instances, covered later in this book, have resulted in much injustice and

| Good legal education   5

billions of dollars in losses. There is now not just a moral reason to revisit good lawyering, but a powerful economic incentive as well. To address this need, a variety of topics are covered, as set out in the next section.

1.4 Coverage of this book

The following sections of this chapter discuss the questions that you should consider asking a law school in order to get an idea of its credentials and capacity for teaching 'goodness'. There is no website that provides the answers. Not surprisingly, just as law firms tend not to proclaim their attitudes to ethics to prospective clients, law schools slip in behind them and emphasise other things, such as their 'commerciality', excellence, and graduate career destinations. All of these claims are possibly true, but they not about being a *good* lawyer. So you need to investigate this issue for yourself, using a questionnaire set out below (at 1.6).

Later, the issues involved in selecting so-called elective subjects are also addressed, along with the hot topics of:

- what is involved in 'thinking like a lawyer' – benefits and disadvantages?
- the essence of how to study law – continuous assessment; on campus or online study
- life-study and part-time paid work – keeping balance
- why volunteering in the law – in addition to undertaking seasonal clerkships – is healthy
- the emotional and physical stress of individual subject demands
- consciousness of depression risks – keeping talking
- the benefits of PLT *versus* a traineeship – pay or be paid
- seeking 'admission to practice' – what it means and what to beware of!

Chapter 2 turns to the moral realities of legal practice. Recent 'headline' cases emphasise the risks and opportunities in the many types of 'lawyering'. The managing partners of large firms and global firms tend to consider law as pure business. They have very different attitudes from other lawyers, for instance criminal and family lawyers. As a generalisation, the larger the firm the more pressure there is for each lawyer to complete daily timesheets – where they must record what they do in *six-minute* intervals.

6 The Good Lawyer

There are other particular ethical issues associated with larger legal practices, especially a degree of nervousness among new lawyers about exercising ethical choice in the face of the business priorities of the firm.

Chapter 2 also explores a range of economic and structural challenges to lawyering, including so-called legal process outsourcing. This trend became prominent in India, where lawyer–IT entrepreneurs saw an opportunity to industrialise and automate transactional and litigious legal work with the aid of artificial intelligence, to the point where the lawyer's contribution in major transactions – ethical judgment – is not as obvious as it used to be. Now many large and mid-tier Australian law firms are sending slabs of routine commercial legal work to India in an effort to cut their local lawyer labour costs. Over time, this may reduce demand for local commercial lawyers. The financial challenges to good lawyering are also considerable, because no one can afford to be a good lawyer at the cost of going broke.

Chapter 3 addresses the core complexities of values, ethics and virtue arising from a choice to be a good lawyer. The major systems of *general morality* (*consequentialism*, *Kantianism* and *virtue ethics*) are analysed and compared in a large table (Table 3.2) for their potential to cut through these debates about what is 'legal' or 'ethical'. In the face of all the 'system' challenges which lawyering throws up to income, wellbeing and our personal relationships, being a good lawyer is just smart. But that does not mean it's easy to do. Ethical concepts are often difficult to 'see', and if seen, are then avoided because the essence of goodness involves making a judgment. Exercising judgment is hard because it's difficult to reduce any particular situation to a formula or rule. Superficially, we often prefer to work with legal rules because they give the illusion that no judgment is required. Law students are known for saying in ethics classes 'just give me the rules'. But rules can only rarely be applied without judgment – that is, without ethical awareness and conscious choice. There is judgment involved in acting intentionally in all ethical decision making, rather than just lazily 'going with the flow' or doing what one is told (that is, following a command or rule without thought). Here, the major challenge for some commercial lawyers is their appreciation of the difference between something that is legal but unethical, a point eloquently emphasised by Abraham Lincoln[13] but not so often taken to heart. In our communities, proposals for new development projects versus the need for environmental sustainability frequently throw up this difference.

| Good legal education   **7**

In Chapter 4 general morality is tied into sub-frameworks of legal ethics that have been developed to help lawyers decide what to do in difficult cases. General morality can seem remote to lawyers, but is made more accessible when considered alongside other frameworks. For this reason, a four-part category popularised by Christine Parker – so-called zealous advocacy, responsible lawyering, moral activism and the ethics (or relationship) of care[14] – helps us appreciate general morality and make difficult ethical choices. Such choices have to be truly intentional rather than based in fuzzy thinking or feelings, or unthinking obedience to whatever a superior might tell us to do.

While Chapter 4 also suggests that virtue and character are a more stable foundation for modern legal ethics, the temptation to simply adopt virtue ethics as the framework of choice and not bother with consequentialism or Kantianism is resisted. It may be that virtue alone is sufficient to guide all decisions, but as will be seen, our tolerance and judgment are important virtues in themselves. Our capacity to make the truly good decision is likely to be enhanced if we allow ourselves to compare, in each case, what each of these three approaches – virtue, consequentialism and Kantian methods – would suggest is appropriate. But it is still important to identify the virtues as they are known and attempt a justification of virtue ethics in response to the criticism, often (erroneously) made, that something as apparently amorphous as a virtue can hope to provide a practical guide to action in tough situations.

While Parker's four types (see Appendix A) are easily understood and therefore useful for increasing awareness of your own preferences as a lawyer, they were not intended to provide an active guide for decision making in complex and ethically confused situations. The comparison of virtue ethics, consequentialism and Kantian ethics provides a framework for doing this.

Prominent among these traditional categories is the concept that Luban was so critical of: zealous advocacy, or role morality. Role morality, also known as the 'dominant' form of legal ethics, allows lawyers to say and do things on behalf of a client that they might not be able or willing to say or do in their private lives. Some have described role morality as nothing more than licensed lying and cheating,[15] but a milder description tones this down a bit to merely passionate advocacy and involves the justification (in its simplest form) that lawyers on both sides of a dispute should *properly* put their client's case as strongly as possible. For example, a criminal defence lawyer may – and sometimes must – hassle, accuse and even trick prosecution witnesses in an effort to make sure they are not lying. A zealous advocate does this because

8 The Good Lawyer

they are confident in the knowledge that a sensible judge (and sometimes jury) will work out which version of events and which interpretation of the law is most credible. Role morality is accepted throughout Australia and New Zealand as important for the defence of criminal charges because the state (that is, the prosecution) often has greater power to pursue a defendant than he or she has to defend themselves. Role morality is a balancing mechanism that has stood the test of time over the last several hundred years of English criminal trial history.[16] But it is not appropriate for all lawyers in all situations. This book does not discount the importance of role morality, but it is insufficient for a good lawyer. When a zealous advocate subjects themselves to the scrutiny of general morality, even better lawyering will result.

Chapter 4 then covers the relatively recent insights of positive psychology, which is not the same as the increasingly discredited notion of 'positive thinking'. Positive psychology provides a respectable method to connect us to our own sense of general morality and allows us to be – and remain – 'positive' about life as a lawyer. Chapter 4 concludes by centring the whole debate about morality and law inside the special case of the large law firm. These are the workplace settings where it seems that new lawyers are under the most pressure to conform to a culture that is intrinsically profit focused.

Chapters 5 to 8 deal sequentially with specific areas of legal ethics that provide you with many opportunities to demonstrate general morality, even though few will see you functioning in this holistic manner. Since good lawyering tends to be less visible, these chapters must unfortunately make use of examples of bad lawyering in order to get the point across. In each of these chapters, the choices open to us in determining a course of moral action are illustrated with specific cases and analysed according to the three general moral approaches discussed above, in the light of the *Australian Solicitors' Conduct Rules* (ASCR).[17] These cases also refer to the four legal ethics sub-categories, where appropriate. The method used to analyse the illustrations in each of these chapters involves reflection on the contrasting ethical approaches in order to discern the mature decision.

Chapter 5 tackles the painful agendas of truth and deception, often in a criminal law context. It might be said that role morality justifies just enough deceit to ensure a fair criminal law trial, but the concept still fails to satisfy almost every non-lawyer. Coping with the disguised suspicion you will receive at parties when you say you are a lawyer is just the start of it. Perhaps more than in any other area of legal ethics and lawyering, we need to combat the

| Good legal education   **9**

popular idea that as lawyers we are intrinsically crooked or dodgy and are profoundly unable to tell the truth. Key situations where this challenge must be taken up are discussed, including the difference between active and so-called passive deceit, the concealment of embarrassing documents, the disguising of the true purpose of a legal action, 'knowing too much' and evading tax.

Chapter 6 then explores the idea of professional secrecy, which can both support and confuse the subtleties of truth and deception by providing a justification for saying as little as possible. Lawyers' secrets now come in two varieties: the fairly bland concept of legal confidentiality, and its altogether sharper sub-category, client privilege. The former is said to underpin everything a lawyer does, which is accurate as far as it goes, but in practical terms it's really the narrower idea of client privilege that is vital. It is only privilege that allows a party to litigation to keep something secret from a court. Nevertheless both confidentiality and privilege have their limits, and in defining those limits general morality is useful, particularly where the ASCR prove again to be simply a set of rules, albeit rules that are enforceable by regulators. Three central examples are explored, where our capacity to keep quiet is linked to murder, corruption and finally to protection from the consequences of a hit and run killing.

Although truth-telling and secrecy are high in the public profile, there is a largely undiscussed underbelly of legal practice that has a more insidious effect on our character – conflicts of interest. Chapter 7 explores these conflicts of loyalty and interest as a recurring and sometimes nightmare challenge to large firms. We are constantly conflicted by our desire to do the best for our client but also to charge them enough for us to earn a living. Here the rules say we can charge a 'reasonable amount', but try working out what is reasonable without some wider general moral framework to guide you. Conflicts are also a challenge when we find ourselves suddenly acting for two clients who are in an argument with each other or who could be in such an argument – or a current client finds themselves opposed to a former client. Do we not owe some loyalty to the former client, or at least an obligation to keep their secrets secret from our newer and current client? The temptation for large firms to earn double fees by keeping all parties in-house in these situations is often seductive, but just as often the seduction leads to tears all round, and then winds up in public.

Chapter 8 addresses professional competence, something that is often taken for granted until you make your first significant mistake as a lawyer

10   The Good Lawyer

and it becomes necessary to claim on your employer's professional indemnity insurance policy. Remember that mistakes are inevitable for us as much as for anyone; they are not a sign of moral failure. Negligent advice is offered every day in the most respectable of firms, but at the same time, morality still plays a subtle role. If your attitude to the quality of your work is one of 'close enough is good enough' or you are untroubled that you are habitually late in meeting work-related deadlines, then it's likely that you will make more than your quota of mistakes and you may not care that much.

General morality, and particularly virtue morality, values a conscientious approach, and in this sense, competence requires morality. There are many implications explored in this chapter. In practical terms, we need to be competent despite the let-out clause of 'advocates' immunity', because individuals' carelessness will mean all of us must pay much higher insurance premiums even if our clients cannot always successfully sue us for negligence because of the immunity. We are required also to be financially competent by making sure we know how to keep our own money separate from our clients' money. Historically, failure to recognise this point has often led to theft and then jail – with all that that means for our families and our reputation. Over-charging and bribery are also challenges to competency, and there are several dimensions to this particular risk. For example, each of us will benefit from continuing professional development (CPD) training on a regular basis and will adopt risk management procedures so that we recognise an invitation to bribery when we encounter it. If we cannot connect our competence to morality, we may well recognise corruption as an opportunity rather than as something to be resisted.

Finally, Chapter 9, 'Practical wisdom', explains how lawyers are regulated and how the regulators deal with those of us who go off the rails, depending upon whether we are anxious, depressed, addicted, mentally unwell, careless or (for a few), just crooks. Most of us are not in any of these categories, but many of us will encounter one or another of these issues if we have a long career. If we are so affected, recovery is always possible. One can even be personally redeemable after criminality, and we need to remain resilient and positive about legal practice as one of the most important and even noble of human occupations. The book concludes with a review of emerging technological and cultural challenges to lawyering and a specific ethics assessment scale. This scale can be used by all law students and lawyers to expand and refine their knowledge of who they are and what they may become. Other appendices set out the features of our various professional safety nets – professional indemnity insurance, professional standards schemes and so-called fidelity compensation funds. Each of these schemes is the creation of lawyers who have gone ahead of us and who have recognised the importance of backing up the virtue of client care with the practical wisdom of prevention and client compensation, where necessary. Meantime, we return to the beginning: identifying what makes a good law school.

1.5 Identifying a good law school

There are several online rankings of Australian law schools. A prominent example is that of the Australian Education Network,[18] which aggregates data from a variety of local and international research-based surveys. Only the 'top' 12 law schools[19] from Australia's total list of 36 law schools appear in this ranking. Many developments are occurring in this area, but at present the quality of law *teaching* does not figure significantly in these rankings. However, the arrival of the federal government Tertiary Education Quality Standards Agency (TEQSA) will progressively improve the situation.

There is no way in which a potential law student can easily compare law schools on any basis except these rankings.[20] However, ranking and reputation do not really matter because the current criteria are too narrow and they can be incorrectly measured. It is what goes on in the law course that really matters. But as a prospective law student you will need to know what you want from a law school and if you want the goal proposed above – to be a 'good' lawyer emerging from a 'good' law degree. You therefore need some other basis upon which to decide which law schools will take you in this direction. A 'good' law school is one that develops your character or professionalism: the mix of your better values, skills and attitudes that will make you a (morally) good lawyer – and one whose reputation will last.

'Good' law schools develop character by providing the cultural and technical power for graduates to improve social functioning, through law reform and through better access to justice. Among these attributes are:

- the depth of your theoretical knowledge about the way in which the law works and does not work, on a day-to-day basis. This means the capacity of the law school not just to teach the law 'as it is' (which is of course essential and is described broadly as a legal positivist approach[21]), but to balance that with a critique of what law should be or ought to be (a normative or natural law approach[22]), having due regard to legal theory and its attempts to reconcile these two divergent but necessary approaches to understanding law.

- the extent to which your interest in law as a discipline has been excited or 'dumbed-down' by the experience of going to law school. 'Did you learn to love the law?', as former High Court judge Michael Kirby has asked.[23] Conventional law teaching (associated to some extent with positivist approaches) can be satirised as 'bulimic' because it asks you to swallow a great deal of information in a short space of time and then disgorge it hurriedly in periodic 'vomits' of memory. This approach to the process of learning involves little incentive to understand the connections of the curriculum to justice or to the overall purpose of law: that is, to come to love it. In contrast, progressive Australian law teaching[24] is normative and emphasises more considered reflection on the purposes of law and the development of personal judgment, two virtues which follow on from the central quality of love of the law, which successful lawyers need to have and to demonstrate.

- your own emotional intelligence, client sensitivity, understanding of how the law works in practice, ethical judgment, and, through a *real* personal experience of social inequality, a sense of compassion for victims of injustice.

- all of these qualities are developed by best practice clinical legal education (CLE) – a form of workplace-integrated learning (WIL, also known as 'service learning' or 'learning by doing') that puts law students in a position of responsibility for real clients who are facing immediate and demanding legal problems. CLE has been endorsed by the Council of Australian Law Deans (CALD) and *Best Practices for CLE* have been identified for law schools that offer such programs.[25]

- your capacity for seeing (recognising) ethical danger and for clearer thinking about law and ethics: leading to inclusive and appropriate ethical judgment – as discussed in Chapters 3 to 7. What is legal is not always ethical, but both legal and ethical thinking requires capacity to see the ethical issue despite apparent legality and then to make intentional decisions about what to advise a client and what to do. This process requires both rationality and emotion. A good lawyer will know how their emotions are affecting them, will take their emotional state into account in all their actions, and will try to decide difficult ethical issues not by simply succumbing to an unexamined 'gut' feeling.

| Good legal education   13

- US scholarship shows that when legal ethics content is taught both as a stand-alone subject and integrated into other subjects such as Criminal Law, Contracts and Torts, the overall impact of ethics on students (your 'professionalism') is enhanced.[26]
- your developing approach to the rule of law debate. In general terms, the rule of law maintains that all of us are primarily subject to the rule of law above and before, when necessary, the rule or dominance of governments or parliaments. For example, a dictator who arbitrarily imprisons or executes political opponents commonly does so after going through the motions of changing 'the law' to allow this to happen. But the rule of law denies him/her legitimacy in imprisoning or executing people unless the *proper* processes of law are first followed. Depending on the interpretation of the rule of law issue by a law school, deciding what is 'proper' may be a circumstantial and principled matter of ethics, or just a narrow matter of the law 'as is', so to speak.[27] It is important that both perspectives are covered respectfully in law school. They are normally dealt with in the first year of law study and the depth of that coverage is significant for the development of your ethical judgment.[28]
- your capacity to understand if the overall orientation of the law degree is towards socio-legal change and human rights or commercialism (or all of these). A law degree with a strong human rights orientation and little commercial focus may fail to take due notice of the critical importance of money and financial knowhow in the translation of rights into realities. Similarly, a commercially oriented law degree may not equip you for doing enough justice. A balance between the two is a key objective of a good law school.
- a developed research capacity, since the ability to research effectively (and to know how your own research habits are best accessed and nurtured) is a core skill supporting the depth of your legal knowledge now and in your future legal practice. This is the only criterion where the current Australian law school rankings are useful.
- your developed desire to do justice, at the end of the whole experience of law school. This may sound shallow or trivial when stated as simply as this, but the kernel of the issue is important for the good lawyer: will you (or did you?) come out of law school with a desire to make a just difference to the community, or are you content to just have a job?

14   The Good Lawyer

Diagram 1.1 summarises these attributes:

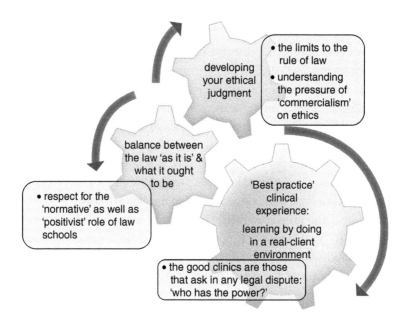

Diagram 1.1 What makes a law school good?

1.6 Questions to ask your preferred law school

Most, if not all, law schools are unused to interrogation about what and how they teach. Some will be very surprised that you might want to know something about content, approach and the underlying values represented in their teaching, before you decide whether or not to take up an offer of a place. But as a prospective law student who will pay either a modest amount or a great deal of money to study law (and in either case), you are entitled to be an informed consumer. If after you explain what you are interested in and why you are interested, a law school declines to provide you with any useful information in response to your queries, then that response would be eloquent.

The following list of questions can be put to a law school to ascertain whether or not it is likely to prepare you for good lawyering:

1	In what year and subject is the rule of law taught? Is that content in the 'must be assessed' category?
2	Is legal ethics taught as a stand-alone subject or integrated into other subjects, or both? If integrated in whole or part, is the law school able to tell you how the ethics content is divided up between different subjects and year levels?
3	Does the law school offer a clinical legal education program? If so, is that program an elective or a compulsory subject? If it is an elective, are there sufficient places available for all those who wish to enrol in the elective? Does the program provide for you to take responsibility, under supervision, for a real client with a real legal problem? Does the program meet the Best Practices endorsed by the Council of Australian Law Deans? If the program does not meet *all* Best Practices so identified, in which ones is it deficient?
4	In what subject(s) are the contrasting emphases of positivist and normative understandings of law taught? Is this subject (or subjects) compulsory?
5	How does the law school conceive of the balance between the socio-legal and commercial emphases of the law? What is the view of law school leadership as to the balance between these orientations?. Or indeed is there any view at all?
6	Does the law school organise legal volunteering ('pro bono') opportunities for its students? If so, what is the mix of such placements, as between law firms and NGOs?
7	In what subjects are the concepts of emotional intelligence, interpersonal skills and wellbeing taught? Is a knowledge of this material in the 'must be assessed' category?
8	Were you referred to people in the law school who were willing and able to take your queries seriously?
Questions for yourself . . .	How did the law school respond to your questions? Was it engaged and aware of the significance of your enquiries, or confused and struggling to come to grips with the concepts, or dismissive and unable/unwilling to help? Are you clearer about whether your preferred law school will help you to be a good lawyer, or merely a competent lawyer?

1.7 Choosing electives

As mentioned at 1.1, there are 11 compulsory areas of law that must be covered in an Australian law degree. You will usually have an opportunity to choose additional subjects (electives), commonly another 8 to 10. In a small law school, the available electives will be limited and may be biased towards either commercial or socio-legal offerings. There are also categories of electives which cover both these descriptions, for example international law, family law, consumer law, environmental law, succession law (determining what happens to property after death), trial practice and professional practice. The wider the range of electives available to you, the better. In general terms, and assuming you have a choice,[29] it is desirable to choose between a third to a half of your electives from commercial categories, even though you may think that they do not reflect your priorities as a good lawyer and you do not intend to practise that type of law.

You are likely to find as much to stimulate you intellectually and morally in commercial law fields as in any others, and you may well discover that good commercial lawyering becomes your objective. For example, Corporations (or Company) Law is a compulsory subject that lays the foundations for a range of contemporary commercial-related electives that are typically attractive to good lawyers.[30] The good lawyer may just as readily be a commercial or corporate lawyer as any other type of practitioner. Chapter 4 sets out how as a general group, commercial lawyers in large firms face extra challenges as good lawyers, but the good commercial lawyer is a much-valued member of the community and a critical contributor to corporate stability and productivity.

Common examples of commercially focused electives	taxation, banking law, insurance law, the law of employment, media law, petroleum law, aerospace law, commercial remedies, patents and trademarks, copyright, cyber and internet law
Examples of socio-legal related electives	gender and feminism, indigenous law, legal philosophy, medical negligence, forensic medicine and law, sentencing, migration and refugee law, privacy and surveillance

1.8 Essentials in the process of law study

There are many online how-to-study guides for law and secondary students who succeed in entering law school typically have well-developed ideas and awareness about how they are best able to study. Yet first-year LLB students are often challenged by the lack of the close discipline and teacher attention they had become used to in their final year of secondary education. Law concepts are also frequently new to students who did not pursue legal studies at school. And opportunities for distraction in law school are legion. Mature-aged JD students may have life experience which usually offers advantages in self-knowledge about balancing competing demands on their time, but even they are commonly working full-time or nearly full-time in business hours and can find that they need to use their time very carefully in order to stay up to date. The result for both categories of student can be stress.

Severe stress is dealt with below at 1.9, but 'ordinary' stress is normal and there is only one generally applicable approach to it: ration (reduce) activities and manage your time. However, while that sounds easy in theory, the practice can be elusive. Inevitably, the techniques that apply to properly managing your time are those that are also important in stopping the development of severe stress.

1.9 Managing your mental health

Even 10 years ago there would not be a section on this topic in a book for law students and new lawyers. Recognition that the legal profession (and law students) are exposed to mental health risks is recent but nonetheless real.[31] There is research which shows that lawyers are significantly more likely to suffer serious depression than any other professional group.[32] It is not entirely clear why this is the case. Affluent societies may be experiencing more anxiety (in proportion to their increasing wealth) in any event, regardless of any occupational stressors. There may, however, be a particular combination of circumstances that adversely affect law students and lawyers more than other professions and occupations. The causes are not just the emotional and physical stress of managing lectures, tutorials, research and constant assessment (or of clients, 'matters', court cases, budgets and deals, after you are admitted to legal practice). The constancy of these tension-creating deadlines provides the backdrop, but these deadlines are common to many occupations and are unlikely to be the real problem.

Law school and legal practice have a certain aura that is both powerful and, for some, unhealthy. As you know only too well, you need high to very high marks to get into law school. So you already have a history of working hard and are known to work hard. Your friends, parents, extended family, spouses and even children will be proud of you and expect you to do very well, even if you have already shown your ability in Year 12 or are successful in another occupation. There will be a strong expectation of continued and 'ever upward' success, even if that expectation is only there in the background and rarely articulated to you. The goal is prestige, and unfortunately, the default way in which law school culture commonly measures prestige is by your prospects of work in a very large law firm – not just any law firm. And many other students in the law school are working to the same agenda[33] with

18   The Good Lawyer

the same hopes, even when everyone knows that the number of jobs in such firms is increasingly limited. One estimate suggests there are law jobs for perhaps less than half the number of annual graduates in law.[34]

The point is: students know they are in a paper chase (for a graduation *testamur*[35]) and that in the race for an offer from such a firm, many – if not most – of them must lose. But knowing that failure is likely does not lead all students to adjust their expectations, because (and to generalise) this group of students have never known significant defeat or failure. If you are in this group then you will recognise that you cannot be assured of success, but you will not be prepared to give up. Why should you? Your chances are as good as anyone's, even if large law firm traineeships are few in number. And this is where personality comes in. If your underlying personality is resilient, you will eventually adjust even if you are unhappy about it, but in the process, you may be inclined to anxiety and vulnerable to depression. This is why many law schools are now either engaging counsellors or psychologists, or facilitating referrals, to help students manage the adjustment from dream to reality. This transition is a good thing, even if the process can be hurtful and disillusioning. Many law graduates do not find the very large law firm a great place to be, even as they welcome the relatively high income.

So what is different from the pressure exerted on students seeking entry to other sought-after professions? The difference is that law (and to some extent medicine), as professions, have overactive self-esteem. Law students soak up the mystique of law and its power even if they do not particularly want high-powered commercial careers. Collectively, law students and lawyers are prideful (not so much a virtue as a vice) to a degree not afflicting other professions. The irony is that law students are (another generalisation) trained to win even as the law school seeks to pick up the pieces of students whose emotional resources are not up to the stress of such relentless competition.

1.10 A 'structural' connection between legal education and student health: Rationality but not emotion

Some law students reflect on the competitive realities of legal education and are, to put it mildly, somewhat critical. An extreme but articulate view of a former Australian National University law student, Melanie

Poole, is that conventional Australian legal education, in seeking to help students 'think like lawyers', focuses on developing students' 'rationality' (understood as male, white and ordinarily heterosexual), to the exclusion of emotion.[36] Poole considers that the disdain for emotion among law teachers colours their approach so much that their default position is to teach 'the law as it is', with negative consequences for students' wellbeing:

> It is clear that 'rationality', with its focus on ethnocentrism, property and profits, precipitates the seepage of corporatism into law school culture. But it is the degradation of emotion and, correspondingly, students' human connections with self-worth, which drives them to repudiate their ideals.[37]

Poole is one voice, and it is unfair to label all legal education and all law teachers as unwilling to acknowledge the close connections between rationality and emotion in everyday decision making. But she puts a broadly credible argument (and is supported by empirical research[38]), sufficient for you to be justified in asking how your preferred law school's culture will contribute to or undermine your health and wellbeing? And she foreshadows something important about the role of emotions in balanced ethical decision making (explored further in Chapter 3):

> We should scrutinise the role of emotion in determining the law. But the rigid version of rationality taught in law school does not achieve this. As philosophers have demonstrated, regardless of how influential emotions *should* be, the reality is that they affect the way that humans reason.[39] (italics in original)

The recommended response of those who have studied the issue closely is to change first-year curricula to include sufficient recognition of the value of 'experiential' learning, to counter the rationality emphasis.[40] But law schools that attend only to improving first-year experience (with another 2–4 years of teaching taking the older, opposite approach) are unlikely to make sustained progress in turning things around. Students will still graduate with an over-developed regard for 'thinking like a lawyer' and less capacity to attend to their own emotional health or that of their friends and future clients.

20   The Good Lawyer

Consider this situation:

> Your elder sibling, to whom you are close, is also a law student. She drinks a bit too much but tells you that she thinks it's under control. It doesn't appear to be affecting her study or part-time work yet, but friends' reports about erratic behavior are becoming hard to ignore. Last week she was found very unwell, half in and half out of her car, after a party. She demands that you keep silent about it while she works it all out. In particular, she insists that your parents must not find out about what's happening until she is 'out the other side'.

Is it likely that your law school experience will give you the tools and resources to deal both with your sister and your own reactions to her possible addiction? Will you be more inclined to 'think like a lawyer' and keep her out of a vehicle at all times, or to argue with her about the importance of getting more help, or tell your parents in an effort to get immediate help anyway, or simply shut up for the sake of the relationship? Above all, will you be able to keep your own anxiety and distress in check so that you remain effective in her interests?

Some research suggests that the depression situation among law students is pervasive and may not, realistically, be reversed, even in law schools that are aware of the issues. In a survey comparing Melbourne Law School JD and LLB students' experience, Larcombe and colleagues found no significant differences in the degree of psychological distress suffered by the two groups. Program features that try to improve students' experience do not automatically improve their wellbeing.[41] And the curious suggestion is that you may be 'satisfied' with your law course while still being unhappy generally: 'it appears that law students can be "happy" with their course while experiencing considerable levels of psychological distress'.[42] But Larcombe has also found that students' personal distress can be ameliorated and their wellbeing improved by law lecturers' attitudes to their students, 'in particular the level of autonomy-support they provide'.[43]

Law schools, to their credit, are increasingly attempting to offer students education and training in emotional resilience and wellbeing,[44] and the more these caring programs are available, the stronger will that law school be. Even if these initiatives deal rather more with symptoms than causes, they can still be enormously helpful in their focus on quiet reflection, on the balance in life–study activity and between recreation and part-time paid work, and particularly in their strong encouragement of regular sport.

In the end, though, the good law school is one that not only cares for its students' emotional wellbeing, but actively teaches goodness, a quality which must pay equal regard to reason and emotion and does not seek to subordinate justice to the myth that law is value-free and is addressed only through rational processes.

1.11 After you graduate: Practical legal training (PLT)

Although it takes some years to progress through law school, that is not the end if you want to practise law. There is a final 'pre-admission' stage in which you are exposed to more practice-related activity designed to translate your law school knowledge into practical skills. Some law schools provide practical legal training (PLT) at the end of the law degree or as a postgraduate program.[45] But most graduates go to external providers for their PLT training. Unlike a law school live-client clinical program, PLT does not allow you to acquire actual lawyering experience, but PLT does a comprehensive job of simulating same. For example, if you have covered Succession Law in law school, you will know that a will gives each of us a chance to say what will happen to our property after we die. If Succession Law is taught energetically and having regard to the Threshold Learning Outcomes (TLOs), then you may have not only seen a real will in your law school class but also had a chance to draft one. But the likelihood is that that will be the limit of your practical skill in this area.

In the PLT phase, you will not only draft a simulated will, but also draft the accompanying Probate application to the Supreme Court of your state, draft the accompanying Affidavit of Executor and Inventory of Assets and then lodge all of them with a simulated court official, before all your drafting is assessed and either passed or rejected. If you do not do as well as you should, resubmission is required. PLT students rarely fail, but resubmission of assessable modules is common. Theoretically, you will have a choice to undertake PLT inside a law firm (as a part of your employment and at the cost of the law firm, described as supervised workplace training (SWT) for 12 months), or as an enrolled student with a commercial PLT provider, at a cost varying between $6 000 and $10 000.

22 The Good Lawyer

Commercial PLT courses commonly take 4–6 months to complete, can be full or part-time and, within some limits, are increasingly available online.

In Victoria, SWT is not a complete substitute for a formal PLT course. There are a few areas where law firms are not, in effect, trusted to deliver certain training. One of these is the PLT version of ethics and professional responsibility, which must be taught by a PLT provider.[46]

You will be attracted to a traineeship because you get into the paid legal workforce immediately and can undertake your PLT program part-time while employed. However, traineeships are extremely hard to get. Formerly known as 'articles of clerkship', they are offered by only a small number of firms [47] so few are available.

The reality is that it is the elite or larger firms that offer most traineeships, and they tend to reserve their limited number of places for graduates who have worked for them during their law degrees, as part of short-term seasonal programs. Often, the key to a traineeship place depends on a successful prior seasonal placement, and *that* opportunity can in turn depend as much on 'who you know' as on your innate ability and inter-personal skills. In this niche, the informal Australian class system makes its presence felt. Most law graduates are now compelled to enrol with a commercial PLT provider at their own expense. After completion of PLT, you can apply for admission to practice. When 'admitted', you become a lawyer in your own right and can generally appear before courts 'as of right', without seeking the permission of the court. After a 2 year period of supervised practice, you can practise law as a 'sole practitioner'. But all that comes after admission, which is a process that can be quite difficult for some, as we shall see below.

1.12 Seeking admission to legal practice

Not everyone wants to practise law or can get a job as a lawyer,[48] but most graduates want at least to be admitted, so that they are legally able to practise law at some point, assuming they can find the right law firm. Admission is a serious process. The documents required of you when applying for admission are all designed to testify to your suitability for admission to practice, having regard to what is known as a 'fit and proper person' test. That test emphasises personal character and particularly the virtue of honesty.[49] The following description of the reason for the test is from the judgment in a Victorian case:

> The requirement for admission to practice (sic) law that the applicant be a fit and proper person, means that the applicant must have the personal qualities of character which are necessary to discharge the important and grave responsibilities of being a barrister and solicitor. A legal practitioner, upon being admitted to practice, assumes duties to the courts, to fellow practitioners as well as to clients. At the heart of all of those duties is a commitment to honesty and, in those circumstances when it is required, to open candour and frankness, irrespective of self-interest or embarrassment. The entire administration of justice in any community which is governed by law depends upon the honest working of legal practitioners who can be relied upon to meet high standards of honesty and ethical behaviour. It is the legal practitioner who is effectively the daily minister and executor in the administration of justice when advising clients, acting for clients, certifying documents, and making presentations to courts, governments, other professionals, and so on. The level and extent of trust placed in what legal practitioners say or do is necessarily high and the need for honesty is self-evident and essential.[50]

The character test exists in all Australian jurisdictions, with slightly different practical emphases. In New South Wales, for example, an application for admission need only be signed, while in Victoria, an affidavit is necessary. The difference is important. If you make an affidavit, you are saying to the court and to society at large that you are telling the truth and understand that if you are found later to be lying, you will have committed the criminal offence of perjury ('lying under oath'). A signed application for admission does not carry the same consequences as an affidavit if it contains a lie.

If you have in your background a criminal history – which includes any finding by a court of 'offence proved', even if no conviction was recorded and a good behaviour bond was ordered – it is essential that you disclose that in your application. Disclosure, not deceit, is the best strategy. Failure to disclose can result in either the rejection of your application for admission or, if the omission is discovered after admission, in your being 'struck off' and unable to practise law again. Where a supporting affidavit was required, you may also face a prosecution for perjury.

The problem, however, can sometimes be whether or not to disclose minor problems from the past, such as parking fines. It is best practice to disclose *unpaid* parking fines, because their unpaid status shows a lack of interest in complying with the law. In addition, unpaid fines will often have escalated into enforcement proceedings and have resulted in some sort of court record. But satisfying the disclosure test is never a walk in the park and considerable care should be taken, as you will see from Table 1.1, which sets out the disclosure requirements in Victoria.[51]

It is important to appreciate that being a good law student involves the idea of academic integrity and of the connection between your private life and your professional life. The fact that admission to practice is discretionary ought to make law students cautious in their private lives and in the way they study law and submit assignments. However, the reality is that very few law students understand the significance of these avoidance and disclosure requirements until they are near the end of the law degree. By that time, it's too late to change anything, but the past must still be disclosed.

The 2007 case of *Re OG*[52] is a well-publicised example of what can happen years later if these principles are disregarded:

A barrister (already in practice) who was found to have deliberately misrepresented to the Board of Examiners the circumstances under which he was awarded a zero mark for an assignment at law school (because he had collaborated with another student), was struck off the role of practitioners by the Full Court of the Supreme Court (14 December 2007).

Interestingly, the Victorian Chief Justice circulated the *OG* decision to all law school Deans as soon as it was published. Diagram 1.2 shows how all this theory became important in an unusual Tasmanian case which also involved an allegation of undisclosed collaborative work among law students. Here the point was not that collaboration was inherently bad – indeed, legal practice is usually built around lots of necessary collaboration between lawyers – but that it was kept secret in order to cope with individual assessment requirements.

Together, *Richardson*'s case and *OG* received so much negative comment that they seem to have played a role in introducing mandatory

Table 1.1 Disclosure requirements for admission to practice

Required document	Significance	Source
1 an affidavit of disclosure	This is the primary supporting document for your application. If in your past you have any incidents of breach of the law or other acts which show a lack of good character, they should be disclosed in this affidavit. Disclosure in most cases will support your claim to be honest. Lack of disclosure points to the opposite. There is a long list of other things that should be disclosed (see *Source* opposite), including: • general misconduct (in a workplace, educational institution, volunteer position, club, association) including offensive behaviour, workplace or online bullying, property damage, sexual harassment or racial vilification • making a false statutory declaration • social security overpayment or other social security offences • tax offences • corporate insolvency or penalties. If in doubt, seek advice from the Board of Examiners, your law school ethics lecturer or your PLT ethics teacher, before you swear of affirm your affidavit.	*(Practice Direction No. 2 of 2012* – Disclosure Requirements for Applicants)
2 two affidavits as to character in the form set out in Schedule 9 of the Rules, each made by an acceptable deponent	These affidavits need to be made by a class of persons (see *Source* opposite) not related by blood or marriage and who has known you for 12 months, *or* someone who has taught you at a secondary or tertiary institution for at least 12 months.	*(Notice No. 10 of 2008* – Character Affidavits)
3 a criminal record check	This check is redundant if you have fully disclosed your background, but the Board of Examiners requires a criminal record check in any event, since it is not in a position to know if it can trust you or not.	*(Practice Direction No. 1 of 2008* – Police Record Check)
4 academic conduct reports from each tertiary institution or PLT provider at which the applicant has studied	Law schools *must* report conduct infractions by students to the Board of Examiners. Most commonly, students who have plagiarised, that is, passed off others' written work as if it were their own, during law school assessments – will be reported to the Board.	*(Practice Direction No. 3 of 2009* – Academic Conduct Reports)

Plagiarism

- In *Law Society of Tasmania v Richardson* [2003] TASSC 9, Crawford J considered the impact of a case of academic plagiarism at law school on the fitness of an applicant to be admitted.
- Richardson was a University of Tasmania law school student in 1999 who worked cooperatively with another student on an assignment and submitted a paper that was nearly identical to the other student's. He was charged with plagiarism by the law school but for reasons peculiar to the disciplinary process and the cycle of events, no real penalty was imposed on him, though that failure to impose an effective penalty appears to have been accidental, rather than by design, as far as the law school was concerned.

Discovery

- When Richardson applied for admission, he relied only on an affidavit from his father (a Hobart criminal lawyer), that he was of good fame and character and made no reference to the law school plagiarism proceedings. Crawford J was inclined to the view that the other student had plagiarised Richardson's work (rather than the other way around, as found by the law school), but this was by then immaterial, except as an apparent explanation for the silence of the father as to the disciplinary proceedings and his advice to his son that the plagiarism proceedings did not need to be disclosed.
- Richardson gave evidence that a law school lecturer had advised him that he did not need to disclose his disciplinary history in his admission affidavit, but the lecturer denied this and said that while he could not remember the conversation, he would have said that the proceedings would need to be disclosed, even though the law school could not compel this and the decision was his as to what he should do. [para 51] The applicant's mother, also a lawyer, and one who had assisted her son in the preparation of the relevant assignment, gave evidence that she had been told by the law school head that it was not necessary to disclose the history when applying for admission.
- The Law Society of Tasmania sought an order from the court, after Richardson had been admitted to practice, that he be struck off for failing to disclose his disciplinary history.

Result

- Crawford J refused the order, finding that Richardson knew that he had not plagiarised anything, and had sought advice from his parents and the law school as to what he was obliged to do. Crawford J found that the law school academics might merely have advised him that he would have to decide for himself what to do, 'which he interpreted as meaning that they did not regard him as being under an obligation to do so'. [para 85]
- Crawford J found that at the most, Richardson had made an error of judgment based on the advice of two experienced practitioners who were also his parents and that this did not justify his removal from the roll. The result of this case is that while it is not in all circumstances necessary to disclose a university disciplinary history, not to do so still involves considerable risk. Much seemed to depend on the reliance he placed on his parents for advice on all matters legal. Richardson was an immature and cosseted male who was still, at 22 years of age, helped by his mother to complete assignments.

Diagram 1.2 Disclosure during admission

disclosure by law schools to admitting authorities of adverse academic disciplinary histories, as discussed above.

The only conclusion that anyone could reach after thinking about these cases is that regardless of what you may have done in your past, always disclose that past and never seek to argue that something that was dodgy was not. And even if you do not intend to seek admission in a state or territory that does not require an application to be supported by an affidavit, behave as if you will have to make such an affidavit. A process that requires applicants to disclose all sorts of events and infractions will always lead to over-disclosure, but that is not such a bad outcome if the objective is to demonstrate good character. Good law students far outnumber the not so good, and go on to become the good lawyers who make a difference every day. Chapter 2 discusses how to make that difference, beginning with identifying and choosing a good law firm.

Notes

1. The so-called Priestley 11, named after the judge who chaired the Committee which first determined which compulsory subjects must be taught to and passed by all LLB/JD students. The 11 areas are: Criminal Law and Procedure, Torts, Contracts, Property, Equity (including Trusts), Company Law, Administrative Law, Federal and State Constitutional Law, Civil Procedure, Evidence and Ethics and Professional Responsibility. See, for example, The Council of Legal Education, www.lawadmissions. vic.gov.au/admission_requirements.
2. Ethics (Greek), meaning the study of morals in human conduct (moral philosophy). *The Australian Oxford English Dictionary* (2nd edn), Oxford University Press, Melbourne, 2004, 429.
3. Abbreviation for *Legum Baccalaureus* (Latin). See *The Australian Oxford English Dictionary* (2nd edn), Oxford University Press, Melbourne, 2004, 744.
4. The Australian Qualifications Framework is the national policy for regulated qualifications in Australian education and training. Levels of qualification range from the basic Level 1 to highly advanced, at Level 10. See www.aqf.edu.au.
5. Some students undertake a general studies bachelor's degree and then undertake a specialised law degree. Such programs are available at a number of law schools, including those of the Universities of Melbourne, Western Australia, Monash and RMIT. Many students now combine Law with a degree from another discipline as a 'double degree'.
6. The cost of high-quality law degrees is likely to increase because of increasing reliance on the expensive JD model.
7. The exception is Newcastle Law School in New South Wales, which has for some years been accredited to offer an LLB which integrates a significant level of practical

legal training into its academic subjects. A graduate of this degree is able to seek admission to practice without completing additional PLT studies.

8. Rowman & Allanheld, Totowa NJ, 1983.
9. See Joseph P. Tomain, 'The legal heresiarchs: Luban's *The Good Lawyer*' (1984) 9(3) *American Bar Foundation Review* 693. Tomain admiringly described Luban and his co-authors as heresiarchs ('arch heretics') because they were profoundly dissatisfied with conventional approaches to legal ethics.
10. Aristotle, *Nicomachean Ethics* (trans. W. D. Ross) (e-book edn), University of Adelaide, 2012. See ebooks.adelaide.edu.au/a/aristotle/nicomachean.
11. It is easy to find contemporary laments for legal education and US lawyers, showing that not a lot has changed in that country. See, for example, Eli Wald and Russell G. Pearce, 'Making good lawyers' (2011) 9 *U. St. Thomas L. J.* 403.
12. Tomain, n 9, 694.
13. Many have cited Lincoln's famous quote. Here it is: 'One morning, not long before Lincoln's nomination – a year perhaps – I was in your office and heard the following! Mr. Lincoln, seated at the baize-covered table in the center of the office, listened attentively to a man who talked earnestly and in a low tone. After being thus engaged for some time Lincoln at length broke in, and I shall never forget his reply. 'Yes,' he said, 'we can doubtless gain your case for you; we can set a whole neighborhood at loggerheads; we can distress a widowed mother and her six fatherless children and thereby get for you six hundred dollars to which you seem to have a legal claim, but which rightfully belongs, it appears to me, as much to the woman and her children as it does to you. You must remember that some things legally right are not morally right. We shall not take your case, but will give you a little advice for which we will charge you nothing. You seem to be a sprightly, energetic man; we would advise you to try your hand at making six hundred dollars in some other way.' Undated manuscript, about 1866, in William H. Herndon and Jesse W. Weik, *The Project Gutenberg EBook of Abraham Lincoln*, Volume 2 at www.gutenberg.org/files/38484/38484.txt.
14. Christine Parker, 'A critical morality for lawyers: Four approaches to lawyers' ethics' (2004) 30 *Monash Law Review* 49.
15. See, especially, Daniel Markovits, *A Modern Legal Ethics: Adversary advocacy in a democratic age*, Princeton University Press, New Jersey, 2008.
16. See, generally, Gino Dal Pont, *Lawyers' Professional Responsibility* (5th edn), Thomson-Reuters, Sydney, 2013, Part 4. For a dramatic and informative television series that charts the key English development of 'innocent until proven guilty' in early criminal trial practice, see *Garrow's Law*, inspired by the life of pioneering 18th century barrister William Garrow: *Garrow's Law*, BBC One at www.bbc.co.uk/programmes/b00w5c2w.
17. See *Australian Solicitors' Conduct Rules* 2011 (ASCR), Law Council of Australia. See www.lawcouncil.asn.au/lawcouncil/index.php/divisions/national-profession-project/australian-solicitors-conduct-rules. These rules are likely to be adopted with minor modifications as a part of the regulatory framework provided by the Legal Profession *Uniform Law*. See Ch. 9.3.
18. See www.australianuniversities.com.au/.
19. In 2012, these law schools were 1 University of Melbourne, 2 University of Sydney, 3 Australian National University, 4 University of New South Wales, 5 Monash

University, 6 University of Queensland, 7 University of Western Australia, 8 University of Adelaide, 9 Macquarie University, 10 Griffith University, 11 Queensland University of Technology and 12 University of Technology Sydney. See www.australianuniversities.com.au/ratings/law-school-rankings.
20. The current Australian bias of law school ranking towards research productivity and reputation is understandable. Law schools currently receive only modest federal government funding per law student enrolled in an LLB. They can charge significant fees for places in their JD degrees (and underwrite the cost of delivering an LLB), but only if their overall reputation is such that JD students wish to come. Reputation is measured according to the international criteria of research productivity, not teaching quality.
21. See, generally, Jeremy Bentham, *A Fragment on Government; or, A Comment on the Commentaries* (2nd edn), W. Pickering, 1823; John Austin, *The Province of Jurisprudence Determined and the Uses of the Study of Jurisprudence*, Weidenfeld & Nicholson, 1954; H. L. A. Hart, *The Concept of Law*, Clarendon Press, 1961; Joseph Raz, *The Authority of Law*, Oxford University Press, 1979.
22. See generally, Ronald Dworkin, *Taking Rights Seriously*, Duckworth, 1978 and *A Matter of Principle*, Harvard University Press, 1985; Richard A. Posner, *The Economic Analysis of Law* (2nd edn), Little, Brown and Co., 1977; John Rawls, *A Theory of Justice*, Oxford University Press, 1973; Roberto Unger, 'The Critical Legal Studies Movement' (1983) 96 *Harvard Law Review* 561; John Finnis, *Natural Law and Natural Rights*, Oxford University Press, New York, 1980. A very useful overview of the whole debate about the proper role of law ('jurisprudence') is contained in Raymond Wacks, *The Philosophy of Law: A very short introduction*, Oxford University Press, New York, 2006.
23. Jane Lee, 'Graduates shun legal profession', *The Sunday Age*, 20 May 2012, 6.
24. The Threshold Learning Outcomes for Law (TLOs) are a best practice statement for Australian law schools. They contain a number of detailed statements about how law students should learn and be assessed. They are normative in tone and intent. TLO2(a) is particularly strong as a legitimising statement for normative approaches and rejection of purely rote learning of lawyers' professional conduct rules: 'Graduates of the Bachelor of Laws will demonstrate . . . an understanding of approaches to ethical decision-making.' See the Learning and Teaching Academic Standards Project, Bachelor of Laws, *Learning and Teaching Academic Standards Statement*, December 2010, Office of Learning and Teaching, www.olt.gov.au and Chapter 3.
25. See www.olt.gov.au/project-strengthening-australian-legal-ed-clinical-experiences-monash-2010. See also Lori M. Graham, 'Aristotle's ethics and the virtuous lawyer: Part One of a study on legal ethics and clinical legal education' (1995–96) 20 *Journal of the Legal Profession* 5; Maksymilian Del Mar, 'At the lectern: Moral education in law schools and law firms' (2009) 59 *J. Legal Educ.* 299, which discusses a series of exercises in which law teachers, practitioners and students participated and notes that the participants 'discussed the limitations of text-based teaching in legal education' and the need for a more deliberate moral pedagogy in law schools, one that goes beyond reproducing the ordinary professional environment – as in clinical legal education.

30 The Good Lawyer

26. See William M. Sullivan et al., *Educating Lawyers: Preparation for the profession of law*, John Wiley & Sons, Inc., San Francisco, 2007 (hereafter The Carnegie Report).

27. The debate centres on the notion of a 'thick' as opposed to a 'thin' concept of the rule of law. See, for example, Adrian Evans and Michael King, 'Reflections on the connection of virtue ethics to therapeutic jurisprudence' (2012) 35(3) *UNSW L. J.* 717, at 727.

28. If rule of law debates are taught in law school in a manner that trivialises or devalues the contribution of ethics to lawyers' decision making, that can have a negative impact on students' subsequent views about the relevance of legal ethics.

29. Most law teachers teach only 1 or 2 of the Priestley 11 areas and (realistically) specialise in only 1 or 2 elective areas. Law school staffing pressures mean that in any one year, the available teachers will rarely match up perfectly with students' preference for particular electives. As a consequence, many electives tend to be offered once every 2 years.

30. For example, corporate social responsibility, taxation policy, climate change and sustainable development law, environmental law and not-for-profit corporate entities.

31. Beaton Research and Consulting and beyondblue, Annual Professions Survey 2007, at www.beatonglobal.com/pdfs/Depression_in_the_professions_survey.pdf.

32. Larcombe, Malkin and Nicholson report that Australian law students have high or very high levels of distress (35.4%), compared to medical students (17.8%) and the general population (13.3%) in the 18–35 age group. See Wendy Larcombe, Ian Malkin and Pip Nicholson, 'Law students' motivations, expectations and levels of psychological distress: Evidence of connections' (2012) 22(1&2) *Legal Education Review* 70.

33. This is not just an issue for students. Among law teachers, the prestige associated with being appointed to a large law firm consultancy is considerable.

34. This guesstimate comes from a very informal comment by the Council of Legal Education, for Victoria alone (email of 17 June 2013 on file with author). There is no verified national data on the number of graduates who have jobs at the time they leave law school, but there were 6890 Australian law students set to graduate in 2012. See Lee, n 23.

35. The testamur (Latin *testari* for 'we testify' or 'certify') certifies your proficiency as a graduate. It is commonly printed on thick paper in an ornate font and given to graduates at graduation ceremonies.

36. See Melanie Poole, 'The making of professional vandals: How law schools degrade the self' (2011) Legal Scholarship Network, SSRN abstract #2029993. See ssrn.com/abstract=2029993.

37. Ibid., 56.

38. See, generally, Larcombe, Malkin and Nicholson, n 32.

39. Poole, n 36, 19.

40. See Larcombe, Malkin and Nicholson, n 32, 72–73.

41. Wendy Larcombe, Letty Tumbaga, Ian Malkin, Pip Nicholson and Orania Tokatlidis, 'Does an improved experience of law school protect students against depression, anxiety and stress? An empirical study of wellbeing and the law school experience of LLB and JD students', *Melbourne Legal Studies Research Paper*

Good legal education 31

No. 603, 30. See ssrn.com/abstract=2147547. Larcombe reports that the key issues of distress were 'assessment anxiety, lecturers' lack of understanding, an exclusive law school culture and course inflexibility (JD)' (at 31).

42. Ibid., 30–31.
43. Ibid.
44. Resilience is best understood as the ability to recover quickly from setbacks.
45. So far, Newcastle law school is the only one which combines academic knowledge and clinical experience throughout their law degree.
46. Ethics and Professional Responsibility must be taught by an approved PLT Provider. See, for example, *Legal Profession (Admission) Rules 2008* (Vic), Rule 3.09(1)(c).
47. See n 33.
48. A Graduate Careers Council survey of 1300 recent law graduates showed that 64% were not practising between 2010 and 2011. As there were 6890 Australian law students due to graduate in 2012, that percentage, if repeated, would mean over 4000 would not immediately work as lawyers. See Lee, n 23.
49. Character is also impacted upon by mental health. An applicant for admission whose mental health has been compromised in the past will need to show that they are mentally well in order to be admitted. See Mary-Jane Ierodiaconou and Roberta Foster, 'Telling admissions: Disclosing mental illness among lawyers' (2013) 87(1/2) *LIJ* 32, at 35.
50. *Frugtniet v Board of Examiners* [2002] VSC 140, per Pagone J. This quote from his Honour's judgment in *Frugtniet* is accepted by the Law Admissions Consultative Committee (LACC) as the reason behind the testing of character prior to admission. See *Law Admissions Consultative Committee, Disclosure Guidelines For Applicants For Admission To The Legal Profession*, Practice Direction No. 2 of 2012.
51. The Board of Examiners (Vic) is effectively a division of the Supreme Court and administers the admission process for the Court. Similar organisations perform this role in other jurisdictions. The documentary requirements in Victoria are available at www.lawadmissions.vic.gov.au/admission_requirements. It is necessary for a candidate to satisfy the Board of Examiners that he/she is a fit and proper person to be admitted to practice (s 2.3.10 of the former *Legal Profession Act 2004* (Vic)).
52. *Re OG, a lawyer* [2007] VSC 520.

Chapter 2

THE LAW PRACTICE LANDSCAPE: CHOOSING TO BE A 'GOOD' LAWYER IN A GOOD LAW FIRM

2.1 The connection between good lawyering and good legal communities

Good lawyers need a credible, practical framework to be good *in*, so to speak. So where you practise law and who you practise it with are important in supporting your good lawyering. Even barristers, who are comfortable working alone and who are independent in the sense that they have no employer except themselves, are commonly co-located in 'chambers' for a reason: so that they can seek support when they need it. Lawyers' reputations matter because there is a fundamental two-way connection between being a good lawyer and being in a good (that is, morally sustainable) legal practice. This reality is supported by a small but comprehensive pilot study of 11 new Australian lawyers in the ACT, which emphasises that first-year lawyers learn what is expected of them as professionals, for good or otherwise, from the legal community in which they are first operating.[1]

The sum total of how you see your role as a lawyer will define you as you advance through the law. This is where you begin to develop your reputation: the hard-to-pin-down mix of what others think of your knowledge and skills, your trustworthiness, your willingness to prepare thoroughly and your sense of appropriate ethical behaviour. Notice that this list begins but does not stop with your intelligence. High IQ will not be enough to mark your professionalism or determine your success, because they depend on the harder things – the virtues (trust, diligence and judgment) – which must be demonstrated just as convincingly as your intelligence.

So the environment where you start being a lawyer needs to be ethically healthy: it should provide good role models or mentors, help you manage your stress, encourage clear thinking about ethics and carefully expose you to the wider realities of professionalism. This chapter addresses the ethical challenges posed by different types of legal practice and law firms in an Australian setting. The case studies, practice lists and questions are there to emphasise that you can decide to choose a healthy legal ethical community, where you are most likely to find a nurturing, meaningful future as a legal practitioner.

The difficulty with identifying the good environments to work in is that while they are far more numerous than dodgy workplaces when assessed across the profession as a whole, there is not any easy way to distinguish them from the others. The contents of law firm websites and marketing campaigns are unhelpful because they focus on attracting clients, not lawyers. There is a buyers' market for legal talent and that will continue as long as student entry into law schools keeps growing and is uncapped. And firm websites invariably emphasise '24/7' availability to clients rather than the fact that their clients are likely to receive more considered, value-adding comprehensive service from lawyers who are happy, engaged and have a life away from the office; in short, from lawyers who feel they have a meaningful future ahead of them. So while knowing which particular firm could be good to work for and with is not easy, we do know a fair bit about what issues to consider in avoiding the not-so-good lawyers, law firms and corporate employers. Even these have something to teach us. In the following cases (Table 2.1), some consistent themes show what to be wary of.

2.2 Common themes in major examples of poor lawyering

Table 2.1 Themes in poor lawyering

Case, incident or research report	Themes of the ethical danger zone
1. The creative tax lawyer	
Jenkens and Gilchrist (J&G) was a mid-tier firm in Chicago that grew very rapidly after an incoming partner, Paul Daugerdas, was allowed to quickly build up an extremely large tax haven practice. That practice failed spectacularly after the basis of the build-up was undermined by US Internal Revenue Service (IRS) investigations, leading to the collapse of the firm in 2007.	What is the dominant culture of the firm?

34 The Good Lawyer

Table 2.1 (cont.)

Case, incident or research report	Themes of the ethical danger zone
J&G took on Daugerdas in the late 1990s after he promised the then partners an additional $5 million per annum in profit from his tax shelter practices. This was not a huge sum, but was enough to get him a partnership. He insisted on, and the firm agreed to, a remuneration deal where he was entitled to a set percentage of the profit he brought in to the practice, contrary to the normal practice, whereby all partners equally shared the profit of all practice areas.	Over-attraction of partners to law firm profit.
Despite this warning sign, the firm went ahead with the arrangement. Daugerdas' *modus operandi* was to prepare and market tax sign-offs or 'rulings' on certain tax shelter schemes to investors who required such rulings if the schemes were to be considered IRS-compliant. IRS compliance meant that if the scheme in question was later ruled to be non-compliant, the earlier taxes would still need to be paid by the client, but there would be no tax penalties. His rulings became highly sought-after by numerous clients of the major accountancy firms and J&G revenue received quickly climbed to over $80 million per annum, a sum far in excess of Daugerdas' initial projections. When the schemes were declared illegal by the IRS, a group of investors began a class action against the firm and the Justice Department commenced a prosecution of J&G for tax evasion.	Importance of the values and culture of the firm's leaders in deciding the behaviour of the whole firm.
The J&G partner who had almost solely objected to the arrival of Daugerdas was, at the end of the day, finally responsible for negotiating the closure of the firm in 2007, in return for an end to the prosecutions. The profession responded to the collapse, not with a sense of recognition of cultural or systemic culpability, but with the comment '[they were] a rogue firm'.[2]	Incapacity of the firm or the wider profession to do more than assert that the tax lawyer alone was responsible for the moral failure.

2. The vanished documents

In early 2002 Rolah McCabe, a terminally ill victim of lung cancer, sued British American Tobacco Australia Services (BATAS), alleging that her cancer was a result of her childhood addiction to nicotine acquired from smoking and that BATAS was responsible because it had known of the toxic and addictive qualities of tobacco at the time they were marketing their cigarettes to her as a child.	What was the dominant motive of the client corporation?
Mrs McCabe succeeded in persuading Justice Geoffrey Eames that the defendant, knowing that litigation by someone addicted to nicotine and suffering from lung cancer was imminent, had destroyed its own historical documents; documents which presumably showed that it knew of the toxicity of nicotine at the time of its cigarette marketing.[3] BATAS' defence was struck out by Justice Eames on the basis that a fair trial had been denied to the plaintiff when the defendant (having destroyed its records) failed to provide sufficient discovery.	What was the dominant culture of the law firm?
Eames J also decided that BATAS was assisted by its lawyers, Clayton Utz, in developing a 'document retention policy' which was in fact designed to systematically destroy incriminating documents, noting that they had 'advised Wills [BATAS] on the wording of the policy, [ensuring] that words were inserted into the written policy document to which reference could be made in order to assert innocent intention and to disguise the true purpose of the policy'.[4]	Importance of the values and culture of the firm's leaders in guiding the behaviour of the whole firm.
In December 2002, the Victorian Court of Appeal comprehensively reversed the judgment of Justice Eames and exonerated Clayton Utz,[5] asserting that destroying documents was not unlawful unless it amounted to an attempt to pervert the course of justice or was a contempt of court. The appeal court effectively affirmed Clayton Utz's behaviour, but ... public distrust of the profession was again boosted when *The Age* published a critical commentary on the appeal court decision and its implications for document destruction ...[6]	Initial reluctance of the firm to do more than assert that the individual lawyers were responsible for the moral failure.

In July 2003 ... [i]n an affidavit, a former executive of BATAS asserted that it was in fact the company's practice to destroy documents that might have been embarrassing.[7] Clayton Utz responded by asserting that the NSW and Victorian regulators had withdrawn investigations into any alleged wrongdoing by the firm in relation to the 'document retention policy'.[8] In October 2006, an internal draft report by Clayton Utz

2 The law practice landscape　　**35**

Table 2.1 (cont.)

Case, incident or research report	Themes of the ethical danger zone
on its own behaviour was leaked to the press by another former partner and appeared to confirm, despite the firm's own previous denials, that a small number of its partners and staff were involved in deceiving the Supreme Court.[9] Subsequently, all those involved left the firm.[10]	

3. Recent Australian research

Lillian Corbin investigated the attitudes of 16 Australian practitioners, who were asked about their perceptions of professionalism,[11] that is, about their adherence to ethical practices.[12] These Queenslanders were divided into two groups of eight; half had been in practice for two years and half for more than 15 years.[13] Semi-structured interviews were conducted to ascertain if [they] broadly agreed with the ethical culture of the firm, or not.	Importance of the values and culture of the firm's leaders in guiding the behaviour of the whole firm.
The older group tended to consider their firm's professionalism to be satisfactory (since they tended to determine those policies themselves[14]), while those who had been more recently admitted to practice were not comfortable because they were 'experiencing dissonance . . . [believing that their firms were] pressuring them to "fit in" by following . . . prescribed policies and procedures'.[15]	Firm leaders, who are commonly older than their employee lawyers, favour 'commercialised professionalism'.
The older group promoted a 'commercialized professionalism' culture (that is, expert service designed to enhance peer perceptions) while the younger lawyers were more interested in traditional professionalism, with elements of altruism and public service strongly represented.[16] The recent graduates felt tension because 'their understanding of professionalism [was] being undermined by the "firm" view to which they are being required to conform.[17]	

4. The Reserve Bank of Australia

Two Reserve Bank of Australia (RBA) subsidiaries – Securency and Note Printing Australia (NPA) – were required by the RBA to obtain contracts to print plastic polymer bank notes for other countries. Brian Hood was the Company Secretary of NPA. He discovered over some years that NPA had been paying bribes disguised as commissions to foreign sales agents who were well connected to governments, in order to obtain the plastic note printing contracts.	What was the dominant motive of the client corporation?
Hood shared his concerns verbally in 2007 with various senior RBA executives, including its in-house lawyer, and then wrote a memo setting out a number of warnings of likely corruption, which included this description:	Could the in-house lawyer afford to behave independently of the client corporation?
The rates of commission agreed to be paid have at times, without substantiation, greatly exceeded what I understand to be industry averages, and do not seem to me to be commensurate with the effort expended by the agent to secure the order. They also seem to me to be inconsistent with the returns made by NPA on the relevant export contracts. For instance, the Indonesian agent was paid a commission of AUD$7.4m, and the Malaysian agent was paid at rates of 17% (AUD$2.2m), and 10% (AUD$950,000) a year later, on a top-up order.[18]	
Nothing of substance occurred in response, so in 2008, Hood sent an email to an NPA executive asking for his concerns to be acted upon. *The Age* reported that Hood was told 'his position had become "untenable" and [he was] offered . . . a redundancy which he accepted'.[19] The RBA did not call in the Australian Federal Police until two years later, in 2009, when *The Age* printed the first story about the bribery.	If you were the RBA in-house lawyer, what would you have advised the RBA to do?

2.3 Failures of lawyers' regulation, not just of lawyers' character

The cases and situations mentioned above are just some of those that have laid down a broad trail of breadcrumbs for the good lawyer to avoid, though that should not be hard for anyone who reads the literature. Writers and researchers are inclined to describe the dominant lawyer pathology set out above as terminal for both lawyers' professionalism and their social utility (for example, see Anthony Kronman's *The Lost Lawyer*[20]), but this is a simplification. There are structural faults at work here that go beyond individuals' bad lawyering.

While there is plenty of disciplinary prosecution of sole practitioners and small-law firm misbehaviour, there is little discipline of those involved in the large corporate scandals.[21] For example, there has been a complete lack of any prosecutions or disciplinary proceedings against *any* professionals in respect of the failure of the global financial system in 2007–08. That near collapse was triggered in no small way by the 'packaging' of US housing doubtful debts as worthwhile marketable securities by certain capital markets lawyers.[22]

The prosecution imbalance is a condemnation of the structure of Australian lawyers' regulation, which requires a directly affected client victim to make a complaint to a regulator, something which the mainly corporate clients of large law firms are reluctant to do.[23] Legal regulators are unenthusiastic about tackling large law firms' bad behaviour because it is hard to gather the evidence in the absence of that client complaint. When public interest complaints are received from non-clients, there is still the problem that these complainants are outsiders and generally lack direct evidence. Real improvement would depend upon legal regulators acquiring the power to coercively investigate a suspicion even if no formal complaint had been received and no witnesses were willing to give evidence.

There are informed US critics who say that corporate regulators prefer, out of laziness, to target corporations' bad behaviour with civil penalties alone and either ignore or 'let off' the individual directors, managers and in-house counsel concerned with a slap on the wrist.[24] That criticism has not been made of legal regulators, but that might only be due to the lack of enforcement, civil or criminal, in relation to the misbehaviour of large law firms.

Of course, many lawyers and law associations would be concerned to block such structural reform for self-interested reasons, but that is not the whole story. They would also assert, very reasonably, that coercive investigation of lawyers is a direct assault on the rule of law. And it is unlikely that the wider community would support coercive investigative power, including wire-tap capacity for legal regulators, unless it were very clear and publicly accepted that failure to prosecute corporate or securities lawyers was and is linked conclusively to major social instability. Evidence of that link is tenuous, with negative public attention focused on financiers rather than lawyers. So it is far less likely that there will be any public clamour for legal regulators to become more assertive even if, in the meantime, the moral worthiness of some powerful individual lawyers continues to be suspect.

Disciplinary enforcement of legal professional responsibility will probably remain a marginal operation affecting (for the most part) the smaller law firms and lawyers. So some other strategy is necessary if the public interest in 'good' lawyering is to be supported. Better and pre-emptive ethics education emerges as central to change and social growth. Moral regeneration, clichéd and naïve as it sounds to many, may nevertheless be important in that education. Ethics education raises awareness of the high stakes for society when lawyers are not trusted and offers a path, though admittedly a difficult and narrow one, to individual lawyers – one that provides a useful moral template for practising law responsibly.

Chapter 3 explores the ethical knowledge and courage needed on that path. But first, it will help to understand more of the specific ethical opportunities and challenges faced by particular types of legal practice. The following table (Table 2.2) has three columns: column 1 categorises lawyers according to their general area of work and in column 2 these are divided up according to the ethical opportunities and challenges associated with each area. Opportunities represent your chance to be and do good. The challenges are just that: they are present some or all of the time and must be faced up to. Column 3 contains a number of boxes which categorise the practice type associated with Column 1 lawyers.

The best way to use this table is to select what type of lawyer and what type of practice you see yourself connecting to. Then consider the associated opportunities and challenges. Ask yourself: 'What area of law and type of practice will best enable me to be a good lawyer?'

2.4 The ethical environment in different areas of law and types of legal practice

Table 2.2 Ethical challenges and opportunities faced by different types of legal practice

Broad descriptions of lawyers' work[25]	Ethical opportunities and challenges – the pros and cons	Organisational categories and types of legal practice

Criminal defence solicitors
 	
See Ch. 4
	• You will concentrate on defences and pleas of 'guilty' in local and County/District courts, rarely in Supreme courts.
	• You will have a heroic role and do much to safeguard the *Rule of Law*.
	• You must withstand client pressure to bend truth and hide guilt.
	• You will need to navigate detailed advocacy rules about permissible deception, for example:
	  • the rule that allows a solicitor to be silent if another party or witness makes a misleading statement (ASCR[26] 19.3)
	  • making excessive attacks on witnesses' credibility
	  • should you disclose to the court a mistaken omission by a prosecutor to raise details of your client's prior convictions?
	• You will need to deal with prosecutor pressure on your client to plead guilty to lesser charges to avoid trial on more serious matters, where defence will be difficult but not impossible.
	• The reducing availability of legal aid means less time and capacity to prepare thoroughly.
	• On occasion, you will be doubtful as to the legality of sources of funds which clients intend to use to pay your legal fees.
	• You will need to guard against risks to your independence arising from too close an association with some clients, leading to compromising substance abuse and eventual personal criminality (for example, Andrew Fraser[27]).
		sole practitioner, suburban and rural practices – SMALL

Family lawyers See Ch. 7 See Ch. 8	• You are caring, often compassionate, but also personally determined by nature; family lawyers need to find a small team of supportive colleagues to work with. • You will need high-level emotional intelligence and resilience in order to deliver your best work; this is highly satisfying for an appropriate personality motivated by compassion and a love of justice. • You must withstand client pressure to 'hide' assets, to be aggressive and to delay settlement as a punitive strategy in dealing with their estranged partners. • Client pressure to 'sue the bastard' immediately can be difficult to moderate and divert into appropriate alternative dispute resolution. • Your clients have limited appreciation of the time needed to prepare a case and, due to their understandable stress, can project their grief, anger and frustration onto you in complaints about delays and overcharging. • You must be verbally clear and confirm in writing the level of your likely fees, in advance of commencing any work. • You will need to deal with pressure to reduce fees where your clients are impoverished.	regional and larger regional firms – CUSP

2 The law practice landscape   39

Table 2.2 (cont.)

Broad descriptions of lawyers' work[25]	Ethical opportunities and challenges – the pros and cons
See Ch. 5	• Threats of violence are sometimes received from ex-partners of clients or made by clients against the lives of the other party or their own lawyer. Very occasionally, these threats are acted upon. You will have to consider if such threats should be reported.
General practitioners (GPs – in conveyancing, minor crime, civil debt, family law, minor civil litigation, wills and estates, miscellaneous)	• GP lawyers are often highly experienced, wise and well respected. ← sole practitioners – to regional and larger regional firms • As a conscientious GP, you can develop a wide and deep knowledge of your clients as individuals and make a major contribution to their success and welfare, but your own financial future may be stronger as a GP if you work in a regional centre or rural area. • Fees received in suburban general practice can be just adequate to cover your costs of practice, with capacity to make modest income. • In rural and regional areas, the economics of legal practice tend to be better than in small urban practices and significantly higher incomes are possible. • The economics of urban practice mean that GPs do best in work areas where there is limited competition and longstanding reputations are intact, but this can lead to conflicts of interest arising from pressure to act for both sides in some property and commercial transactions. (See Ch. 7) • Relative isolation, fewer support staff and bank overdraft pressures mean that corners can be cut in client care and communication and in staying up to date with the law. Depression is therefore increasingly a problem.[28] • More disciplinary prosecutions occur in this area than for other categories of lawyer, for a range of offences surrounding misappropriation of clients' funds (the client trust account challenge), overcharging, delay and 'gross negligence' leading to client financial loss. ↖↙ sole practitioners and members of other firms
Mediators and collaborative lawyers[29]	• They are most common in family law but increasingly in commercial practice as well. • Mediating lawyers achieve great satisfaction in helping people resolve disputes and in some cases, preserve relationships. • You can also limit harm and lower costs to your clients in civil claims, thereby increasing individuals' access to justice. • In resolving individual disputes confidentially and therefore without creating a precedent, your efforts at mediation will in some cases avoid confronting larger issues of injustice with publicity ('justice must be seen to be done, as well as done'). • You will encounter some tension with civil litigation specialists as to the point at which mediation has failed and litigation should begin.

40 The Good Lawyer

Table 2.2 (cont.)

Broad descriptions of lawyers' work[25]	Ethical opportunities and challenges – the pros and cons
Civil litigators; commercial and corporate/ transactional lawyers; mega-corporate 'enablers' See Ch. 3	• You will 'add' ethical value to a transaction or case, in the sense that your real expertise is in your ability to provide truly independent, strategic, ethical judgment,[30] so that a business plan that is financially and environmentally sustainable is advised, rather than any less stable or shorter-term plan. • There is opportunity for real character development for you, as a contribution to value-adding judgment. • You can adopt an Incorporated Legal Practice (ILP) model to entrench better ethics in your firm.[31] • 'Ethical infrastructure' – the collection of informal policies and formal guidelines that determine how a law firm behaves in ethically difficult situations – is a part of the ILP environment and will guide better practice: • ILP 'solicitor-directors', alongside all law firm principals, become personally responsible for the behaviour of other solicitors.[32] • The rapid growth of international and particularly Indian legal process outsourcing (LPO), assisted by artificial intelligence ('sausage-machine law') will contribute to some role redundancy for traditionally oriented transactional lawyers in large firms.[33] This means fewer jobs for lawyers who are just technically competent. • LPO pressures will encourage more firms to greater specialisation, so that they are less vulnerable to foreign LPO providers taking their work. This trend means you may need to be clearer about your own specialisation and have some relevant voluntary or clinical experience before you apply for a job. However, if you specialise too early, you may be less flexible in your longer term career. You can manage these risks in law school by undertaking both a general clinic and then a specialised clinic, before you graduate. • You can expect an increased use of psychological profiling before a job offer to you as a new employee lawyer is confirmed. The profile typically desired is one of 'conscientious' work habits, politically conservative or centrist values, and a psychological openness to being 'moulded' by firm culture. • Despite such profiling, you will also need to show psychological balance, so that you do not fit the profile of the so-called typical person attracted to law, who has 'high IQ', but 'low accessing EQ'.[34] • You will need to be aware of an apparent priority of business profit over ethical behaviour, where the two are in conflict. NSW Chief Justice Bathurst has said: 'Young lawyers have little or no interaction with clients. They are motivated to bill as much as possible in the interests of career advancement. This conflicts with their professional duties to act honestly and efficiently ... Their duties as lawyers are superceded by personal gain.' He added that firms who rely on the billable hour for commercial reasons may end up paying a higher price in the end. '[Young lawyers] will avoid firms that are governed

An ILP has the same status as an ordinary company and is subject to 'ethics audits' by regulators

See Ch. 4

mid-tier firms – LARGER 2nd tier firms – LARGE

1st tier national firms – LARGE

transnational firms – VERY LARGE

2 The law practice landscape   41

Table 2.2 (cont.)

Broad descriptions of lawyers' work[25]	Ethical opportunities and challenges – the pros and cons

by the billable hour. They won't stay long, so it's not a [good] commercial strategy in the end ... The courts now attract the brightest graduates, and the one thing they have in common is a desire to avoid the mega firms. It is a problem, and one thing that these firms are going to have to confront [lest they] end up with mindless drones adding six minutes here and there, to the general dissatisfaction of clients.'[35]

- Be aware that lawyers can experience reduced independence because of their identification with their large clients' causes, plans and strategies,[36] or more independence if they are respected for their willingness to question the wisdom of some plans and strategies.

- You will likely be inside a firm that faces pressure to act for corporations with legal, but morally compromised businesses (for example, tobacco, alcohol and arms manufacturers, gaming operators).[37]

6 minute time intervals are used because they equate to 0.1 of 1 hour and are easily managed by digital time tracking systems

- Working days of 8–9am to 7–8pm will be common (though not universal), leading to resentment, life–work tension, relationship stress at home and an attitude that 'others should also work hard if I have to'.

- You will face 'budget' pressure to bill a minimum fee level every month – regardless of whether the firm uses 6 minute timesheet intervals or versions of fixed price to measure value and therefore the size of the client's bill.

global firms – ULTRA LARGE

- There continues to be pressure to 'round up' hours on timesheets (that is, to overcharge clients) to achieve budget targets.[38]

- You will need courage to confront work cultures inside some larger firms that rationalise poor (unethical) behaviour so that it is normalised and becomes acceptable.[39]

Large law firms present special challenges – see Ch. 4

- New lawyers in larger firms can face repetitive work in their early months, leading to boredom and hyper-competitiveness to escape such work by billing more.

- Recommendations: if you know you prefer a commercial or corporate legal practice environment:

  - First seek out the 2nd or mid-tier and niche firms and assess their capacity to deliver a balanced, 'good' life.
  - Prioritise your conscience, because that draws on your character.
  - Consider using the list of questions at 2.5 (below) in order to identify the right firm for you.
  - Take a longer view, so that if the first firm you work for is not the best fit, be prepared to move after 18 months to 2 years.
  - Unless you are absolutely desperate, try not to move earlier than this, because doing so will not allow you to make a balanced assessment of the first firm's strengths and weaknesses and you may get a reputation for being too precious.

42 The Good Lawyer

Table 2.2 (cont.)

Broad descriptions of lawyers' work[25]	Ethical opportunities and challenges – the pros and cons	
	• You may need to move firms 2 or 3 times as your experience grows and you get better at working out which of your key character attributes and values are shared by the firm.	
Corporate/in-house counsel **See Ch. 5**	• With less pressure to work ultra-long hours, you will have more time to assess and consider the nature of your work, and better life–work balance. • This offers you the capacity and opportunity to ethically guide your employer on a safe course of conduct.[40] • However, you may experience a lack of independence from your employer/client[41] – especially in respect to lawyer–client privilege. • You will have no other client, no other income source and little collegiality in a small legal department and will therefore encounter pressure to do what your corporation requires, regardless of morality.[42]	Corporations MEDIUM to ULTRA LARGE

Government lawyers (including parliamentary counsel)	• You will have a relatively stable if lower-paid career compared to some commercial law peers, but over time you will have the chance to mould good law making and will often be able to achieve a better life–work balance than peers in private practice.
	 • You will occasionally face powerful pressure to do what government requires, regardless of morality. For example, consider these extreme historical cases:
	   • the German government lawyers who set up the legal structure behind the Nazi Nuremberg Laws[43]; and
	   • the US lawyers who authored the Pentagon 'Torture Memos'.[44]
		Govts and agencies of govts

Prosecutors and case-managing (instructing) solicitors **See Ch. 4**	• You will be trusted to prosecute crime and seek justice on behalf of the people and in so doing, strengthen society. • You are not supposed to be too zealous because the state (or state authority) which you represent is generally more powerful than a defendant, but you will often feel an emotional pressure to aggressively 'go for the jugular' in the interests of victims; such pressure must be tempered according to advocacy rules that mandate a fair presentation of the case for the prosecution.[45] • You must balance the discretion not to prosecute someone by weighing up competing public interests: that is, by balancing the likely prospects of a successful prosecution (in the interests of individual victims or government revenue) against the substantial cost of mounting a case which fails to prove a sufficient offence. • You will also have to manage a sub-category of discretion to negotiate 'deals' with defendants for 'guilty' pleas to lesser charges and consider what victims will think of such deals.	

2 The law practice landscape 43

Table 2.2 (cont.)

Broad descriptions of lawyers' work[25]	Ethical opportunities and challenges – the pros and cons
Community lawyers	• As a community lawyer working in a community legal centre (CLC) you will be paid modestly but can salary package very effectively. • You will have quite a lot of autonomy in your everyday work and, because you do not need to bill your clients, will be able to choose cases and clients that interest you as well as those that have some potential to influence the course of the law. • Most importantly, you will be able to represent clients who have no one else to stand up for them, since their cases will often be unattractive to private lawyers. • If you are a government legal aid lawyer (for example, working for a legal aid commission), your salary will often be higher, but you may have less autonomy than a CLC lawyer and be required to handle the same types of cases over a long period. • Whether in community or government employment, you will on occasion have an opportunity to work for law reform and perhaps in community (legal) development (CD), as well as casework. As a CD lawyer, you will creatively facilitate legal and social reform – not through your own direct advocacy for change, but by identifying a group of individuals (the 'community') who have a similar socio-legal problem and helping them develop their own capacity to advocate for change. CD is perhaps the most powerful tool of legal reform because it organises the community to act for itself. The ability of community lawyers to act in 'CD mode' is very attractive to many new law graduates. • Community lawyers working in CLCs are subject to increasing political control as government legal aid boards and attorneys' general seek to confine CLCs to more casework and less law reform and CD. As a CLC lawyer, you will need determination, resilience and a clear sense of 'mission' to be effective in this environment. • CLCs and legal aid commissions have on occasion sought relaxation of conflict of interest rules so that they can act, for example, for both a husband and wife in a family dispute and seek to resolve their problems in a 'one stop shop' approach. Although these attempts are usually motivated by a desire to reduce stress and increase convenience for such clients, they are misguided.
NGO lawyers	• Non-government organisations (NGOs) are essentially lobby groups for all manner of special interests: for example, overseas aid providers, political parties, law foundations, health-related charities and conservation–environment groups. Many NGOs operate overseas and play critical roles in global sustainable development. But some are formed to frustrate good objectives and advocate for selfish interests.

Community legal centre and govt legal aid lawyers

See Ch. 7

Nominally independent

44   The Good Lawyer

Table 2.2 (cont.)

Broad descriptions of lawyers' work[25]	Ethical opportunities and challenges – the pros and cons
	• NGO lawyers play vital CD roles within the sectors relevant to their organisation, are often in the media spotlight, achieve significant justice gains and develop powerful reputations in civil society. Many 'successful' NGO lawyers go on to more conventional careers in higher paid jobs, on the strength of their experience and notoriety gained in their NGO roles. • Your role as an NGO lawyer is likely to be intensely stimulating, functionally autonomous, progressively influential, always too demanding on your time and energy but also, if the NGO is small or not well run, often underpaid. • As with community lawyers, you will need to be utterly convinced of the merit of your NGO work to compensate for these realities, while trying at the same time to seek some balance between your public high profile and a lower profile, sustainable private life.
Barristers[46]	• You will have a certain amount of prestige, independence and opportunity to concentrate in areas of work that interest you. ◄— Independent • You will appear in all courts and tribunals and face challenges similar to those of criminal defence solicitors. • You will encounter the 'cab-rank' rule, which nominally requires you to appear for a client even if you do not like or believe them,[47] and you must resist the temptation to abuse the rule: by, for example, being 'unavailable', or declining the work if your 'normal fee' cannot be met.[48] • It has been asserted that some barristers use the cab-rank principle in order to justify their representation of morally questionable clients in civil cases,[49] but other barristers reject this criticism and ask 'Why is there such pressure for the advocate to identify with their client?'[50] • You will face continuous client pressure to distort truth and hide guilt, even though it may be subtle in many cases. It is rarely easy to decide where the line is between putting your client's case forward in a properly zealous manner (see Chs 3 and 4) and consciously obscuring the truth. • As with criminal defence solicitors, there is also constant pressure to navigate detailed advocacy rules about permissible deception (see Ch. 5). • You must deal with prosecutor pressure on your client to plead guilty to lesser charges to avoid trial on more serious matters, where a successful defence will be difficult but not impossible. • Ongoing reductions in the availability of legal aid may mean that you have less time and capacity to prepare thoroughly. • On occasion, you will be doubtful as to the legality of sources of funds which your client intends to use to pay their legal fees.

2.5 Questions new lawyers can ask law firms when assessing their worth

After reflecting on any preference you have for a particular type of legal practice, you can start to think about how to approach a particular law firm. Compiling a list of questions to put to a potential employer is hardly new. Many of us are coached before job interviews on how to present ourselves and what to say in order to perform as well as possible. Coaches and family also advise on issues we ought to ask about – for example, leave arrangements, professional development, child care availability and even the ability to work at home some of the time. It's not necessary to list all those issues here since there are plenty of places where that information will be available when you need it, but it is possible that the policies and practices which constitute the moral worth of the workplace will not be readily accessible, and so a checklist of such material could be useful.

Some employers will think it presumptuous that you wish to ask searching questions about ethical issues, but the firms worth working for will adjust quickly enough and be ready to provide meaningful answers, or agree to provide them later if the partner or HR person interviewing you does not know the firm's position in detail. Obviously, the way in which your questions are answered will also tell you quite a lot.

It's best to start by providing an explanation for your queries. Partners will be immediately curious as to why you want to know about ethics, and will be understandably defensive if you don't seem genuine. You could be a plant for another firm, a sort of mystery shopper out to do some damage! They may also think you are joking, given the relatively small number of lawyer jobs available at any one time and the huge number of applicants for positions. But you won't be joking, because there is little point in going to a firm that is not going to engage your integrity and stimulate a deserved loyalty. The salary does not make up for any workplace 'hygiene' issues, as we know from the high 'churn rate' of lawyers who enter the legal profession – many are gone within a few years.[51] The partner interviewing you should know about the churn rate too. They will usually prefer to employ a new lawyer who will stick around, considering the time and money that must be spent to integrate you into the firm. In effect, you are re-establishing the scene: the interview becomes not so much one of you as an employee but of your potential employer; not so much a buyer's market as a seller's market.

46 The Good Lawyer

So it's reasonable and realistic to explain that you are *not* trying to be arrogant or patronising or even over-confident: you are looking to build a reputation not just for skill, but also for ethics and professionalism – and all of these are important to you in deciding who to work for. Explain further that you've done your homework and have tried to ask around about what it's like to work for the firm and that you have some queries arising from the feedback you have received. Indicate that you've looked at the *Survive Law*[52] website and talked with the young lawyers' sections of your local law society. And make sure you actually do this, because this is how you will learn about the firm you are about to interview.

If that is all received and accepted well enough, consider asking some of these questions, depending on the type of firm you are talking to and your sense of the personalities of your interviewers. Start with easier issues:

1. 'How does the firm support *pro bono* work?' 'What is the firm's attitude to my professional development?' 'Would I be encouraged to undertake a specialist accreditation in due course?'
2. 'What practices or policies does the firm have in place for life–work balance?'
3. 'Does the firm have a written policy on handling ethical issues when they come up?' 'For example, if I were to come across a client who wanted to know if I or we had ever acted for another named individual or another corporation, is there an office manual or database program that will guide me on what to do?' [If the answer is 'Just tell your partner and let them handle it', see Ch. 6 and be cautious.]
4. 'Based on what I've heard, I'm wondering are there any real differences between the actual practice of the firm and what the ethics manual sets out or what the firm's policy is?'
5. [In a large firm] 'What approach does the firm have to acting against a former client?'
6. 'How does the firm resolve difficult ethical issues if one partner wants to do one thing and another has a different view: for example, as to how much to bill a particular client?'
7. 'How is the firm's public reputation, as far as you can tell?'
8. 'What do you generally expect your employees to do in looking after clients and attracting new ones? For example, am I expected to socialise with them or bring in a new client a month, or what?'

9. 'Does the firm use time sheets to work out clients' bills, or some form of value adding in addition to time sheets, or what? How is that process typically applied in a [standard matter]?'
10. 'In relation to my own time sheets, am I required to complete and sign off on them daily, weekly or monthly? If I can't recall precisely how much time I spent on a particular file, what do I do?'
11. 'What processes does the firm go through if I don't meet budget?'

As you will appreciate, the very direct nature of these questions will be more easily handled by a 'good' partner working for a good firm, but they will be harder for others. It could be suggested that it's unrealistic to expect you to ask these sorts of questions because many new graduates just won't have enough confidence to do so, but if you've read this book right through, you will have developed enough bottle to front up in this way. Consider this: if you have just read this list and decided that you are *not* going to ask any of these questions (because you don't think you will get the job if you do), will you still be happy not to know any of the answers?

If you've already explained that you want to know about the firm's 'ethical culture' because you want to contribute to a supportive and healthy climate, you can't do much more to show your own integrity. Good firms have thought about these issues and will take these questions seriously. The best firms will be intrigued because you are standing out from all the other people they are interviewing. But if the interview proceeds badly because the interviewers feel offended or embarrassed, move on until you find a firm that wants good lawyers.

Alternatively, you may decide not to be so confronting at your next interview at another firm. But will you be content not to know about their attitudes to these things and their attitudes to your questioning, next time around?

2.6 Inside the ideal commercial law firm

Once you have the job, staying 'good' and, in due course, contributing to the firm being better (as in good, better, best!) will be a rewarding and invigorating ride. But while you will be intensely stimulated, being on the inside of the ideal law firm does mean work, and a lot of it. This journey will not just be one of value-adding ethics to the firm's whole strategic direction.

We have already mentioned NSW Chief Justice Tom Bathurst's highly disputed warning,[53] but consider also Diagram 2.1, which offers a sobering

48   The Good Lawyer

2013 US assessment of the professionalism *versus* commercialism debate from New York District Court Judge Jed Rakoff,[54] who made several comments about what it means to have the courage to be truly independent:

in-house or external? 'The lawyer in America is ever more a business person, ever less a professional. Just to give you an example, the single biggest growing part of the legal profession are in-house lawyers. There are now something like 80,000 in-house lawyers in the USA. That is, I'm told, a 500% increase between 1970 and 2010. This has come about largely for economic reasons; it is a lot cheaper to use in-house lawyers than outside lawyers. But it's much harder for an in-house lawyer to be an independent professional. He is so dependent on the people he is giving advice to. They are his bosses, they determine his salary, they determine his perks, they determine his career. You can pass things like s 307 of the *Sarbanes-Oxley Act*, which says that if in-house counsel sees severe illegality they have to report it all the way up to the Board. That's fine, but on a day-to-day basis their situation is never (or very rarely) 'shall we do something illegal?' It is 'here are two choices and they're both arguably legal. One really is pushing the envelope, while the other is much more consistent with the spirit of the law.' A real professional will say that the right thing to do is the latter, but for a guy who knows that he's dependent on the people asking [for] that advice, and who desperately wants to have that new widget or new approach? It's much harder for him to say no.

independent? The related aspect is that because so much of the ordinary work has gone in-house, outside lawyers are now much more specialised; they do not have the long-term relationship with the client that they used to; and they are always looking over their shoulder at the other guy who has that specialty. Where they used to have the independence and security to say 'no' to a client, now they can't. Just in the time I've been practising law, I've seen that development go from a small problem to a major problem, and, frankly, I don't see any solution to it.

the power to be independent It is a function of who you are working for and what your power is, vis-à-vis that person. If you have the power to walk away, you can be independent. The legal profession has done its best – in a certain way – to try to combat this, by having more professional responsibility requirements, and things of that sort. But in the end, I think the power relationship has changed and not for the good.' [emphasis added]

Diagram 2.1   Arguably legal

The ideal firm for a new lawyer is one where your partner will support your need to say 'no' to a client from time to time because they realise that the firm's longer term reputation will be swinging in the wind and could easily be undone at some future point should someone like Judge Rakoff look at why you did not say 'no'. The ideal corporation (if you are an in-house lawyer) likewise realises that its share price is intricately linked to its brand and reputation and is therefore attracted to longer term share stability. Your boss (general counsel inside the corporation) will be aware of Enron,[55] of the global financial crisis and perhaps even of the corruption inside the Reserve Bank of Australia[56] – and will not want their firm's name raised in court or in the media.

There are also difficult decisions to be made in representing the relatively few corporations (or individuals) that may be considered 'bad'. There may be no truly bad companies or people and, just as it is said that everyone is a mixture of good and bad, so also must be companies, which are made up of highly complex individuals. As a good lawyer, you may consider it your role to act for such companies in order to modify their behaviour from the inside. Tobacco lawyers, both in-house and external, could say this, and if they did, they would be entitled to a hearing. But they would also assert that someone has to act for tobacco manufacturers. This second claim can be challenged.

> Regardless of whether you are in a private firm or are an in-house corporate lawyer, are you independent enough to say 'no' to a client when your professionalism requires it?
>
> **Are you ready for the next time you will be faced with this challenge?**

Most lawyers have a choice about who they represent,[57] and there are always some lawyers who will properly act for unpopular clients. Society is generally the better for it. But there is no solid moral basis for saying we ourselves must act for an unpopular or bad client in a civil case when we know that others will. If our conscious ethical judgment is that in so acting, we would support immoral or unethical behaviour, any compulsion to act is itself immoral and certainly nonsensical. There is no law and no compelling ethic which says that solicitors (as opposed to barristers) must act for

50 The Good Lawyer

anyone who comes along. So if we choose not to, how is that offensive? When four men and one minor were charged with the repeated rape and murder of a young woman on a bus in Delhi in 2012, the local bar association declined to endorse any legal representation for the defendants. But some lawyers came forward regardless.[58] The idea that an alleged 'bad' individual or corporation will go without civil representation because all lawyers reject them as clients is factually incorrect.

And there are some other trends to keep in mind. Personal anxiety tends to be increasing for lawyers as much as for anyone. If being anxious about the future is just a sign of being more or less sane, perhaps it is anxiety rather than depression that we all need to watch? Will your ideal law firm get on board with mindfulness training? And is your ideal boss attentive enough to you to understand when you need to get some help for over-anxiety?

Global warming is also not going away, but there are still a few corporate clients who are hoping that it will and that they will not need to adapt. It's possible that too few of the world's important governments will be willing to make the tough decisions needed to cap the process, and business generally is still focused on the short term, or is unwilling to accept what is likely to happen and completely restructure in favour of truly sustainable operations. All this implies much lower economic growth on a global scale and that is frightening to most, but not all. With the exception of insurers and reinsurers, corporate business plans are likely still to be underdone and not yet resilient enough to cope with more environmental disruption, public health challenges, greater debtor delay in paying invoices and (if this is possible?) less predictable business cycles. All of this flows through to your law firm as well. So there is much for you to do in adding value to clients' business planning and doing it ethically. More than ever, sustainable commercial activity will have to be ethically sound.

For similar reasons, the connections between lawyering as assisting private commercial relationships (transactional law) and as promoting justice through ethical dispute resolution could become more obvious. There does not need to be a big gulf between the two. Some law firms, for example the global partnership Baker and McKenzie, are already preparing for this more integrated scenario.[59] Try to locate and attract those clients whose priorities recognise environmental and political sustainability and get to know, as thoroughly as you can, how those businesses operate, how they organise themselves financially and how you can add to their stability. If you are doing all this, then you cannot do more, and you can be generally confident that you are living up to your ethical obligations. Legal regulation and legal regulators will also leave you alone.

In the final part of this chapter, the impact of the rules about mental health and general conduct are discussed. Just as law students have challenges with mental health and substance abuse, so too do lawyers, even more. Unhealthy legal practice environments can fertilise instability and offer considerable opportunity for ill-health, as the lists of disciplinary tribunal cases make clear.[60] Diagram 2.2 summarises what happens when things get out of balance in a lawyer's life.

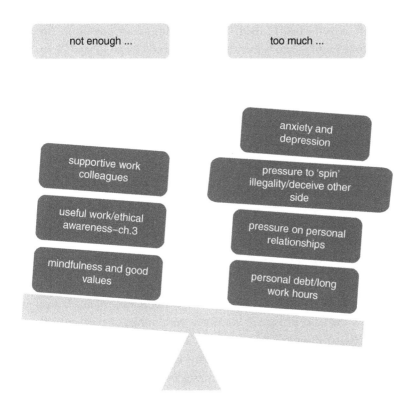

Diagram 2.2 Life balance

52   The Good Lawyer

2.7 The regulation of not-so-good lawyering

If admission to legal practice is difficult for those who cannot meet a fairly high standard of virtuous character,[61] it is easier for lawyers, once admitted, to stay admitted even when their behaviour slips. But there are a few provisos. The regulators – and, if necessary, the courts – take a moderately understanding approach to any mental health or substance abuse issues of practising lawyers, providing you have not:

- stolen or 'borrowed' your clients' money.[62] Pinching clients' funds will usually ruin your career.

    (There are, unfortunately, many lawyers who have become addicted to gambling and 'borrowed' from their clients' funds or who have unknowingly been depressed and, facing a need to top up their business overdraft, have turned to their trust account and systematically fleeced clients over months and sometimes years. Nearly all go to jail.[63])
- actively misled, lied to or refused to cooperate with a court or tribunal,[64] or
- committed an act of general misconduct that tends to bring the profession into disrepute (for example, drug importation or other serious criminal activity).[65]

> Clients' funds must be deposited immediately in a trust account and kept separate from your own money, must be independently audited and must only be withdrawn with your client's permission, or to pay their bill to your firm.[66]
> If you breach these rules, even temporarily, the fact that you are mentally unwell will not save you from report. If the case is serious, prosecution will follow.

Outside this list of 'do nots', the principal regulator in each of the Australian jurisdictions can also prosecute you for a wide range of misconduct and (the less serious) unsatisfactory conduct. Most of these offences relate to clients: for example, overcharging, delay and breaches of the rules of conduct (see below). But apart from these, and even despite these prosecutions, regulators will make an effort to help you get back on the rails if depression or substance abuse overcomes you for a period.[67] If your mental health is at risk, you will need to make an effort to get on top of things and you will need to be candid about what you are doing to get on top of them.[68] There is now enough knowledge of substance abuse issues in the legal community to say fairly confidently that you will get help from regulators, law societies and bar associations if you ask for it, or get someone to ask on your behalf. The point is, in theory, simple: let others know what is going on and they will want to help you. And remember, the obligation for candour is continuous – it is especially apparent when you apply to renew your practising certificate, which occurs every 12 months.[69]

From time to time, you will also need to take note of the local professional conduct rules, as discussed in the following section.

2.8 *Uniform Conduct Rules* (UCR)

In this important area for good lawyering there has been some progress towards uniformity. Various states and territories have different sets of 'conduct rules', as they are generally known, but a common set of rules has recently been agreed upon by Victoria and New South Wales and is likely to be described as the *Uniform Conduct Rules* (UCR).[70] The UCR is based on the *Australian Solicitors' Conduct Rules* (ASCR), which was developed by the Law Council of Australia (LCA), the national body which represents Australian solicitors' political and professional interests.[71] The LCA developed the ASCR in conjunction with law societies in the states and territories over some years. The process was complex and the result is not entirely satisfactory, but there is no other body that could have led the process.[72] The LCA hopes these rules will eventually become law across the country, but they only have effect in each state or territory when that jurisdiction agrees to adopt them. With the Victorian and New South Wales decision, the provisions of the ASCR are likely, over time, to become the default standard for conduct rules across the country (Queensland[73] and South Australia[74] have already adopted them). For this reason, the ASCR are referred to extensively in Chapters 4 to 7, though not with any great enthusiasm, for the reasons that follow.

The ASCR (UCR) remain subject to a hierarchy of general (common) law, statute and regulations, as Diagram 2.3 indicates.

Each time you consider a conduct rule such as that set out in the ASCR, it is imperative to consider whether there is a wider principle or statutory

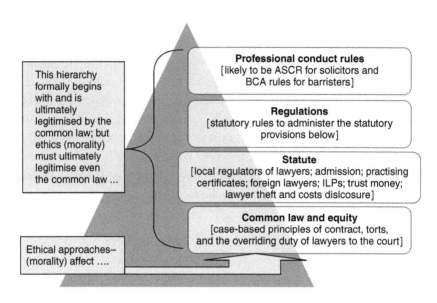

Diagram 2.3 Moral illegitimacy and conduct rules

provision that affects the area you are specifically interested in – and, indeed, even a wider common law or equitable provision. There is nothing contentious in this statement. But it is David Luban's argument that you ought also to consider fundamental moral positions before you make a decision and, if necessary, defer to morality where it is in conflict with 'the law'.[75] Chapter 3 explores the issue in detail and supports Luban, arguing that common law and equity are not enough to guide lawyers' judgment in all situations.[76] But for the moment it is still important to dig down a bit further into the ASCR.

Consideration of underlying ethical principle is important when interpreting the ASCR because, just as all conduct rules are formally *inferior* to common law and statute, this particular set of rules is also internally confusing and unsettling. The ASCR is a composite document which provides both statements and a number of detailed exceptions to those statements, followed by a number of commentaries for some rules, but not others. The general effect is to give a set of very mixed messages to lawyers. Conduct rules are supposed to represent the profession's collective opinion as to the moral standards expected and to give a reference point for deciding whether disciplinary proceedings should be commenced for inappropriate conduct.[77]

They are supposed to provide guidance to newer lawyers, but at the same time can never represent the last word on our ethical obligations.[78] In fact, the ASCR offers false security to anyone who is hoping to get immediate, definitive guidance as to their wider obligations. Nowhere is this clearer than in two particular rules – Rules 10 and 11 – which refer to conflicts of interest. Where moral principles ought to be obvious, there are only tortuously stitched together provisions designed to make it easier for the largest of firms to tolerate certain conflicts and simultaneously represent two or more clients whose interests would morally be thought of as quite different. Similarly, some firms will be able, according to the ASCR, to act against their own former clients in some circumstances, regardless of any loyalty their former clients might think they were still owed (see Chapter 7).

Large firms are large because they tend to command sufficient expertise and reputation to dominate the legal advice and representation available to entire industry sectors. To give one example, it is common for large firm partners over their careers to act for several corporations inside the one business sector, such as mining. But these companies subdivide operating divisions or are taken over by new companies on an ongoing basis. New companies tend to look to the larger firms for their lawyers and naturally, the large firms want that work and want to keep smaller firms (which have fewer conflicts problems) out of the picture. So these partners must constantly check to see that they have not previously acted for a corporation that might have interests that conflict in some way with those of the new player. The conflicts checking process is expensive and irritating for the large firms, and globally, they have been interested from time to time in arguing that they should be separately regulated from all other lawyers (with more relaxed rules about conflicts).[79]

It is important to the large firms to keep looking for ways and means to take on clients who do have current, opposing interests or who are opposed to a former client, even though both strategies strike many other lawyers as offensive and as undermining both the independence of lawyers and their loyalty to their clients. It is generally understood that the large law firm group (LLFG) inside the LCA has been so influential in the rule drafting process that they have been able to ensure that Rules 10 and 11 (see Chapter 6) will meet their commercial need to simultaneously represent clients who are opposed to one another. The detail in these two rules and the attached commentaries is extreme, but it does not make them any more precise or

56   The Good Lawyer

effective. As the rules specifically acknowledge, they do not exclude the common law:[80] that is, they cannot allow what the common law considers to be contrary to the proper administration of justice. Rules 10 and 11 attempt to water down the ethical priorities created by the common law. They cannot offer any guarantees that a court will agree that a large firm has been fair to its two (or more) opposed clients in any particular situation.

Although the ASCR is imperfect, its in principle acceptance by New South Wales and Victoria means that it will have an impact on many other ethical areas. These will be covered in succeeding chapters. In managing that impact, the safest course is to adhere to a contextualised conduct approach. Chapter 3 provides this framework.

Notes

1. See generally, Tony Foley, Vivien Holmes, Stephen Tang and Margie Rowe, 'Practising professionalism: Observations from an empirical study of new Australian lawyers' (2012) 15(1) *Legal Ethics* 29.
2. Mitt Regan has documented these events in 'Taxes and death: The rise and demise of Jenkens and Gilchrist'. See citation.allacademic.com/meta/p_mla_apa_research_citation/2/3/6/7/3/p236739_index.html. See also blogs.wsj.com/law/2009/06/09/gone-but-not-forgotten-jenkins-gilchrist-trio-indicted-for-tax-fraud. This is an edited extract from Adrian Evans and Helen Forgasz, 'Framing lawyers choices: Factor analysis of a psychological scale to self-assess lawyers' ethical preferences' (2013) 16(1) *Legal Ethics* 134, n 3.
3. *McCabe v British American Tobacco* [2002] VSC 73.
4. *McCabe* [2002] VSC 73, [289].
5. *British American Tobacco v McCabe* [2002] VSCA 197.
6. Jonathan Liberman, 'Do judges now admire corporate connivance?', *The Age*, 11 December 2002, 17. Liberman was a legal consultant to VicHealth, the NGO which stood behind the plaintiff and her family throughout the ordeal of the litigation. Liberman argued that 'the only winners will be corporations with much to hide, their $500 an hour lawyers and the makers of industrial size shredders'.
7. William Birnbauer, 'Tobacco insider tells of files "cull"', *The Age*, 19 July 2003, 1.
8. Marcus Priest, 'Clayton Utz says it's in the clear on BAT', *Australian Financial Review*, 25 July 2003, 58.
9. William Birnbauer, 'Cheated by the law', *The Sunday Age*, 29 October 2006, 1, 16–17. See also Marcus Priest 'Informer smoked out over McCabe papers', *Australian Financial Review*, 2 February 2007, 69. At the time this book was finalised, these matters remained unresolved.
10. Edited extract from Adrian Evans, *Assessing Lawyers' Ethics*, Cambridge University Press, Melbourne, 2011, 7–9. Clayton Utz subsequently did much to restore their reputation. The firm announced, in the interim between the initial finding of Justice

Eames in April 2002 and the appeal court reversal in December 2002, that it would cease acting for tobacco companies and that it had appointed former High Court Chief Justice Sir Anthony Mason to head a 'professional excellence committee'. See Bill Pheasant, 'Appeal court to rule on landmark tobacco case', *Australian Financial Review*, 6 December 2002, 14. In other words, lessons were learned.

11. Lillian Corbin, 'How "firm" are lawyers' perceptions of professionalism?' (2005) 8 *Legal Ethics* 265.

12. Ibid., 274.

13. Ibid., 275.

14. Ibid., 274.

15. Ibid.

16. Ibid., 288.

17. Edited extract from Evans, n 10, 202–03.

18. Memo, Brian Hood to Ric Battelino, June 2007. See 'The June 2007 RBA Memo' at www.smh.com.au/national/the-june-2007-rba-memo-20120822-24llm.html?rand=1345598937818.

19. Nick McKenzie, Richard Baker, Maris Beck, 'Whistleblower told to shut up', *Business Day, Sydney Morning Herald*, 14 September 2012. See www.smh.com.au/business/whistleblower-told-to-shut-up-20120913-25v8t.html.

20. Anthony T. Kronman, *The Lost Lawyer*, Harvard University Press, New York, 1993.

21. An exception was the successful prosecution of the former company secretary and general counsel of James Hardie Limited, Peter Shafron, who was instrumental in deceiving the ASX and wider stock market of the extent to which the company had underprovided in its accounts for the money that would be needed to compensate dying victims of the company's decades of asbestos mining and distribution. See Leonie Lamont, 'Hardie verdict puts directors on notice over due diligence', *Sydney Morning Herald*, 4 May 2012, at www.smh.com.au/national/hardie-verdict-puts-directors-on-notice-over-due-diligence-20120503-1y1uh.html.

22. For an overview of the reasons for this failure, see 'The Untouchables', *ABC Four Corners*, 18 March 2013, at www.abc.net.au/tv/guide/abc1/201303/programs/NC1304H007D2013-03-18T203319.htm.

23. Except in rare cases, corporate clients of large firms are reluctant to 'go public' when they are dissatisfied with a large law firm, because their own commercial reputations, their business strategies and their executives' egos are then all on display. Large, unhappy corporate clients prefer to negotiate privately with the law firm for compensation: for example, as fee reductions. They are successful because big firms do not wish to lose such clients and do not wish to see complaints lodged externally.

24. For example, US District Court Judge Jed Rakoff, who complains that individuals make the decision to do the wrong thing, not the abstract corporations who employ them or whom they direct. See Tom Wicker, 'Judicious activism', *IBA Global Insight*, International Bar Association, February/March 2013, 19 (at 20).

25. This list contains some overlap of categories. Lawyers often have a main area of practice and spend less time in a few other areas, as client demand requires it and available time permits. Categories of Practice are as follows: sole practitioners,

58 The Good Lawyer

suburban and rural practices – SMALL (1–5 partners); regional and larger regional – CUSP (5–10 partners; mid-tier firms – LARGER (10–20 partners); 2nd tier firms – LARGE (20–50 partners); 1st tier national – LARGE (50> partners); transnational – LARGE (50> partners, operating in more than one country); global – VERY LARGE (100> partners, with more than 50% of partners located outside home jurisdiction of the firm).

The AM Law Global 100 list of global mega-firms establishes the extent to which these firms dominate the planet in legal services. These firms are not transnational (10–50% of lawyers working away from home jurisdiction of the firm) or national (more than 90% of lawyers employed in home jurisdiction) firms, but form their own class. The global class comprises those firms where >50% of lawyers work outside the firm's home jurisdiction. See Kath Hall, 'Global law firms lose ties to home', *The Australian, Legal Affairs*, 26 October 2012, 1.

26. *Australian Solicitors' Conduct Rules* 2011 (ASCR), Law Council of Australia. See www.lawcouncil.asn.au/lawcouncil/index.php/divisions/national-profession-project/australian-solicitors-conduct-rules.

27. Andrew Fraser was a criminal lawyer in Melbourne. His book is instructive for its insights into the risks of criminal practice for some lawyers. See Andrew Fraser, *Lunatic Soup*, Hardie Grant, Melbourne, 2010.

28. Depression among lawyers is as serious as it is for law students. See Samantha Bowers, 'Lawyers work too hard for their own good', *The Australian Financial Review, Legal Affairs*, 10 February 2012, 49.

29. Collaborative lawyers are often family lawyers who contract with a client to try to settle a claim by actively and fully disclosing all evidence to the other side, where the other side is similarly represented, and collaboratively seeking a principled settlement. The contract provides that if the collaboration fails to settle the dispute, both parties will retain completely new lawyers for the following litigation. See, generally, Tania Sourdin, *Alternative Dispute Resolution* (4th edn), Thomson-Reuters, Sydney, 2012 and Christine Parker and Adrian Evans, *Inside Lawyers' Ethics*, Cambridge University Press, Melbourne, 2014, Ch. 6.

30. Tony Greenwood, 'Ethics and avoidance advice' (1991) 65(8) *LIJ* 724.

31. *Legal Profession Uniform Law Application Act 2014* (Vic), Sch 1, Part 3.7 (*Uniform Law*). This Act is expected to implement the *Uniform Law* in NSW and Victoria as from 1 July 2014 – covering 72% of Australian lawyers. See Chapter 9.3.

32. *Legal Profession Uniform Law Application Act 2014* (Vic), Sch 1, ss 34 and 35. See, for example, *Wise v Law Institute of Victoria Limited* (Legal Practice) [2012] VCAT 1518. See, generally, Christine Parker, Adrian Evans, Reid Mortensen and Suzanne LeMire, 'Ethical infrastructure of legal practice in large law firms: Values, policy and behaviour' (2008) 31(1) *UNSW L. J.* 155–88.

33. Personal conversation with Prof John Flood, University of Westminster, 2 March 2013. See also *Lawyers' Weekly*, 'Mega firms teach greed over ethics', 17 April 2012, 1. Concern about commodification of lawyers' functions has been echoed by former Federal Court judge Ray Finkelstein (at Monash University on 5 June 2012), who identified specialisation as defeating lawyers expertise because they cannot see the wider picture.

34. Rachel Nickless, 'Mental aid course is a know-brainer', *Australian Financial Review*, 22 June 2012, 43.

2 The law practice landscape **59**

35. *Lawyers' Weekly*, n 33, 1. Bathurst CJ was speaking at the 2012 Commonwealth Lawyers Association Regional Law Conference, Sydney. See also Michael Bradley, 'The time sheet shuffle', *The Australian, Legal Affairs*, 4 May 2012, 43.
36. Peter Gordon, former senior partner of Slater and Gordon, address at Monash University on 28 February 2013. Gordon was referring to so-called defendants' (large) firms, but the same could also be said of so-called plaintiffs' firms. The independence of lawyers is always contentious, particularly outside democracies. Chinese lawyers are reportedly now required to swear an oath of allegiance to the CCP (as opposed to more conventional oaths in Western jurisdictions). See P. Wen, 'Chinese lawyers told to pledge loyalty to party', *The Age*, 23 March 2012, 8.
37. Alex Boxsell, 'Fighting for big tobacco is not all plain sailing', *Australian Financial Review*, 18 May 2012, 42.
38. Stephanie Quine, 'New billing software "dehumanises" clients', *Lawyers Weekly*, 11 November 2011, 9. Quine reported that Corrs have introduced an automatic time billing program 'Time Builder' (by US developer IntApp), designed to record for each lawyer, all their software and document usage, email, calendar, texts and phone calls, in a timesheet format and sent as a draft to the lawyer each day, to 'jog their memories' as to what they did and to confirm or alter the output.
39. To the point that challenging that culture can itself be seen as unethical (that is, disloyal). Parker and Rostain have attempted to get beneath the argument about whether business or professional ethics are to blame for lawyers 'poor moral behaviours, beginning with the example of the James Hardie's external lawyer' (Allens), who insufficiently identified the importance of fully funding the corporation's asbestos compensation fund. Their conclusion is that large firm lawyers' networks are monochrome, narrow and few and that they are simply withdrawing socially, psychologically and personally, to the point that they do not automatically recognise any alternatives to purely business imperatives in their decision making. See Tanina Rostain and Christine Parker, 'Law firms, global capital and the sociological imagination' (2012) 80 *Fordham L. Rev.* 2347.
40. Sascha Hindmarsh and Martin Meredith, 'In-house counsel's ethical choice' (2013) 87(3) *LIJ* 39.
41. Ibid.
42. Ibid.
43. Nazi lawyer Wilhelm Frick and his colleagues created the Final Solution through the use of law and official policy. In 1933 the Law for the Restoration of the Professional Civil Service banned Jews from government jobs. Other laws followed, culminating with the Nuremberg Laws, the Law for the Protection of German Blood and German Honour, and the Reich Citizenship Law. See the US National Archives – Nuremberg Laws, at www.archives.gov/publications/prologue/2010/winter/nuremberg.html. For a 2005 film which dramatises the Nazi courts' suppression of Germans' internal resistance, see *Sophie Scholl – The Final Days* (Dir. Marc Rothemund).
44. See Robert K. Vischer, 'Legal advice as moral perspective' (2006) 19 *Georgetown Journal of Legal Ethics* 225 and more generally, Ch. 3. See also Carol Coulter, 'Public confuse solicitor with client – Assange lawyer', *Irish Times*, 4 October 2012.
45. See Parker and Evans, n 29, 148.

46. There are a number of other more specialised categories of lawyers who are not treated separately here, as it's necessary to draw the line at some point. This group includes informal and accredited specialisations in any number of areas (see for example www.liv.asn.au/Professional-Development/Accredited-Specialisation), commercial litigation funders (who are often staffed by lawyers), specialist legal advocacy groups and niche firms – for example, media lawyers, sports lawyers, patent attorneys and wills and succession lawyers.
47. See Dal Pont, *Lawyers' Professional Responsibility* (5th edn), para 3.140.
48. Ibid., paras 3.150–175. A recent UK report has recommended its abolition. See www.legalfutures.co.uk/latest-news/end-line-cab-rank-rule.
49. Alan Myers QC has been criticised for his representation of British American Tobacco in respect of the Federal Government plain packaging legislation. See Jill Stark, 'Peter Mac denies tobacco conflict', *Sydney Morning Herald*, 2 September 2012, at www.smh.com.au/national/peter-mac-denies-tobacco-conflict-20120901-257h2.html.
50. Comment by Robert Richter QC, at Monash Law School forum on the cab-rank rule, 28 February 2013. See, further, Adrian Evans, 'A polemic on not acting for tobacco companies', McCabe Centre for Law and Cancer, www.mccabecentre.org/downloads/Adrian_Evans_A_Polemic_on_not_Acting_for_Tobacco_Companies_and_Identifying_who_to_Act_for_.pdf.
51. See Lee, 'Graduates shun legal profession', 6.
52. See survivelaw.com.
53. Bathurst, n 35.
54. Wicker, n 24, 23.
55. Enron Corporation, a Texas-based oil and financial markets conglomerate and once the 7th largest corporation in the United States with revenue of over $100 billion, collapsed because of essentially immoral re-classification of massive corporate debt as 'off-balance sheet', allowing the company to, in effect, trade while insolvent and dig itself even deeper into debt. The circumstances surrounding Enron's collapse generated a wealth of commentary. See, for example, D. Rhode and P. Paton, 'Lawyers, ethics, and Enron' (2002) 8 *Stanford Journal of Law, Business & Finance* 9, and other contributions to the 'Symposium – Enron: Lessons and implications' (2002) 8(1) *Stanford Journal of Law, Business & Finance*; Robert W. Gordon, 'A New Role for Lawyers? The Corporate Counselor after Enron', in Susan D. Carle, *Lawyers' Ethics and the Pursuit of Social Justice: A Critical Reader*, New York University Press, 2005.
56. See 2.2: Common themes in major examples of poor lawyering.
57. See n 48. Formally, the 'cab-rank rule' or principle obliges barristers to represent any client who can pay their fee, providing they are 'available' and competent in the area of proposed work. See *Australian Bar Association, Barristers' Conduct Rules*, Rule 21, at www.nswbar.asn.au/circulars/2010/feb/rules.pdf. This rule is often honoured in the breach and is little enforced.
58. See www.firstpost.com/india/delhi-rape-three-accused-finally-find-lawyers-to-defend-them-581454.html.
59. Baker and McKenzie developed one of the world's first climate change practices and are well positioned to advise on other connected challenges to business.
60. See, for example, the Victorian Civil and Administrative Tribunal (VCAT) online case reports – in particular, for its subsidiary Legal Practice list, at www.austlii.

edu.au/cgi-bin/sinosrch.cgi?method=auto;meta=%2Fau;query=%22legal%20practice%20list%22;results=20;rank=on;callback=on;mask_path=au%2Fcases%2Fvic%2FVCAT;view=date;submit=Search;sfield=full.

61. See Ch. 1.9: Managing your mental health.

62. *Legal Profession Uniform Law Application Act 2014* (Vic), Sch 1, s 148.

63. See, for example, the historical cases catalogued in Adrian Evans, 'A concise history of the Solicitors Guarantee Fund (Vic): A marriage of principle and pragmatism' (2000) 26 *Monash University Law Review*, 74–154 and Alex Boxsell, 'Qld lawyer struck off roll', *Australian Financial Review, Legal Affairs*, 15 March 2013, 33.

64. Depending on the circumstances, misleading a court can amount to perjury or contempt and is punishable at the discretion of the court. See www.theaustralian.news.com.au/story/0,25197,23175701-26103,00.html.

65. See Fraser, n 27.

66. *Legal Profession Uniform Law Application Act* 2014 (Vic), Sch 1, s 144.

67. Mary-Jane Ierodiaconou and Roberta Foster, 'Telling admissions: Disclosing mental illness among lawyers', 87(1/2) *LIJ* 32–5.

68. Ibid.

69. See, for example, the Victorian renewal form, at www.lsb.vic.gov.au/publications/forms. Similar disclosure is required in all Australian jurisdictions and will progressively harmonise as the advantages of a nationally uniform approach to licensing lawyers gradually become accepted.

70. *Legal Profession Uniform Law Application Act 2014* (Vic), Sch 1, s 423.

71. The national body representing barristers is the Australian Bar Association (ABA), which has both individual members and each of the state and territory Bar Associations. The ABA is much smaller and is less politically visible than the LCA, but the ABA Barristers' Conduct Rules 2010 perform the same function for barristers as does the ASCR for solicitors. See www.austbar.asn.au/index.php?option=com_content&view=section&layout=blog&id=4&Itemid=28.

72. The ASCR comes out of the significant activity of the LCA in the area of conduct rules for many years. The LCA intends that earlier Rules will be superceded by the ASCR in due course.

73. Legal Profession (Australian Solicitors' Conduct Rules Notice) 2012 (Qld) (from 1 July 2012).

74. Adopted by the Law Society of South Australia as from 25 July 2011.

75. See Ch. 1.

76. Chs 4 to 7 provide a method or approach to incorporating morality into your decision making.

77. See Dal Pont, n 47, 27.

78. Ibid., 28.

79. See, for example, Joan Loughrey, 'Large law firms, sophisticate clients and the regulation of conflicts of interest in England and Wales' (2011) 14(20) *Legal Ethics* 215 and John Flood, 'Solicitors regulation authority balks at separate city regulator [blog: Random academic thoughts]', 18 October 2010, at www.johnflood.com/blog/2010/10/solicitors-regulation-authority-balks-at-separate-city-regulator.

80. See ASCR 2.2.

Chapter 3

VALUES, ETHICS AND VIRTUE IN LAWYERING

3.1 Inside the law: First do no harm?

Good law schools and good law firms are important to sustain the good lawyer, but good ethics are also needed. What is involved in talking about good legal ethics? For a start, mere knowledge of legal ethics does not automatically produce goodness. Ethics is the study not just of morality and moral systems, but of its day-to-day practice as goodness. Morality is more than just knowing what is good. Legal ethics provides the opportunity, framework and encouragement to be moral, but at the end of the day lawyers have to choose to be good and act on that choice, rather than do nothing or actively behave badly. Certainly, lawyers who steal money from their clients' trust accounts,[1] or even delay paying genuine creditors[2] are not choosing to do good.

Many lawyers would not automatically think that we need to focus on goodness. 'Obeying and applying the law' tends to come up more often. And applying the law will always command respect. But if applying the law causes harm rather than good (or, sometimes, more harm than good), the law has no automatic mechanism to correct itself. An expensive court case must first be commenced by someone or governments must bring in new legislation. And the law itself does not always help by explaining precisely what governs its underlying moral purpose in any one case. Lawyers' promises on admission are of limited use: they oblige us to conduct ourselves 'well and honestly',[3] and while these are noble virtues, they are not quite enough.

If, for example, we were required to make a promise equivalent to the medical Hippocratic oath,[4] more motivation could be available. If applied to lawyers seeking admission, such a promise might say:

> I promise to this Court that I will, in all my professional activities, seek first to care and second to do justice, above all other obligations.

Such a promise would not be directly enforceable,[5] but it would make a strong aspirational statement and encourage us to seek goodness and not be content with what appears to be injustice, or indeed to ignore the interests of others. The point is this: obedience to the law cannot in itself reliably ensure that what occurs is good. The US case of Alton Logan illustrates the importance of this wider obligation.

Logan was released from an Illinois prison in 2009 after being imprisoned for 26 years for a murder he did not commit. The fact that he was innocent was known by two lawyers, who had no doubts about that issue. At the time of Logan's original trial these lawyers were acting for another man who confessed to them that he was the murderer. They knew from the circumstances that this confession was completely accurate, but they kept their knowledge secret for the next 26 years because they considered themselves bound by the local Illinois bar rule of attorney–client privilege (or client confidentiality).

The lawyers were concerned for the life of their own client, who had been convicted of a different murder and had been sentenced to death. They quite properly feared that he might be executed if the separate crime for which Logan had been falsely convicted were to be correctly attributed to him. Subsequently, the lawyers said they would have spoken up much earlier if a future serious crime was intended by their client because that disclosure was permitted as an exception to the rule,[6] but could not bring themselves to make their own exception in relation to this past murder – for which an innocent Logan remained in prison – even after their own client's life had been saved by the commutation to life in prison of his death penalty. They eventually spoke and allowed Logan's release, but only after their own client had died.[7]

Logan's innocence was in the 'too hard' category because the lawyers thought they had to choose the lesser of two evils. But once the life of their own client was no longer threatened, their silence would seem to have

64 The Good Lawyer

breached some sort of underlying obligation to care, even a little bit, about what was still happening to Logan. What sort of an obligation might this be? If there was such an obligation, it ought to have trumped the local bar rule which they said required them to stay quiet and leave Logan in prison.

This chapter explores the territory beyond the law and examines the underlying pull of morality on our behaviour, particularly where the law itself does not necessarily allow for anything but obedience. As we shall see, there are countless examples of laws that require us to choose to use our moral sense if care and justice are to have any chance at all. But we must first consider if we can actually choose to be good, or if our genes decide this for us.

3.2 Do we have a choice about our behaviour?

The advance of neuroscience over recent years has led to an interesting debate about the dominance of 'nurture versus nature' in our moral functioning. The question is: 'Can we humans exercise moral choice and control what we do, or is our neurological wiring such that what we do is largely controlled by our genetic inheritance?'[8] If the latter is true and unchangeable in the short term, can we actively strengthen our moral engagement with lawyering?

We may know some of the answer in years to come, but just as the debate between science and philosophy is often popularised as the difference between 'how' and 'why',[9] so the reality or otherwise of our moral autonomy is more a matter of 'why' than 'how'. How we function appears to be intertwined with why we function and for what purpose. To put it another way (and in so doing, to co-opt the reasoning behind the God versus science argument), if science is correct then the mind that does science is the end product of a mindless, unguided process of natural selection. Yet we trust that process and in so doing apply a moral, philosophical or religious stance to it. In effect, our choice to trust science ought to give us the confidence to trust that we have a choice in our behaviour.[10] English philosopher Roger Scruton describes this interaction between neurology and morality in this way:

> The picture [given] of the fragile 'I' riding the elephant of grey matter while pretending to be in charge of it, misrepresents the nature of self-reference.

The word 'I' does not refer to some conscious part of the person, the rest of which is a passive and hidden 'it'. The word 'I' is one term of the I-You relation, which is a relation of accountability in which the whole person is involved. To use the first person pronoun is to present myself for judgment. It is to take responsibility for a host of changes in the world and in particular for those for which you can reasonably call me to account by asking 'why?'[11]

In distinguishing between our species and our individuality, it is likely that we can and do choose our behaviour:

> We are human beings certainly. But we are also persons. Human beings form a biological kind, and it is for science to describe that kind. Probably it will do so in the way that the evolutionary psychologists propose. But persons do not form a biological kind, or any other sort of natural kind. The concept of the person is shaped in another way, not by our attempt to explain things but by our attempt to understand, to interact, to hold to account, to relate. The 'why?' of personal understanding is not the 'why' of scientific inference. And it is answered by conceptualising the world under the aspect of freedom and choice. People do what they do because of events in their brains. But when the brain is normal, they also act for reasons, knowing what they are doing and making themselves answerable for it.[12]

In the end, Scruton describes the issue of responsibility versus predetermination in terms of mystery: 'Even if we accept the claims of evolutionary psychology, therefore, the mystery of the human condition remains. This mystery is captured in a single question: how can one and the same thing be explained as an animal, and understood as a person?'[13] Because this debate exists, there is a reasonable basis for arguing that morality is capable of development. And as lawyers we cannot retreat from making moral decisions even when the rules seem to be clear.

3.3 The legal limit: Why 'law' and 'rules' are not enough to produce good lawyering

The number of misconduct and discipline cases is tiny in relation to the total number of lawyers,[14] but the number is not a reliable guide to the levels of good lawyering, because someone has to formally complain before bad lawyering is noticed. Where poor lawyering is undetected or even recognised and privately compensated, or where there is no victim but justice, no complaint is recorded. While there are many reasons to believe that overall, most lawyers try to be and are effective in their clients' interests, there is still the hard question of ethics: do we do the right thing when no one is looking? Or, taking the silence of the two lawyers in Alton Logan's case as an example,[15] are we being good enough when no one is looking?

The everyday struggle to make law something more than just a set of rules – to make it 'just' – has been debated by legal theorists for centuries. In very broad terms, those with a positivist perspective consider law to be sufficient to guide action because of its innate authority,[16] while those with more normative leanings are sceptical of that authority because of the mistakes, lack of resources and even corruption that affect the way the law works in practice.[17] These debates now require more attention.

When it comes to what lawyers actually do (and not just what the law requires), the contest of theories becomes more personal. On the one hand, writers such as Brad Wendel follow in the positivist tradition and are eloquent in their view that lawyers are required by law to assist their clients to do anything that they are lawfully entitled to do.[18] This formulation has almost no external moral content and relies on lawfulness for legitimacy. So if a lawyer's act in this context is lawful, that lawfulness is a good enough proxy for morality and no further enquiry into the lawyer's acts or motives is needed. The real attraction of this 'authority of law' perspective is its apparent coherence, its conceptual clarity and, particularly, its appeal to stability in the face of the constant unpredictability of the normative view – a lawyer who is genuinely confident of the legitimacy of the authority approach is not worried by whether something is moral or not, so long as they never go beyond their client's legal entitlements.

The notion of agency (that the lawyer is no more than the lawful agent of the lawfully acting client) is the foundation of this dominant approach to legal ethics or role morality. Otherwise known as zealous advocacy and sometimes as adversarial advocacy, a lawyer's capacity to stand outside morality but inside the law is a fundamentally different view of goodness from that of the rest of society. This does not mean that role morality is essentially bad. There are reasons for role morality that make sense (and are good in a certain way), but critics of the 'authority conception' or role morality are numerous. They have their allies in normative thinkers, in particular David Luban.[19] Their insistence on defining the proper role of lawyers in opposition to Wendel and others is put forward with conviction. Trevor Farrow, for instance, starts with a question: 'By what standard should lawyers ultimately be guided when answering the question of how they should act: the law only, or the law and something else?'[20] Below is a paraphrased compilation of his views, in which he outlines two problems with the 'clients' entitlements' justification for lawyers' actions:

1. The reference to clients' entitlements is a 'necessary but not a sufficient guide'. If we take 'a robust theory of moral deliberation off the table', Wendel provides nothing for lawyers to make sense of those entitlements.[21]

'If the law were perfectly determinate [and entitlements were clear], then we would not need to worry', but it is not.[22]

'[T]here are ... laws that, by their nature, require a [heavy] amount of interpretation and – potentially – moral deliberation in order to understand and apply them in any given context.' For example, what does it mean for a director to have to act 'in the best interests of the corporation', or to 'negotiate in good faith'?, or to insert a 'reasonable' contractual term? These provisions do not just allow for a moral component in interpretation, they require it.[23]

And if a lawyer were to say, OK I will have a moral conversation with my client, and stop at the boundary provided by law, how will they deal with the fact that 'finding that boundary is not an easy task and in many cases requires a very active and deliberate moral conversation'?[24]

'As such, in all but the clearest of cases (involving the clearest of laws), morality is not incidental, but is rather central, to the lawyering role.' In that sense fidelity to law is necessary, but not sufficient to the lawyering role.[25]

2. For an 'entitlements' sufficiency approach to work, law must exercise lawful rather than just raw power. In other words, in today's world, where access to justice is driven by money and power, 'might' pretends to be 'right' more often than not. And lawyers re-enter the discussion here because they play a big role in what laws get made. The reality is that lawyers, particularly in self-regulatory regimes, get to decide things and cannot do so on a value neutral basis, given the inequalities represented by money and power.[26]

Other writers echo Farrow's reluctance to limit the role of lawyers simply to administering and being faithful to law. The number of these normative viewpoints and the consistency of their perspective are compelling.[27] When weighed against the need to achieve justice in the face of injustice – despite law – lawyers' moral disengagement is unattractive:

68 The Good Lawyer

Through consistent and considered moral deliberation, lawyers are engaged in a much grander enterprise [than fidelity to law] – not only the protection of the rule of law, but also the creation of a just society.[28]

3.4 Determining a priority between law and ethics

In Chapter 1 the differences between legal behaviour that is or is likely to also be unethical behaviour were illustrated by the anecdote from Abraham Lincoln's days as a practising lawyer.[29] He was clear that just because we can do something as a lawyer (within the law), that does not mean that we should do it. Assuming you agree that the law is not enough and that you ought to exercise moral judgment as a lawyer, the situations where your moral sense ought to be clearly outraged are not as infrequent as you might think. You might not be asked to write a memo to government justifying torture on an everyday basis,[30] but as a government lawyer you may be asked to prepare a coal mining lease under land that supports viable dairy farms, where that mining will drain the underground water from the water table and force those farmers off their land.[31] Or you might be asked to help draft legislation which sends likely refugees who arrive by boat to 'camps' in neighbouring countries. Or as a corporate lawyer you could be required to submit to a parliamentary committee that your employer should be allowed to make cluster munitions or sell cigarettes with corporate-logo packaging in neighbouring countries, using the often-cited argument that 'overseas competitors are doing so and we are missing out on this business'.

If you think these situations seem extreme and unlikely for new lawyers, consider these more everyday occurrences:

- you are asked by a client to witness their affidavit without first 'swearing' them;[32]
- you are asked to play 'hard ball' in negotiations to settle a case and oppose an adjournment, or shower your opponent with irrelevant documents and keep your clients' real offer secret right till the end, in the hope of wearing down their willingness to continue with their case;

3 Values, ethics and virtue **69**

- at the end of a long day you are tired and have not had time to finish a real estate lease, so you ask your client to sign the last page and tell them you'll complete the rest tomorrow;
- you get your client to sign something and later on, change the date of the document, to make it look as if it were signed earlier than it was; and
- if you discover too late that someone else may know that these events have occurred, you decide to make a backdated note and insert it into the file, so it appears as if your client has understood and agreed to these processes.[33]

The everyday humdrum of legal practice throws up these and other ordinary ethical challenges constantly. All are capable of getting you into trouble, so even if you have the most worthy client in the world, your tiredness or laziness or disorganisation can lead to an attitude of 'whatever'. Your willingness to allow minor infractions can lead to a sort of moral insensitivity which, over time, allows some complacency and makes it easier for you to permit or commit major ethical failures.

You will also be in situations where it's hard to decide if a particular act is inside the law or not and issues will be presented to you not as obvious breaches of law but as 'potentially compliant' with the law. Judge Rakoff warned (Chapter 2) that when a boss or a client wants something from you that is likely to be legally (and morally) dodgy, it will be presented as 'arguably legal'.[34] The boundary between law and crime is particularly hazy in some areas of law, for example taxation law, where structuring a business to pay less tax is either legal (and classified as 'avoidance'), or as illegal (and called 'evasion'), depending on the exact nature of the structure and the artificiality of the methods used.[35] You will have real difficulty in determining legality in situations such as this and it is certain that your values and your moral sense will be needed to sort out one from the other.[36]

In all these situations, our understanding of the subtle differences in ethical choice is an issue of thought and intention. Intentional decision-making around ethical choice is responsible, and a sign of the good lawyer at work; just being lazy about our decisions, taking unthinking direction or even preferring our unexamined 'gut' reaction, is not. The best way to start being 'intentional' is to learn how others have categorised options for ethical thinking.

70 The Good Lawyer

3.5 General morality: The three major systems of ethical thought

As discussed in Chapter 2, it is useful to understand something of our values and ethics and how they interact before we try to interpret legislation, make sense of case law and comprehend professional conduct rules. In this process, a useful approach is first to consider the three major competing ethical frameworks – or ethical methods[37] – that underlie all approaches to professional ethics in the Western tradition.[38] We talk about 'methods' here because ethics is as much a process of thought as an outcome.

Together, these broad approaches make up general morality. They guide us, knowingly or otherwise, in judging what is ethical. Their broad connections to one another can be compared, as follows:

Table 3.1 General morality

Ethical method	Basic description of approach	Differences from other approaches
Kantian or 'deontological'	'Right' actions or policies are those that primarily enhance and respect individual autonomy by treating persons as 'ends' rather than 'means'. The deontological approach emphasises the rightness of 'process' rather than the ultimate consequences. **'Fairness'**: see for example, *R v Nerbas*.[39]	Kantian methods are concerned to refute the notion that 'the end justifies the means' – arguing that the means, since they often involve what happens to individuals, are at least as important as outcomes. Kantian ethics are therefore usually wary of consequential approaches. Kantian ethics suggests that individuals' human rights cannot be sacrificed to larger national policies or 'the greater good'.
Consequential or 'teleological'	'Right' or morally good actions or policies are those that bring about good or better consequences than any of the other realistic alternatives. **'Necessity'**: see, for example, The Torture Memos.[40]	Otherwise known as 'maximising the public good', consequential methods suggest that the 'utility' of an action or policy, even if it might subordinate individual autonomy, is justified because it produces the 'greatest good for the greatest number'. To take an extreme case, a consequential approach might justify, for example, the death of a few people from induced bird flu, in order to save many by helping to develop a vaccine against the virus.
Virtue ethics	The categorisation of an act as ethical or unethical is not determined by its impact as such, but by the quality or character of its actor. Virtue ethics is enjoying a radical return to favour among many moral philosophers because of the emphasis on nobility of motive.	Virtue ethics approaches derive from Aristotle's classical emphasis on 'right character' as a personal virtue. This approach transcends both Kantian and consequentialist approaches because it is simply unconcerned with 'what may happen to . . .' – because that can never be accurately predicted – and looks

3 Values, ethics and virtue   71

Table 3.1 (cont.)

Ethical method	Basic description of approach	Differences from other approaches
	'Character': see, for example, Sir Thomas More, the English lawyer executed by Henry VIII.[41]	instead at how an individual is motivated at a profoundly personal level. Thus, if the actor is 'good', so also will be 'the act'. Notions of 'good and bad', noble and ignoble, deplorable and admirable populate virtue ethics, rather than whether someone is 'for or against' a rule, or considers an action or policy 'permissible or obligatory', etc.

Each of these three methods of ethics has much to commend it. Kantian method is duty-based and places complete emphasis on the duty of humans, as rational beings, to obey what Kant described as the 'categorical imperative' to respect other rational beings.[42] The notion of duty informs the concept of a right and Kantian thinking tends to be well regarded by lawyers because of its emphasis on rights and fairness of process. For example, much of the Western concept of a proper criminal trial is supported by Kantian emphasis on fair process and, in turn, underlies the ideal of the zealous advocate in such trials.

Consequentialism (the wider category in which the more well-known 'utilitarianism' sits)[43] is also a very persuasive and well-developed method of ethics. Although it is not strictly understood as duty-based, it is treated as such here because the process of thinking consequentially has an inexorable sense of logic to it that, for some, compels only one result when a difficult choice must be made. Consequentialism has a rigour about it that seems to command obedience. Thus consequentialists assert that it is our duty to consider consequences in every decision we make and action we take. A consequential approach appeals to many of us as sensible: as just 'common sense'. If as a lawyer you prefer a consequentialist method then you may tend to see the outcome you are working towards as the justification for the approach or method you are taking. Consequentialist methods are often important because they help us to recognise who is likely to be advantaged and who could be hurt by our actions, even if we decide that some hurt is necessary in order to achieve our outcome. Consequentialists need to be clear about the likely balance between hurt and benefit before they decide something. For example, a lawyer working for the Sea Shepherd organisation, which is opposed to commercial whaling, is likely to consider the termination of this hunting such an important outcome that they will actively subvert the laws of countries that engage in the practice.

The third major approach, virtue ethics, can seem strange to lawyers because our professional focus is so much on actions and outcomes that other frameworks seem superfluous or flimsy. Yet we use virtue ethics terms a great deal, though maybe without appreciating where they come from. Take the term 'good', which is central to this book. Goodness is a fundamental concept of virtue and we apply it when deciding whether a law graduate can be admitted to practice, by requiring applicants for admission to be of 'good character'.[44] Admission is the start of your career and the time when the wider profession says: 'We expect you to *be* good.' To this extent virtue is our foundation ethic and is centrally located in who we are at that point in time, not only what we do.[45] But such goodness gets lost as we shift away from who we are towards what we do, to the point where what we do is used as the only measure of who we are. So we tend to ask people we meet about what they do, rather than who they are. Of course, our actions have profound importance – hence the maxim *spectemur agendo* ('we are judged by our actions') – but actions on their own are not enough to testify to goodness.

Just one example of this shift is the recent *Why Good Lawyers Matter*,[46] written for a Canadian legal audience and designed to support the integrity of the Canadian legal profession. The title itself suggests that its focus is the inherent goodness of lawyers as people, but each of the very worthy chapters deals instead with the important roles that lawyers fulfil and anchors goodness in those roles. There is nothing objectionable in that connection, but the book assesses goodness in terms of consequences, not in terms of lawyers' character. Should this matter? Even if our everyday sense of professionalism almost automatically equates doing good things and being a good lawyer without further enquiry, why should anyone be concerned if a lawyer's character is good or not? If actions are good, who cares if the underlying actor is dodgy or malevolent? But virtue ethics maintains that actions that are not motivated by an underlying virtue (that is, by a good actor) are likely to misfire or be subverted, or, to put it positively, that the good actor is most likely to do things that turn out to be good.

Richard Moorhead and others make the point that proper behaviour by lawyers depends on more than our character. After a lengthy survey of the many studies which have addressed professional ethics, they conclude that there are '3Cs' – character, context and capacity – which together are likely to affect behaviour in lawyers.[47] This conclusion is plausible. Character is the primary focus of this book, but capacity (your ability to recognise and reason through ethical problems) runs a close second. Context (that is, the ethical culture of your workplace) was addressed in the Chapter 2 workplace categorisations. All three concepts are implicit in the detailed problem discussions of Chapters 5 to 8.

In the following section, Table 3.2 goes into the details of the three general approaches to ethics and tries to clarify their differences with examples that reflect on lawyering. While the bias of this table generally favours a virtue approach, it is not necessary that you share that bias, or indeed that you have any fixed view about the proper basis for deciding ethical problems. A safe and responsible approach to such decisions is to consider all three methods and consciously weigh up their competing strengths before making a decision. Or, to put it slightly more carefully, what is important is to know which of the three approaches you prefer and to consider the possible contributions of the other two, before you decide what to do in a particular situation.[48]

3.6 Understanding general morality through the distinctions between the ethics of duty and virtue ethics

Table 3.2 below draws extensively from and modifies an earlier table created by Stan van Hooft in his book *Understanding Virtue Ethics*.[49] Van Hooft built on earlier work of Justin Oakley[50] to identify many points of difference between virtue ethics and the ethics of duty (the latter includes, for present purposes, consequentialism and Kantianism). I thank them both for this classification. They wished to help their readers understand the distinctive qualities of each of these components of general morality. In this table, van Hooft's specific phrasing is identified by the reference [UVE x]. The primary differences in approach between the ethics of duty and virtue ethics have been illustrated for lawyers by the addition of specific examples from both Australian and foreign settings.

74   The Good Lawyer

Table 3.2 Distinctions for lawyers between the ethics of duty and virtue ethics

The ethics of duty	Virtue ethics (character, values)
1 Duty defines moral theory There is no moral theory which is not based in duty to act, be it a duty to maximise the happiness and welfare of the greatest number of people, or a duty to identify through rational reflection what is the 'right' thing to do, or a combination of duties. The ethics of duty is initially attractive to many lawyers, and remains so because it identifies morality with law, allowing duty to be located and in some senses confined to written rules of professional conduct, or a combination of those rules, common law and statute. The ethics of duty is attractive to legal thinking which places great store on a perceived certainty of law and its capacity to order human relationships dispassionately and effectively, through the power of its own authority.	**Extends beyond legal duties** Virtue ethics is not confined to the orbit of morality as law or duty, but upturns the territory of morality fundamentally by looking at the actor, not the act. Appropriate character and values give rise to the moral actor and are the well-spring of that actor's moral actions. While these actions may be identical in any one set of circumstances to those that an ethic of duty would prescribe, there is no necessary congruence. For example, a lawyer may choose to represent a morally reprehensible client (a tobacco company) on the basis that that client has a right to representation, and he believes he has a duty to provide it under the 'cab-rank' conduct rule, but a virtuous lawyer might readily consider it unjust to assist that client because tobacco kills people after addicting them. Virtue ethics allows the virtue of justice in that lawyer to override the conduct rule.[51]
2 Duty asks: 'What should I do?' An ethics of duty person tells the truth because they believe it is right to do so. So a lawyer with an ethic of duty approach will tell the truth in court and insist that others do so too, because it is right to do so. But if another rule establishing the rightness of a contradictory action conflicts with the duty to tell the truth, then the lawyer's decision to lie (or commonly in legal practice, to remain relatively ignorant and silent), is as ethically justifiable as is the duty to tell the truth. For example, in the well-known English case of *Meek v Fleming* [1961] 2 QB 366, a lawyer remained silent and allowed his client to pretend (by wearing his previous police uniform in the witness box) that he still held a certain rank in the police force, rather than disclosing that he had been demoted. The lawyer believed, erroneously, that he had the right to remain silent because of a rule which, arguably, permitted such silence (in effect, passive deception) as long as it did not amount to active deceit of a court.	**Virtue asks: 'What should I be?' or 'How should I be?'** 'The virtuous person expresses who they are when acting and, in acting, they develop who they are.' [UVE 11] A virtuous person tells the truth because they love the truth. A lawyer who loves the truth will find it internally difficult to remain silent when a lie is told by another or a deception is practised by another, because their love of the truth is compromised. Their primary virtue of love of truth is central to who they are and is not susceptible to variable rule permission.
3 *Deontic* (Greek, meaning necessity – right, wrong, obligated, forbidden, required, prohibited) [UVE 12] The deontic view of the actions of lawyers forms the basis of teaching in most law courses and is the dominant ethos of legal practice in most Western jurisdictions. Lawyer role models are almost always of financially successful men and women who have	*Aretaic* (Greek, meaning virtue, excellence – virtuous, good, admirable, honest, courageous, modest, friendly) [UVE 12] Virtue ethics' focus on admirable character can contribute outstanding role models to legal practice (for example, the fictional Atticus Finch in *To Kill a Mockingbird*), but it is unclear how many practising and financially well-off lawyers are guided by

3 Values, ethics and virtue   **75**

Table 3.2 (cont.)

The ethics of duty	Virtue ethics (character, values)
applied rationality to rule definition and devised mechanisms that capitalise on imprecise laws in the interests of their clients. Since most law is capable of and requires interpretation if it is to be applied at all, there is endless scope for the deontic approach. What is right or wrong is clear enough to be stated by law. For example, it is forbidden for a lawyer to abuse the process of justice by commencing a legal action on behalf of a client that is based on lies or distorted evidence and is really intended to achieve an ulterior purpose unconnected with the merits of the particular case.	character before the ethics of duty. It is plausible that successful lawyers are attuned to both virtue and duty over the long term. Note that virtue ethics does not insist that virtue always trumps duty: the virtuous lawyer will be aware of their duties under positive legal systems and, in particular, of the rules of professional conduct that formally bind them. Often, what duty requires will be what virtue encourages. But virtue ethics does say that duty without virtue is ultimately barren, particularly for the actor (lawyer). Accordingly, the virtuous lawyer will, when their virtue requires it, disobey a law, and if they do that, must be prepared to take adverse consequences if they arise. For example, Stephen Keim QC represented Indian doctor Mohammad Haneef in Queensland when he was charged by the Australian Federal Police (AFP) with terrorism-related offences in 2007. Glasgow airport had just been bombed by a distant cousin of Haneef. The AFP case against him was weak and, before the case was decided, the AFP leaked to the media selected and misleading extracts of their record of interview with him, in order to sway public opinion against him. Keim faced a rule of conduct which asserted that a lawyer 'must not publish . . . any material concerning current proceedings which may prejudice a fair trial or the administration of justice'. He decided to nevertheless publish the full record of interview (which showed how unlikely it was that Haneef was connected to his terrorist cousin), to balance the adverse effects of the AFP's selective publication, asserting later that his decision was essential to a fair trial and the administration of justice. The prosecution case was withdrawn and although Keim was investigated by regulators after an AFP complaint was lodged against him, he was exonerated.
4 **Duty focuses on action** Since action is important, it does not matter in a strict sense what motives are behind the action. Legal representation is typically available to all clients, regardless of their personal worthiness or corporate reputations. Accordingly, planning lawyers whose firms represent, for example, fast food restaurants, poker machine venues, big tobacco or armaments manufacturers, all of which are legal operations and which are entitled to legal representation, are not obliged by duty-based ethics to examine their conscience as to the merits of their decision to act.	**Virtue focuses on character** 'There is something real within us that comes to expression in our behaviour . . . such that it takes a greater effort to act contrary to our character than in accord with it.' [UVE 13] Character does not involve a uniform and pre-determined moral position. A virtuous lawyer will often represent odious clients or clients who may be exploiting others and will do so because of their love of justice (for example, Stephen Keim QC). There will also be virtuous lawyers whose emotional reaction to a particular case and a possible

76   The Good Lawyer

Table 3.2 (cont.)

The ethics of duty	Virtue ethics (character, values)
Similarly, lawyers who act for accused rapists, accused terrorists, accused paedophiles and accused politicians are not required to justify their decisions so to act, in order that the fair administration of justice is able to proceed according to law (and duty).	client is so strongly negative (even allowing for the fact that allegations made against defendants do not amount to proven behaviour) that they identify their emotional inability to properly represent those clients and decline to take the case. Virtuous lawyers in this position would not be discouraged by a contrary rule of conduct that might apply to them (for example, a cab-rank rule), because their love of justice is such that they know justice is not served if defence counsel are personally conflicted in this way. [They would also know, as a matter of practical necessity, that other counsel will take a duty-based approach and will choose to represent such clients.]
5 **Goodness is defined in terms of rightness** The 'right thing' is the most powerful concept in duty-based ethics. Few can disagree that if the truly right action can be identified, then it ought to be carried out and if carried out, it will be good. A lawyer who 'knows' what is right because of their sense of duty is confident in themselves, in the applicable law and in their decisions. Rightness is understood as the applicable law. For example, a lawyer who hears his client threatening to kill his spouse if she does not agree to his contact with their infant daughter will be properly anxious that murder is not committed. If that lawyer believes his client, or is at least persuaded that his client could be serious, then he will be persuaded that the *Australian Solicitors' Conduct Rules* (ASCR) allow him to breach confidentiality [ASCR 9.1] and report his client to the opposing lawyer or to the police because he considers there to be a real possibility of imminent and serious physical harm to another person [ASCR 9.2.5]. In taking such action, the ethics of duty are facilitative, because a secondary rule allows the lawyer to disregard a primary rule.	**Goodness is defined in terms of excellence** Goodness is first a fundamental personal quality of humans and only in a derivative sense is it an objective and rational concept which describes some aspect of humanity. The goodness of a single human being is a function of the sum total of their personal virtues; that is, of their excellence. The virtuous lawyer who may be known for their selfless defence of those charged with terrorist offences but who is also known for their compassion for others and understands the practical necessity of preventing terrorist attacks, may hear from his client – who is someone charged with conspiring to carry out a terrorist attack – that another terrorist group is also planning an attack. This lawyer may be far from certain that his client is telling the truth about this prospective attack because of his clients' unbalanced state of mind. They also know that if they breach confidentiality their client will likely be faced with additional conspiracy charges whether or not an attack occurs. In the pursuit of excellence, the virtuous lawyer will consider if they are: too emotionally involved because they are anxious for themselves or their family or friends; competent enough to make a decision as to their client's truthfulness (and whether or not they require forensic psychological assistance to make that decision); and then examine (through their compassion and benevolence for their client) whether their client will be able to gain suitable alternative representation if they are forced to withdraw after reporting their client to the AFP. Finally, the virtuous lawyer will seek advice from those they admire for their virtue and only then make a decision, knowing that while that decision might turn out to be 'wrong', it was as 'good' as they could make it – in the sense that the decision was the product of a pursuit of excellence.

3 Values, ethics and virtue **77**

Table 3.2 (cont.)

The ethics of duty	Virtue ethics (character, values)
6 'Practical necessity' (that is, what we feel we must do or ought to do in a difficult situation) **is seen as a matter of obligation and obedience**, based on the command quality of the norm. [UVE 16] Many traditional ethics codes (for example, the Torah-Ten Commandments/the Koran) are law based and therefore command oriented. Reasoning is deductive (what rule binds me here?; or, what rule is likely to lead to the greatest good for the greatest number?) [UVE16–17]	**'Practical necessity' is seen as an expression of character and response to values** The virtuous lawyer will act in a particular way because they want to do what their developing sense of good character pushes them towards. Their values drive them. They are compelled by their passion for or heartfelt commitment to truth. The honest lawyer will tell the truth because they want to. A virtuous lawyer will also be guided by what other virtuous lawyers would do. [UVE 18]
7 Duty is absolute, leading to moral dilemmas If duties are absolute and more than one duty applies in a given situation, how is the conflict resolved? A common duty ethics answer is to assert that duties are only *prima facie* superior to any other duty and then to argue that one loyalty is more important than the other, allowing the inferior duty to be cancelled out. [UVE 19] How, therefore does a lawyer who has two clients in conflict with one another resolve their duty of loyalty and confidence to both clients without in some (even minor) way preferring one over the other? In practice, by trying to avoid choosing between loyalties and avoiding the conflict through some sort of information barrier and by obtaining both clients' consent. However, duty-based ethics would doubt the morality of that avoidance, arguing that one loyalty should dominate the other and that there is no dishonour in one client being sacrificed to the other providing that sacrifice occurs according to law.	Virtue is varying in stringency, requiring judgment Virtue ethics allows the lawyer-agent to decide priority between competing claims on loyalty and other duties. A virtuous commercial lawyer faced with competing claims on their loyalty and confidence would determine if their loyalties to both clients can be truly and faithfully reconciled by information barriers and fully informed consent. Such reconciliation could never be unequivocally ruled out, but if they cannot be so reconciled in the particular circumstances of the case, then the virtuous lawyer would explain to both clients that neither can be preferred to the other and assist them to find other competent lawyers, so that neither client is worse off than the other. If one client is retained and one departs, the virtuous lawyer would recognise the moral cost to themselves in discarding one client, including a possible loss of reputation and self-esteem. [UVE 19] The virtuous lawyer would emerge scarred and bearing the loss of virtue.
8 Duty is based on general principles Lying is wrong in principle and it is therefore also wrong for lawyers to lie. The ethics-of-duty lawyer will know they have done the right thing because they have succeeded in acting in a way that is strongly or even marginally inside and allowed by a law. Their conscience is likely to be clear because they have behaved according to their duty to act within the law. [But assigning personal responsibility for actions to the authority of a principle or rule only attenuates our sense of responsibility. We remain fully responsible despite rules. [UVE 22] The ethics of duty provide a degree of comfort and the illusion of easy decision making, but there is no longer a 'superior orders' defence to moral failure.]	Virtue is responsive to particular considerations Moral duties are not helpfully articulated in a general form. Particular circumstances are such that a virtuous lawyer will need to judge whether to lie or not (for example, to deceive as to the whereabouts of refugees facing oppression and self-harm) and be responsible, and be prepared to take rather than evade the consequences if that judgment, in those particular circumstances, turns out to attract a penalty. [UVE 21] Virtuous lawyers acknowledge moral ambiguity in almost every situation they are confronted with and will feel the tension and risk of choosing to lie or to remain silent when others might say they should speak up. Virtuous lawyers will not be certain of the rightness of their actions but will be courageous in the knowledge that they have tried to act according to their character and values.

78   The Good Lawyer

Table 3.2 (cont.)

The ethics of duty	Virtue ethics (character, values)

9 **Duty is justified by reason**
The ethics of duty asserts that moral thinking must be entirely rational and devoid of all emotional involvement. Only in focused rational reflection can the proper course be discovered. For example, Kant considered 'pure reason' to be the safest of guides in difficult situations and the emotion of love for others to be a distraction in the task of establishing what it is our duty to do. [UVE 23]
    An ethics-of-duty lawyer is concerned first with upholding the law because it is the law and only secondarily with achieving justice, though the rationalism of the ethics-of-duty lawyer will also acknowledge that law which is unfair for too long or with too many adverse consequences (injustice) will be an unstable law and will not be either respected or successfully enforced.
	Virtue is influenced by emotion
	Sentiments of care, love and concern (benevolence) and distress, sadness, appropriate revulsion and a desire for justice are valued by virtue ethics as entirely appropriate considerations when making difficult moral decisions. 'Emotion is part of the dynamic link that connects character and behaviour.' [UVE 23]
	    Virtuous lawyers will be especially concerned for justice because their care for their clients and the wider community cannot be fully achieved without a degree of fairness in outcomes, as between people and as between communities.

10 **Rule logic perspective**[52]
Carol Gilligan's UK studies of early school age children identified that young boys preferred to think of moral issues in terms of 'following rules and receiving what is theirs by right, while girls preferred to compromise so as to maintain friendly relationships'.[53]
    The ethics-of-duty stance makes no comment on a genetic basis for morality, let alone for male v female lawyers, but emphasises that all lawyers should be 'doing the right thing'.
    The ethics of duty is not formally concerned with how acts are perceived or explained, with any pain that may be caused by those acts or with their consequences for humans, providing that they are right, as determined by law or *a priori* reason. For the ethics of duty, right actions become good actions.
	Caring perspective
	Caring lawyers, that is, those exhibiting an ethic of care, may be the same as virtuous lawyers, but need not be.
	    A virtuous lawyer will not shirk a tough or 'uncaring' decision if their good character is such that they feel compelled to choose to act in that way.
	    What distinguishes the caring perspective of virtuous lawyers is their care(ful) attention to how they act, who they impact upon and how their decision is received. Virtuous lawyers are vitally interested in mediating their decisions in a care-filled manner.

11 **Duty is impartial**
If an agent is confronted by a burning house with two people in it (one their aged mother and the other 'a world-famous scientist who will bring great good to the world')[54] and can save only one, who should they choose to save? The consequentialist (utilitarian) agent will choose the scientist because the calculus of greater contribution to the world, based on impartial reason, is clear. [UVE 24] The Kantian agent will acknowledge that one must die but will be morally incapacitated because they cannot (unless they turn to another ethical framework) prefer one to the other, since to do so offends a central Kantian principle (a categorical imperative) that each life is as valuable as another.
    The impartial ethics-of-duty lawyer who authored the Pentagon's *Torture Memos*, which justified the use of waterboarding and other torture of suspected terrorists during the US presidency of G.W. Bush,
	Virtue is partial
	Virtue ethics applauds the agent's decision to save his mother because of their emotional ties, but the virtuous rescuer would feel a sense of regret that the scientist could not also be saved.
	    Virtue acknowledges that it is highly appropriate to be partial in acknowledging 'the web of interpersonal relationships.'[55] [UVE 24–25]
	    A virtuous lawyer in a similar position as the Pentagon author might be appalled at the thought of torture as the opposite of care, and ask themselves if the torture really would produce reliable information, whether the weight of evidence against the suspect was of greater probity than the certain harm that will be done by torture to him and his family relationships, whether the reputation of the US as a just society will be damaged if the torture and its justifications were ever to become public and whether they, as the lawyer proponent of that

3 Values, ethics and virtue **79**

Table 3.2 (cont.)

The ethics of duty	Virtue ethics (character, values)
was and is content in having done their duty to protect as many Americans (and others) as possible from the threat of terrorism. Indeed, such torture may have saved the lives of others and proof to the contrary is unlikely.	torture, ought to take full responsibility for their decision by seeking to personally conduct the torture themselves.

12 **Universal**

The ethics of duty

Moral actions are absolutes because of their universal nature, for example, to tell the truth, show courage and practise benevolence.

Foundational, duty-based ethics avoids the problem of aberrant cultures with deficient moral codes.

A lawyer whose being is grounded in universal duty-based ethics may be less likely to succumb to the perversion of morality that characterised Nazi Germany, or apartheid-era South Africa or even some agencies of government in both conservative and liberal democracies.

But if such lawyers' grasp of universal principles is actually parochial or blunted by nationalism, they may succumb to the blandishments of employers or governments that identify nation-state interests as the proper base of their duty. If that occurs, they may be willing to work on legislation or its enforcement that denies universal values and assists injustice. It is possible that the lawyers who during the 1930s developed the anti-semitic legislation that came to define the Nazi Holocaust, were persuaded that their duty-based ethics were owed to the German state alone.

Culture-relative

Virtue ethics (character, values)

'Virtues are always culture specific. They have moral validity because the culture they have developed within values them.' [UVE 39]

Nazi Germany developed loyalty to the point of unwavering obedience, but such unquestioning obedience was (and is) not perceived as a virtue outside Nazism or similar totalitarian societies. [UVE 40–41]

The corruptibility of a community or state's moral position in the manner of the Nazis (and perhaps of some contemporary fundamentalist religious communities and states) represents a challenge to the authenticity of virtue ethics, because there is nothing intrinsically right about culture-specific virtues. So virtue ethics appeals to the reality that individuals, despite their moral theorising, always make decisions in very precise circumstances and rely on their general connections to others: there is always a 'spark of creativity' that allows individuals to look at intuitions and insights from other societies [UVE 41]; in effect, they are always subject to a wider hermeneutic which judges their morality against the whole of human experience. For example, while slavery was for a long time regarded as entirely acceptable, it gradually became suspect according to wider understandings of human decency and was formally abolished in English-speaking communities. [UVE 41]

Specific cultural contexts for moral actions also extend to MacIntyre's concept of a 'community of practice' [UVE 39]: that is, a group of people who for a particular reason develop and formally agree on a specific moral code.

Lawyers have developed such a culture-relative moral code and their particular code provisions, such as zealous advocacy, can be and are characterised by lawyers as both the essence of lawyering and as only part of lawyering.

The virtue of a code that comes from a community of practice, such as the legal profession, is that it is provisionally authentic for the lawyer community and is in a state of more or less constant development, in order to maintain the approval of the wider community.[56] To that extent the ASCR is likely to be accepted as authentic beyond its borders. And as the ASCR is in the end, founded in character considerations, it can evolve to develop its virtue.

'Character as shaped by community or tradition can motivate such a critique because of its inherent creativity and sensitivity to value.' [UVE 41]

3.7 Conclusion: Strengthening our self-respect

Although virtue ethics is likely to be a more demanding approach to legal ethics than either of the duty-based approaches, it gets us closer to the essentials of good lawyering than the others because it strengthens our self-respect and integrity. As emphasised by the 'good character' test applied when lawyers want to be admitted to legal practice, virtue ethics offers the best fit with what the community wants to see in new lawyers and what the profession wants to encourage through its professional conduct rules. However, duty-based ethics will ground our thinking by reminding us of the objective cautions raised by both consequences and fairness. Good lawyering cannot be harmed and is likely to be advanced by weighing all these approaches in the interests of both care and justice.

In Chapter 4, the connections of virtue ethics to the traditional duty-based role of a lawyer as a zealous advocate are examined in detail. A case is made for a more formal restriction of zealous advocates to just two areas of law: criminal defence in courts or adversarial tribunals and in family law.

Notes

1. See, for example, the case at Ch. 8, Table 8.3.
2. See, for example, *Legal Services Commissioner v Coldham and ors* (Legal Practice) [2012] *VCAT* 74 (with co-defendants, Philip Barton and Donald Brookes), who were partners of the mid-tier firm Anderson Rice in Melbourne. The three were found guilty of common law misconduct and had their practising certificates suspended for 9 months for deliberately delaying the presentation of $300,000 worth of cheques owed to barristers and expert witnesses. The strategy was designed to reduce the level of debt in their practice's overdraft account. They also had to pay $50,000 for the Legal Services Commissioner's costs.
3. See Ch. 2.7.
4. Popularly known as the Hippocratic Oath. See www.nlm.nih.gov/hmd/greek/greek_oath.html.
5. Any disciplinary proceedings brought against practitioners are commenced having regard to principles of misconduct or unsatisfactory professional conduct under common law, statute or regulation, not for breach of a commitment given to the Court. See, further, Adrian Evans, 'First, do no harm . . .' (2008) 82(6) *LIJ* 86.
6. This is also a permitted exception under the ASCR. See Ch. 6.
7. See 'After 26 years, 2 Lawyers Reveal a Killer's Secret', *USA Today*, 13 April 2008, at www.usatoday.com/news/nation/2008-04-13-murder-silence_N.htm?csp=34. See also

Peter A. Joy and Kevin C. McMunigal 'Confidentiality and wrongful incarceration' (2008) 23(2) *Criminal Justice, Ethics section.*

8. See, for example, David Eagleman, *Incognito: The Secret Lives of the Brain*, Canongate Books, UK, 2012. Eagleman argues that ideas such as responsibility and freedom will not retain much meaning as neuroscience advances.

9. See, for example, Victoria Gill, 'Big Bang: Is there room for God?', BBC, 19 October 2012, at www.bbc.co.uk/news/science-environment-19997789.

10. Ibid., adapting the arguments of John Lennox in this BBC debate.

11. See R. Scruton, 'Nature versus nuture: a moral mind field', *Australian Financial Review, Review*, 24 February 2012, 1 and 10.

12. Ibid.

13. Ibid.

14. For example, of the 18 000 lawyers in Victoria in 2012 and huge (but unknown) number of transactions, cases, letters and enquiries undertaken each year by all those practitioners, only 1982 resulted in complaints to the Legal Services Commissioner in the year ended 30 June 2012. See www.lsc.vic.gov.au/complaints/complaints-data.

15. See Ch. 1.

16. See Ch. 1, n 23.

17. See Ch. 1, n 22.

18. See W. Bradley Wendel, *Lawyers and Fidelity to Law*, Princeton University Press, Princeton NJ, 2010. See also W. Bradley Wendel, 'Moral judgment and professional legitimation' (2007) 51 *St. Louis U. L. Rev.* 1071 at 1073; and Tim Dare, 'Virtue ethics, legal ethics and Harper Lee's *To Kill a Mockingbird*', in T. Dare, *A Counsel of Rogues*, Farnham, Ashgate, 2009.

19. See Luban, *The Good Lawyer: Lawyers' Roles and Lawyers' Ethics* and Tomain, 'The legal heresiarchs: Luban's *The Good Lawyer*'.

20. Trevor C. Farrow, 'The good, the right and the lawyer' (2012) 15(1) *Legal Ethics* 163 at 164.

21. Ibid., 169.

22. Ibid., 170.

23. Ibid.

24. Ibid., 171.

25. Ibid.

26. Ibid.

27. See, for example, Alice Woolley, 'Review Symposium: W. Bradley Wendel and *Fidelity to Law*' (2012) 15(1) *Legal Ethics* 41, where she comments that 'the view that the lawyer can set out legal choices for clients while maintaining moral neutrality fails to recognise the necessary moral quality of much legal reasoning.' See also Roberto M. Unger, *Democracy Realized: The Progressive Alternative*, Verso, 1988, 255; Judith Bessant, 'Ethical behaviour more than just following rules', *The Age*, 30 November 2011, 17; and Clare K. Coleman, 'Teaching the Torture Memos: Making decisions under conditions of uncertainty' (2012) 62(1) *Jnl of Legal Education* 81 at 94. In response to his critics, Wendel is matter-of-fact: 'Being a lawyer is a job, not a comprehensive perspective on the human predicament.' See W. Bradley Wendel, 'Putting Morality in its Place' (2012) 15 *Legal Ethics* 175 at 181.

82   The Good Lawyer

28. Farrow, n 20, 172. And Farrow is not anxious that opening the door to lawyers' moral engagement will be counter-productive: 'we will not be opening the door to a tyranny of lawyers who refuse to take on unpopular clients and causes' (173). Failure to launch has not been a problem so far, for many lawyers already take on unpopular causes.

29. See Tomain, 'The legal heresiarchs: Luban's *The Good Lawyer*'.

30. See Ch. 2, n 43.

31. See, for example, 'GAS LEAK!' by Matthew Carney and Connie Agius, *Four Corners*, ABC1, 3 April 2013, at www.abc.net.au/4corners/stories/2013/04/01/3725150.htm.

32. 'Affidavits are documents which set out a list of facts. They are used in court cases to "prove" those facts. But first, the person who says that the set of facts are "true and correct" must sign their name at the bottom of the document. They must then verbally "swear" (as an oath on the Bible or other holy book) or "affirm" (if they have no religious belief), that the signature on the document is their own and that the contents of the affidavit are accurate. Anyone who swears or affirms a false Affidavit commits the criminal offence of perjury. Lawyers and other approved persons are not permitted to witness an affidavit if they do not put their client (or other person) through this process of "swearing" or "affirming" first.' Extract from Ross Hyams and Adrian Evans, *Practical Legal Skills*, 4th edn, Oxford University Press, Melbourne, 2014, Ch. 4.

33. Ibid.

34. See Ch. 2, n 55.

35. See, for example, Stephen Barkoczy, *Foundations of Taxation Law* (5th edn), CCH Australia Ltd, 2013, 752–56.

36. One of the most important and relevant US publications in recent years to recognise the normative realities of teaching law (and by implication, its practice) is The Carnegie Report (see Ch. 1, n 26) injunction to 'enable[e] students to learn to make judgments under conditions of uncertainty'.

37. See, for example, M. Baron, P. Pettit and M. Slote, *Three Methods of Ethics – A Debate: For and Against Consequences, Maxims and Virtues*, Blackwell, Oxford, 1997.

38. There is a case for discussing the contributions of legal philosophers such as John Finnis, who has developed the concept of natural law and goodness in a synthesis which draws on all of virtue ethics, Kantianism and consequentialism and much else (see Finnis, *Natural Law and Natural Rights*).

39. Kantian fairness requires a fair trial process. In *R v Nerbas* [2011] QCA 199, for example, a defendant in a Queensland drugs case was required by his barrister to enter a plea of guilty midway through his trial, after the barrister received what they considered to be a change of instructions sufficient to place them in a 'difficult' position. This information was presumed to be a confession, but the court said that the defendant's appeal against conviction had to be allowed because counsel were not entitled to insist on a guilty plea unless they knew, as opposed to strongly suspected, that the change in instructions represented a change in the factual basis of the defence. In other words, a barrister is not entitled to regard a confession as truthful (without additional convincing information). See also Chapter 5.5 and *Tuckiar v The King* (1934) 52 CLR 335, 341.

40. The 'Torture Memos' were a series of secret Pentagon memoranda prepared after the World Trade Center terrorist attacks on 11 September 2001. The memos were intended to provide a legal justification for torture, particularly the practice of 'waterboarding', which is alleged to feel like drowning to the person being interrogated. The memos were eventually leaked and their purpose was made clear. See Jane Mayer, 'Annals of the Pentagon – The Memo: How an internal effort to ban the abuse and torture of detainees was thwarted', *The New Yorker*, 27 February 2006, 32.

41. Sir Thomas More was Lord Chancellor of England (chief law officer) during the reign of Henry VIII. At one point the King wished to divorce Catherine of Aragon and marry Ann Boleyn, but the Pope would not agree. Papal permission to divorce was then essential under the law of England. More was a devout Catholic and considered he was morally obliged to uphold the marriage to Catherine, unless the Pope decided otherwise. The combined opposition of the Pope and More meant that Henry could only be divorced if he founded his own church and broke with Rome, in effect establishing a new legal order under a new Church of England. He took this momentous step and More was tried, convicted of treason (opposing the King) and beheaded in 1535. See *Britannica – The Online Encyclopedia*, Sir Thomas More.

42. Derived from the work of Prussian philosopher Immanuel Kant, 1724–1804. See Roger Scruton, *Kant: A very short introduction*, Oxford University Press, New York, 2001.

43. Consequentialism is not the same as utilitarianism, but is a general overarching category which includes utilitarian thinking. A consequentialist will hold that acts which promote a variety of overall dimensions of goodness (for example, happiness, knowledge, achievement) are ethical, while a utilitarian is narrower and will tend to prioritise acts which maximise just the happiness of sentient beings. See also Stuart Rachels, *The Elements of Moral Philosophy*, McGraw-Hill International, New York, 2010, Chs 7 and 8.

44. See Tomain, 'The legal heresiarchs: Luban's *The Good Lawyer*'.

45. See further Alice Woolley, 'Tending the bar: The "good character" requirement for Law Society admission' (2007) 30 *Dalhousie L. J.* 27.

46. David L. Blaikie, Thomas Cromwell and Darrel Pink, *Why Good Lawyers Matter*, Irwin Law, Toronto, 2012.

47. Richard Moorhead, Victoria Hinchley, Christine Parker, David Kersaw and Soren Holm, 'Designing ethics indicators for legal services provision', *Legal Services Board* (UK), 5 September 2012. See www.legalservicesboard.org.uk/news_publications/press_releases/2012/pdf/2012_09_04_ethics_research_final.pdf.

48. It might be said that the virtue of prudence is involved in a decision to consider all three methods before acting, because there is no such thing as certainty or correctness in ethical decision making at the margins.

49. Specifically, see Table 1, in Stan van Hooft, *Understanding Virtue Ethics*, Acumen Publishing, Chesham, 2006, 8.

50. See Justin Oakley and Dean Cocking, *Virtue Ethics and Professional Roles*, Cambridge University Press, New York, 2002. They devised a number of categories which van Hooft included in his analysis. See also Justin Oakley, 'Varieties of virtue ethics' (1996) *IX Ratio* (New Series) 128, which in many ways foreshadowed the categories later appearing in van Hooft, *Understanding Virtue Ethics* (n 489).

84 The Good Lawyer

51. See further R. M. Saguiel, 'A virtuous profession: Reconceptualising legal ethics from a virtue-based moral philosophy' (2006) *Windsor Review of Legal and Social Issues* 1; Angela Olivia Burton, 'Cultivating ethical, socially responsible lawyer judgment: introducing the multiple lawyering intelligences paradigm into the clinical setting' (2005) 11 *Clinical L. Rev.* 15 at 19, noting that law schools lag behind other professional schools in incorporating the teaching of judgment-making into the curriculum; Nathan M. Crystal, 'Using the concept of "a philosophy of lawyering" in teaching professional responsibility' (2007) 51 *St. Louis U. L. J.* 1235 at 1240, noting the 'number of approaches' used in the professional responsibility literature to assist lawyers in making discretionary decisions and the 'wide range of discretionary decisions' that lawyers will face in their practice, at 1241; and David Luban, 'Epistemology and moral education' (1983) 33 *J. Legal Educ.* 638, 639, noting that 'judgment cannot be taught in the form of rules'.
52. Van Hooft calls this category the 'justice perspective'. See n 49, 24.
53. Ibid.
54. Ibid.
55. Ibid., 25.
56. Farrow cites these provisions of the American and Canadian codes of professional conduct. They illustrate sensitivity to the importance of lawyers' character. For example, the Federation of Law Societies of Canada (FLSC) *Model Code of Professional Conduct* contains a provision that a lawyer cannot do something on behalf of a client that the lawyer considers 'dishonorable' [FLSC r 4.01(2)(b), adopted 17 March 2011] and the American Bar Association *Model Rules of Professional Conduct* assert that a lawyer must be guided by 'personal conscience' and when representing a client, 'may refer not only to law but to other considerations such as moral, economic, social and political factors, that may be relevant to the client's situation' ['Preamble and Scope', para 7 and r 2.1,1983, as amended]. Compare these provisions with the ASCR 4.1.4: '[a solicitor must] ... avoid any compromise to their integrity and professional independence.' See further Farrow, n 20, 172.

Chapter 4

CONNECTING CHARACTER TO LAWYERS' ROLES

4.1 Introduction: Character-laden law

Previous chapters have explored what a good law school looks like and what a good legal practice environment needs. Chapter 3 then examined several dimensions of our underlying ethics and started to again make the case, just as Luban did, that general morality has a significant part to play in our legal ethics. This chapter continues that theme and connects a central aspect of underlying morality – that of our character – to the role we perform as lawyers.

The quest to develop lawyers' capacity for goodness has never been more important. In the short period since the new millennium, corporate failure around the Western world has focused community and judicial disillusion on the professionals implicated. Accountants, auditors, financiers and lawyers (in-house and external) have all suffered loss of reputation and self-esteem, not to mention jobs. Lawyers were rarely the main drivers of these collapses, but our entrenched role in validating and enabling deals and a wide range of financial products was always crucial. Perhaps it's because we often think of ourselves as only the mouthpiece, never the mouth – in the comfortable lawyer role of agent, not actor – that as a profession, we do not seem to have been interested in offering much by way of apology for those momentous events in 2007–08.[1] But some atonement may be possible by strengthening individual lawyers' character. We may then be able to show enough compassion for the victims of our mistakes (and in some cases our greed), to limit the impact of traditional role morality and the risk of recurrence.

85

4.2 Strengthening underlying character

Character is the essence of reputation, not just its appearance. If we have a developed sense of good character, then that will be increasingly known to our peers and opponents. They may not agree with the values we have, but they will over time respect us and therefore our differences. You may not share the same political or social views as those around you, but if your character is known to be good – that is, if you are known to keep your promises, if you are industrious, if you treat opponents fairly and do not deceive them – then your reputation will not only add to your success in material terms, but it will sustain your self-respect. And self-respect is a key factor in professional 'flourishing', the quality of 'growing vigorously' that Aristotle thought was central to living the full life.[2]

Aristotle insightfully insisted that character does not suddenly appear; it does not just arrive one morning (with the mail). We develop our character by applying ourselves to that task, usually over years. He thought character has to be 'habituated' or worked at in a very conscious manner,[3] because developing our character involves a habit of ongoing reflection on the good and bad experiences we all have and contemplating what each experience meant. If that is correct, then for each of us, the process of character development means reflecting upon what is important, and then at some point being firm enough to make a decision about what to do. As the Danish philosopher Søren Kierkegaard saw it, character development cannot just be cerebral; it means progressively identifying what we believe in most passionately and eventually altering how we act:

> [I]ntellectual reason alone can never motivate action. A decision to end the process of reflection is necessary and such a decision must be generated by passion . . . The most significant passions [decisions], such as love and faith, do not merely happen, they must be cultivated and formed.[4]

4.3 Connecting with your own sense of general morality

If you choose to develop your character in this deliberate way, it will occur more easily if you are reflecting on your experiences not in a vacuum, but in the context of a moral framework. Moral knowledge, all things being equal, translates into moral sense and strengthens character. Eventually, stronger character leads to a developing sense of judgment, which when combined with experience is the really critical quality lawyers need. For our whole profession, the final, essential 'value-adding' ingredient can only be our sense of judgment. But we all have to start with knowledge, not just of law, but of ethics as well. The large table in Chapter 3 was one such knowledge framework and it appears there because our understanding and adoption of ethical methods is foundational and should come first, but there are several general frameworks that serve related purposes in the fields of personality[5] and educational psychology[6] and in other particular disciplines.[7]

There are no instruments that have been developed specifically to help lawyers assess their underlying or general moral positions, though a number of US studies have reached fairly depressing conclusions which bear on the related issue of a typical lawyer personality. These studies have been reviewed and summed up by Susan Daicoff[8] and tend to emphasise competitiveness, ambition, logical rule-based thinking, objectivity in making decisions and fewer interpersonal strengths than the general population.[9] To be fair, these characteristics will be particularly valuable in a number of adversarial contexts and do not prohibit a well-developed sense of underlying or general morality in any way. But mixed with the depression which Beaton has identified in the Australian legal profession,[10] it's plausible to suggest that lawyers, particularly lawyers with unexamined role morality, are to some extent unhappy about their lives as lawyers. So there is likely to be some gain for us in getting closer to our moral core, even if that knowledge is unsettling.

4.4 Being and remaining 'positive' about life as a lawyer

The necessary emphasis in this chapter on some of the negatives of life as a lawyer is not intended to dampen your enthusiasm. The reality of legal practice is a moral mixture of good and bad and there is no intrinsic reason why the good should not prevail, if we each recognise that a choice must be made. 'Forewarned is forearmed' could almost be the subtitle, but once you are prepared, there is every reason why your own lawyering can and will be both emotionally satisfying, morally sustaining and powerfully enabling inside your law firm. You have a tremendous opportunity to improve the culture of your law firm: by showing collegiality, by being fair and honest in your work relationships and by understanding that the quality of these human relationships becomes your 'culture'. We may be a product of our culture, but we are also contributors to it. Cultural leadership by those at the top is naturally important, but being optimistic about your contribution as a new lawyer is part of being a 'good' lawyer. It is also rational, realistic and likely to be effective. One of the reasons for this optimism comes from modern psychology.

In recent years a branch of psychology known as positive psychology has developed considerable recognition. Positive psychology builds on the very broad statement that a life well lived (that is, one which displays a number of good qualities) is one that will be authentically happy.[11] This goal is not to be confused with the over-used concept of positive thinking and its associated pursuit of a shallow happiness. That path is increasingly discredited because of its consumerism, its denial of failure (and of our ability to learn from failure) and, particularly, its avoidance of the realities of suffering.[12] There is a much deeper and more satisfying understanding of goodness, one that strengthens resilience and addresses more of the crucial qualities needed by new lawyers. So what are these good qualities? Christopher Petersen and Martin Seligman have identified a number of so-called character strengths and virtues associated with positive psychology. Three of these (Table 4.1) are of particular relevance to lawyers:

Table 4.1 Key virtues of good lawyers

1. **Wisdom and knowledge**: Cognitive strengths that entail the acquisition and use of knowledge.
- Creativity (originality, ingenuity) . . .
- Curiosity (interest, novelty-seeking, openness to experience)
- Open-mindedness (judgment, critical thinking)
- Love of learning: mastering new skills, topics and bodies of knowledge whether on one's own or formally
- Perspective (wisdom).

2. **Courage**: Emotional strengths that involve the exercise of will to accomplish goals in the face of opposition, external or internal.
- Bravery (valour)
- Persistence (perseverance, industriousness)
- Integrity (authenticity, honesty)
- Vitality (zest, enthusiasm, vigour and energy).

3. **Justice**: Civic strengths that underlie healthy community life.
- Citizenship (social responsibility, loyalty, teamwork)
- Fairness: treating all people the same according to notions of fairness and justice; not letting personal feelings bias decisions about others; giving everyone a fair chance
- Leadership: encouraging a group of which one is a member to get things done, at the same time maintaining good relations within the group; honouring group activities and seeing that they happen.[13]

You may be cautious about this list because it appears simplistic, highly idealised and remote from the everyday life of lawyers. And there should be scepticism about faddish psychology movements and even cults which propose 'self-improvement' but in fact create dependency. Positive psychology is, however, in the mainstream and seems unlikely to be cast in that mould.[14] What does seem clear is that practising members of the legal profession can be particularly prone to depression and substance abuse, and in its central impact on others, this can tend to catalogue failure rather than affirm goodness. The combined effect on us as lawyers can be somewhat negative, so we need some positive models of lawyering up front, as it were, if we are to be 'vaccinated' against illness and flourish.

Positive models for lawyering are discussed below under lawyer 'types'. They need to be preceded by our own awareness of our 'good' (moral) qualities, because positive lawyering builds on that knowledge. There are now several psychological instruments that allow anyone to evaluate where they are in relation to the above list of qualities.[15] It is not feasible to reproduce or explore these general purpose tools in detail, but lawyers will find many of them useful; depending on the results, they may need to seek assistance in their interpretation. And there is a vital goal here. The lawyer who has a well-developed sense of character, an understanding of their own preferences in general morality and a positive perspective on life is better able to manage the special role morality of lawyering.

4.5 Why is role morality (zealous advocacy, the dominant legal ethic) so important for lawyers?

Role morality is a powerful concept, supporting the 'good' of justice to the community[16] because it supports the citizen (and non-citizen) against the power of the state. Role morality is important for lawyers because it justifies our existence in that key area. But its use comes with caveats as well.

The stereotype of the good lawyer in common law countries,[17] particularly outside the US, is of a bewigged Queens Counsel (QC) who stands up in front of a criminal court to defend someone charged by the state with a serious crime. This lawyer is first of all good because of their actions rather than who they may be when not in role. Whether the client is rich or poor makes no difference, because in theory, they do not discriminate between their clients.[18] The lawyer knows that only they stand between their client and imprisonment or, in earlier years, the gallows. In the face of such high stakes and in the strong belief that the judge (who at one point also stood where the QC stands) will know the truth when they hear it regardless of what any advocate says, the QC is determined to take every possible advantage in the interests of their clients' freedom. In this ideal of legal history and many current criminal trials, the good QC or the good barrister is not there to put forward or conceal what seems privately to them to be the truth,[19] but to put forward in their clients' interests what could be the truth or could be the true position, both as to the facts and as to the law. If they know – as opposed to strongly suspect – that the truth is otherwise, they must not deceive the court,[20] but in every other case – that is, where their every sense tells them that their client is lying – traditional role morality still requires them to act as if their client is being truthful. They must not 'spill the beans', and are expected to internally justify their silence as to their misgivings, again confidently leaving it to jury and judge to work out who is really being honest.

QCs and other barristers in this situation are expected to console themselves with the rational thought that they cannot be 100% certain of what really occurred and because that is the case, they may do and should say things that common morality would find outrageous. And the prosecuting barrister has a similar role.[21] The jury, with the judge's assistance, will decide what is most likely to have occurred and the barrister need not be anxious about whatever they said being analysed carefully for truth. So the defending barrister is not just permitted, but positively obligated to exploit every weakness in the prosecution case, including (if necessary) harassing and defaming prosecution witnesses in the interests of forcing or tricking an admission or confession that will assist their client. All this is justified, and reasonably so, because in defended cases, criminal courts are not all-seeing gods and must commonly decide between degrees of probability only. The essential justification for role morality is to allow courts to get close to discovering truth with the help of fearless advocacy: that is, when lawyers love justice and act with courage.[22]

Oakley considers that the key flaw in role morality is still an empirical one: that is, lawyers are seen to go too far too frequently in pressuring or denigrating witnesses, offending not just general morality but even the minimal fairness expected in role morality.[23] He cites the case of a former Victorian Supreme Court judge who, long after the event, considered that he had, as a barrister, been party to (in his own words) 'an appalling injustice' in the manner in which he had questioned a 14-year-old girl in the witness box.[24] This criticism is valid as far as it goes. Advocates who abuse the protection of their role to damage others are ignoring the fact that role morality does not license the infliction of human misery. The ASCR reflects those expectations.

But the cost for lawyers is also an issue here. Every QC and defence barrister or solicitor, advocate or attorney who ever appeared before a criminal court displays as a virtue a profound sort of integrity; because to be in this weird role day after day and yet be able to come home and be truthful and express their emotions honestly to their family and friends is not easy for everyone. Role morality takes a psychological toll on many, particularly if they have no real sense of their moral core outside of lawyering, if they have not developed their underlying virtues and especially if they have not realised that role morality must stay in role and is toxic to their health and relationships outside a court.[25]

Similar issues arise for advocates who work in family law or in the many tribunal jurisdictions that have increasingly been set up to resolve consumer, tenancy, planning, disease compensation or licensing disputes and to determine the outcome of professional discipline cases, to name a few. In each of these environments also, there are complainants (plaintiffs) or respondents (defendants) – or both – who are under-resourced compared to their opponents, but the tribunal still decides by working out whose case is strongest. One party will be disadvantaged if their advocate is not as zealous as that of their opponent.

Advocates who practise in family law are also often dealing with clients on both sides for whom nearly every issue in dispute is bitterly contested and deeply emotional. Family lawyers must often test the claims of the other party with as much determination as any criminal defender.

But outside these environments, the justifications for role morality start to decline and the case for general morality starts to improve.

4.6 Central criticisms of role morality

Role morality can become a problem for some because of its allowable detachment. That is, while lawyers are able to behave poorly according to ordinary moral standards while in role, in the process they can become emotionally detached from any consequences. This self-deception is aided by Kantian conceptions of moral character which emphasise the importance of rights in an institutionally supported context.[26] So a criminal lawyer who has a strong sense of the guilt of their client, though no actual proof, is appropriately required to assist them to plead 'not guilty'. They may then shrug their shoulders when their client is acquitted and despite also feeling some professional pride, they can be faced with a sense of shame – regardless of the justification of role morality.

Even when acting appropriately in role, lawyers need to beware of blaming the adversarial system (as an institution) as a way of psychologically avoiding any general moral responsibility for their actions.[27] Psychological dysfunction arising from too much role detachment is reduced by virtue ethics, which encourages us to internalise our professional roles and integrate them with our personality to the point that we recognise an ultimate moral accountability for all our actions, making it less likely that we will see our in-role behaviours as separate from our private and personal life.[28]

While role morality can be personally costly to its practitioners, it does fulfil a social good in limited adversarial environments. However, it begins to look less good and less socially useful when it is applied to the vast number of transactional and corporate law environments that make up the work of most lawyers. If criminal law, family law and tribunal contests can bring out the best in role morality, then the contracts (financing arrangements, share issues, mergers, housing developments, sales and purchases) that drive economic growth, together with the debt restructuring and insolvencies that mark its decline, can bring out the worst. Contractual (that is, transactional) law occurs on a very different legal playing field from the adversarial trial.

Transactions occur first in private, and while an increasing number of them must be placed before a judge of regulator for subsequent approval, that process is not as rigorous as a contested case conducted in open court. Transactions require no primary scrutiny by a judge and depend for their long-term stability on the good faith of the players. That is, the parties to commercial deals must trust each other to abide by the contract and need to use lawyers who can support that trust. Lawyers can only do that effectively if they are known by the lawyers on the other side for their candour and integrity. Highly adversarial trials need zealous lawyers who have a capacity to keep quiet in the interests of discovering the truth. But none of the corporations involved in major deals, or their transactional lawyers, are well served if they automatically adopt adversarial attitudes and approach their role with secrecy rather than candour.

Transactional lawyering needs lawyers who are motivated by general morality; who see that successful and beneficial corporate enterprise ultimately depends on shared and transparent business goals and the long-term flourishing of their clients' businesses. If business lawyers on both sides of a proposed deal or manoeuvre are able to draw on role morality to convince themselves that they owe no greater loyalty to anyone except their current corporate client, danger is very close. There will be many reasons why they do in fact fail in their responsibilities to their company or client, but at the heart of that failure is the implicit conditioning they acquire over time that it's their job (in role, as it were) to prioritise their client 'at all costs'. The client in these cases owns not just their loyalty but their spirit as well.

This issue of autonomy is at the centre of the large law firm lawyers' dilemma, because they commonly work on transactions, often for only one or two huge clients. If they act for (or are in-house lawyers of) a corporation in trouble and are able to justify fraudulent and technical arrangements that preserve legality but in fact weaken not just their clients but all the sectors with whom they deal, then the ultimate usefulness of their role is diminished and in some cases extinguished. We have seen significant examples of lawyers' perverse role morality in corporate law:

- in AWB Ltd, which drafted and signed false contracts to pay bribes disguised as trucking fees to Saddam Hussein in Iraq, contrary to UN sanctions, to secure contracts to sell wheat,[29]
- in James Hardie Industries Limited, where the company's secretary and general counsel moved the corporate headquarters around the world to try to get away from an obligation to compensate those dying of asbestos-related diseases and when those manoeuvres failed as a part of that restructure, conspired with the CEO to mislead the Australian Stock Exchange as to the adequacy of those compensation arrangements,[30]
- in many cases of document destruction organised by lawyers where there was a concern that those documents would incriminate the company if discovered in later litigation,[31]

94   The Good Lawyer

- in the many cases of tax avoidance by large companies' use of tax havens, and most recently, by global technology companies who produce false transfer pricing contracts between their subsidiaries across many jurisdictions, in order to prevent paying the required tax in high-tax countries.[32]

But none of these was as spectacular or has been so carefully dissected as the failure of Enron Corporation, where both external auditors and external lawyers crafted and maintained a deceitful regime to hide staggering levels of the corporation's debt.[33]

Luban's plea for general morality in lawyering is therefore on its strongest ground in the transactional world and legal ethicists in the US legal system have taken up and developed his themes over time.[34] But role morality remains dominant in common law traditions for all lawyers, no matter the nature of their work, with some of its defenders re-casting the problem of over-zealous lawyers as about their lack of integrity.[35] So it should not be lost on anyone that an appeal to virtue (that is, to integrity[36]) is enlisted by the defenders of role morality. The ongoing recurrence over the last 30 years of cases such as those above is making it easier to recognise that the moral non-accountability of the transactional lawyer is less and less viable.

Of course transactional lawyers are not by definition lacking in moral character. There are numerous examples to the contrary, but the attitude of moral non-accountability that arises from role morality hardly encourages character development. If such lawyers see themselves as only loyal to their current client and without general moral obligations, then their client calls the tune and those lawyers lose their capacity to counsel morally safe courses of action. This is particularly obvious when clients' projects appear to lack any (general) morality and fail.

We need to find a coherent and credible framework to stave off the sort of judicial comment delivered by Judge Rakoff in the Global Financial Crisis (GFC) aftermath (see Chapter 2) or the US District Court in ruling that the tobacco industry had breached racketeering laws in a conspiracy to deceive the public. In 2006, Judge Gladys Kessler made this comment about the role morality of the lawyers involved in that industry:

> Finally, a word must be said about the role of lawyers in this fifty-year history of deceiving smokers, potential smokers, and the American public about the

hazards of smoking and second hand smoke, and the addictiveness of nicotine. At every stage, lawyers played an absolutely central role in the creation and perpetuation of the Enterprise and the implementation of its fraudulent schemes. They devised and coordinated both national and international strategy; they directed scientists as to what research they should and should not undertake; they vetted scientific research papers and reports as well as public relations materials to ensure that the interests of the Enterprise would be protected; they identified 'friendly' scientific witnesses, subsidized them with grants from the Center for Tobacco Research and the Center for Indoor Air Research, paid them enormous fees, and often hid the relationship between those witnesses and the industry; and they devised and carried out document destruction policies and took shelter behind baseless assertions of the attorney client privilege. What a sad and disquieting chapter in the history of an honourable and often courageous profession.[37]

Role morality and even minimal zeal need to recover their position of respect in the wider community. To achieve this, the concept does need to be confined to the limited environments of criminal, family and tribunal representation; that is, where the state or its agencies are prosecuting or where domestic partners are in close combat. Elsewhere, lawyers' integrity and the wider community will benefit if general morality is permitted to assert itself.[38]

4.7 Virtue and character as a more stable foundation for modern legal ethics

Chapter 3 discussed many of the distinctions between the two dominant approaches to general morality – consequentialism and Kantian morality – and virtue ethics.[39] Both consequentialism and the Kantian approach are duty-based ethical frameworks because they regard adherents of either framework as having duties to seek out the best consequences of their actions or to be fair to all sentient beings in their actions, respectively. These are dominant models of general morality because the nobility of their objectives is attractive. Kantianism is especially attractive to lawyers because of its pervasive demand for fairness and, beyond that, the right to fairness. As lawyers, we are conditioned throughout law school to value duty, if only because much of the 'thin' concept of the rule of law[40] requires

96 The Good Lawyer

us to support obedience to law as a duty. So it is a tall order to suggest that there is a third general moral framework and that it ought also be taken seriously by lawyers.

If you agree that general morality is important to your professional role, then consider this: ought virtue ethics be your initial framework? Virtue ethics has a claim to be considered by lawyers before other approaches because justice is the proper[41] and dominant objective of the legal system and because virtue is as much a quality of the person as it is a characteristic or aim of the duty-based ethical frameworks. Duty-based ethics do not in their conventional formulation pretend to examine the character of the lawyer or other actor, but virtue ethics will always say that the virtuous lawyer, out of prudence, will wish to consider what outcomes are at stake and what rights are involved in any one particular ethical problem. In short, virtue ethics is inclusive and the strongest of the three frameworks for that reason.[42] But paradoxically, we cannot be so certain of the power of virtue ethics alone to promote goodness in absolutely every legal situation. Although some virtue ethicists may be confident of that capacity as a general proposition,[43] prudence suggests that you begin with what your virtues tell you[44] and then consider what the duty-based ethical frameworks would have to offer. When deciding, for example, who to act for and who to walk away from, Joseph Tomain puts it this way:

> A lawyer's services should go to those clients the lawyer is most capable of serving. A lawyer's talents should be used to their maximum advantage to serve others and for self-development. It is here, at the confluence of personal growth and development through service to others, that the lawyer makes the most mature moral choice.[45]

But what does it mean to listen to 'what your virtues tell you' and how does such a strategy prevent you from falling into a bottomless pit of ethical relativity? After all, if my first reference point is my virtues but I am deluded and (for added impact) a megalomaniac, I may not be overly virtuous, even if I think I am. The response to this is that, as lawyers, we need to be (and there is no alternative to) constantly examining our own virtue and testing it against morality: that is, against the other duty-based frameworks.[46] Such testing is likely to be difficult and sometimes costly. Consider what ethical method or approach you would think about if you were confronted by this situation:

> Despite long hours and a great deal of work, you have been struggling for some months to make ends meet in your first couple of years as an employee lawyer. You have a HECS debt that you would like to clear and a close friend you are very keen to move in with and set up a house together.
>
> A corporate client of your firm, for whom you have done some useful work, takes the partner responsible, yourself and others in your section to lunch to celebrate (confidentially) the award of a tender. You know that the client is grateful and wants to recognise your collective contributions to this particular success. The client CEO says as much and speculates in an off-handed way that the price of the company's shares is likely to increase to reflect the win once it is all announced.
>
> **Will you buy shares in the company now, in order to (almost) guarantee yourself some extra money when the price rises?**

In answering this question – that is, in examining your responses to this proposed behaviour (which is in fact insider trading, a criminal act) – the good response may not immediately appear, but it will provoke more questions about your virtues, and when those questions occur to you, you will begin to see that general morality 'lies less in concrete answers to moral questions than in the process of asking the questions and attempting to answer them'.[47]

4.8 Identifying virtues

Van Hooft reminds us that the virtues are not pieces of furniture, fixed and unchanging. They are fluid and culturally relative, and they resist categorisation. They overlap, relate closely to the particular situation in which they are expressed and depend for their adequate description on the particular language used to convey their essence.[48]

The virtues are deeply embedded in the language we use to characterise our behaviour as lawyers and can be seen in the propositions, comparisons and examples used in earlier chapters. Restating them may seem repetitive, except for two things: the virtues connect us to the personal qualities that are in some measure examined when we seek admission to practice (see above) and they remind us of the list developed for therapeutic use in positive psychology (see above). The virtues are infused to a great extent in how we ought to practise law, though rarely named[49] as such or invoked after admission (except to a

98   The Good Lawyer

limited extent in some disciplinary cases). Within both law schools and continuing professional development courses, virtue ethics is rarely cited and the virtues remain unconnected to each other or to other ethical frameworks. So there is some point to identifying them here.

In addition to a love of justice, as a good lawyer:

- you will seek out knowledge (that is, will love the law enough to want to know it as thoroughly as you can);
- you will want the best for and show compassion to those around you – clients, colleagues and your family and friends – while not neglecting your own welfare;[50]
- you will seek, prudently, to balance your knowledge of law and the alternative ethical frameworks before making a decision;
- you will learn to develop and value the wisdom and judgment that comes from that balancing process while not losing a sense of humility or humour;
- you will be courageous in taking the actions you believe to be good, even at the risk of being criticised or censured; and
- you will be sufficiently humble to be content with failing, on occasion, to be good.

And other virtues[51] will readily emerge in you as you become, as Aristotle suggested, habituated[52] to looking for them and listening internally to what they say to you.

The process of learning from your internal reflection was called 'practical wisdom' by Aristotle,[53] and is something that becomes easier the more you engage in it. Practical wisdom[54] starts with knowing what the virtues are as intellectual concepts, and leads, as you seek it, to reflection on what they are to you (that is, to identifying what your current strengths are in the virtues), where they are deficient, and then what they could be in you. Look again at the list and reflect on which of these virtues are already strong in you and which are still to be strengthened.

4.9 Can virtue ethics stand up to criticism?

Virtue ethics as applied to law is vulnerable on several levels because it allows and even encourages a degree of subjectivity in the legal process. This is so because virtue asks us as lawyers to integrate our rational and our emotional selves in the interests of strengthening our capacity for justice. But we have been taught, at law school, to be wary of subjectivity because it undermines easy comparability or standard setting: the two outputs of law for which we as lawyers are paid too much, according to our critics. And there is a danger there, but if we do reflect on our virtues – and especially those of wisdom, courage and finally justice – then the risk of too little objectivity in our decisions is controlled.

In liberal democracies, virtue ethics is also capable of leading to paternalism and to being unduly 'holy', substituting for declining religious traditions and intruding excessively into the private realm. In doing so, virtue ethics can be seen as censorious, something that lawyers readily react to – but also support if there are other legitimate interests to consider, such as national security or the protection of children. So intrusion into privacy is something that lawyers both support and resist, depending on its wider purpose. Stronger criticisms may be that virtue ethics undermines the rule of law by encouraging judges to decide cases according to their own whimsy or pet projects or, as we have seen earlier, by allowing lawyers to be guided by their personal moral convictions in discharging a professional role.[55] But as with the earlier response to the claim that virtue permits too much subjectivity in lawyers' decision making, virtue ethics asks us as lawyers to integrate our professional and personal selves inside the virtues, so that our overall guides become the positive values (the virtues) for which law and lawyers are truly affirmed by wider society: that is, wisdom and knowledge, courage and justice.[56]

Perhaps the most serious charge levelled at virtue ethics is that it cannot give adequate action guidance, in comparison to the duty-based ethics frameworks. This criticism is not the same thing as asserting that lawyers feel more at home with the duties of consequentialism and Kantianism. Lawyers are comfortable with duty as a concept because it resonates with their professional obligation to support the rule of law. Both consequentialism, in its focus on the greatest good for the greatest number, and Kantianism, in its concern for fairness, have obvious and consistent attractions for the rule of law. This last and strongest criticism of virtue ethics is not that its reference points are too specific to individual circumstances to be capable of generalisation into a rule, but that a lawyer faced with an ethical challenge will get insufficient sense of direction if all they can do is reflect on what their virtues tell them.

100 The Good Lawyer

Virtue ethics responds to the challenge of providing guidance in a subtle manner, focusing first on the actor and then on the act. The virtues are first and foremost the signs of living life well, in the positive psychological sense we discussed earlier.[57] Virtue is of course about being well and being good in the present tense, but it is also about seeking goodness. The criticism that virtue ethics cannot look forward and provide clear guidance for the future forgets that the virtues are all prospective qualities about living life to the fullest, about flourishing and seeking out the good. A lawyer learning to be virtuous will be seeking to strengthen those virtues that relate particularly to their professionalism – wisdom and knowledge, courage and justice – all of which are powerful guides to future behaviour. They give as much relevant guidance as a duty-based ethic. Consider this typical ethical problem which confronts commercial lawyers from time to time:

> You are a planning lawyer acting for a developer in a long-running planning dispute about a proposed estate to be built very near an old quarry and refuse transfer centre. This developer provides you with the majority of your work, although your last fee invoice is overdue and has been outstanding for several months.
>
> You have engaged an expert consultant in public health to prepare a report assessing the merits of the proposal in relation to public health impacts. When you initially discussed the matter with the expert, their view was that the proposal had no impact on public health. However, when they send their final report to you (prior to its filing with the planning tribunal), their conclusion has been revised and the report says that the development will probably have a fairly minor negative impact on public health.
>
> Your client instructs you not to file the expert report. However, the expert learns of this and calls you to say that their reputation is important to them and that they are a little concerned about the future residents of the estate. You schedule a conference with your client to discuss the issues.
>
> **In conducting yourself in this conference, what guidance would the alternative ethics frameworks provide? What framework would you disregard as of no use?**

Table 4.2 below provides a template response to your dilemma from the perspective of all three ethical frameworks, with the addition of the procedural rules of discovery[58] and the ASCR. This template is used for the case studies in later chapters. The intention is to 'habituate' you to working through those situations using each of the general moral frameworks, before you decide on the ethical course of action in each case. Take note that the last column sets out what the law requires, but rarely does it offer a complete solution on its own:

Table 4.2 Guidance available from different ethical frameworks and conduct rules

Virtue ethics	Consequentialism	Kantian	Rules of discovery/ASCR
Courage would call you to put aside your own desire for ongoing work from this developer and use prudence to 'tell truth to power' by carefully confronting your client and (desiring justice), seek to persuade them to file the report so that the tribunal is able to make a fully informed decision on the application. Your integrity tells you that all this is expected of a reputable practitioner.	The consequences of keeping the report secret are uncertain, but they could include residents' civil action and/or criminal action alleging fraud against your client; disciplinary action against you for deceiving the tribunal (depending on what you say to the tribunal); the expert disclosing their report at a later date and finally your client alleging that you failed to warn them of all these consequences should they keep the report secret.	Fairness suggests that all relevant documents be discovered to the other side so that future residents of the estate, although unidentified and not opposing the current application, receive the benefit of a properly scrutinised approval process. The rights of future residents and their unborn children to a safe and healthy environment are no less than the right of the developer to market and sell their own property.	If civil procedure reforms are enacted in the jurisdiction and apply to planning tribunals, then failure to disclose the report could invalidate the planning process and require a re-application for planning approval, with considerable delay and cost to the developer. ASCR 19.1 states: 'A solicitor must not deceive or knowingly or recklessly mislead the court.' This rule does not compel the solicitor to do or say anything about the report, providing they can avoid making *any* statement about the health impact of the proposed development.

Beginning with virtue ethics, all of these ethical frameworks and the applicable rules have a contribution to make in resolving this dilemma.[59] They all help a good lawyer to be good and reflection upon them is likely to help you make your decision.[60] However, none of them compels or predicts good behaviour, and no system, framework or structure[61] including those offered here, can guarantee such an outcome, particularly if you are sceptical about the future of the profession.[62] Hopefully, the above frameworks provide a deliberative structure to help you be good.[63] Remember that this dilemma is transactional in the sense that you are not yet in the planning tribunal and you are not operating under the constraints of an appropriate role morality. In this scenario, it is general morality that has a claim on you, and one of those claims encourages you to be 'good'. The virtue of courage to make that decision and act on it is the ultimate test of such goodness in this case.

4.10 Role morality versus the rest: Connecting character and attitudes to positive and preferred lawyer 'types'

Almost as soon as you decide to explore virtue ethics as a lawyer you will come up against a problem, and it's powerful. Oakley and Cocking recite Nicolo Machiavelli's old warning:

> [A] man who wants to act virtuously in every way necessarily comes to grief among so many who are not virtuous. Therefore if a prince wants to maintain his rule he must learn how not to be virtuous and to make use of this or not according to need ... A prince must not flinch from being blamed for vices which are necessary for safeguarding the state. This is because, taking every-thing into account, he will find that some of the things that appear to be virtues will, if he practices them, ruin him, and some of the things that appear to be wicked will bring him security and prosperity.[64]

It is true that some corporations will use lawyers who are overly comfortable with role morality to achieve what they would prefer not to do or cannot do themselves.[65] The fact that these moral misadventures sometimes fail and enter public knowledge does not seem to deter many. But the alternative view, contrary to Machiavelli and possibly Daniel Markovits, is that there are desirable, successful and powerful clients who require counsellors with wider frameworks than mere obedience and who value commercial lawyers who offer courageous, independent advice and representation. These clients may not immediately come to you until, through your conscientious work and resilience, you acquire a reputation for these qualities, but they will come in time. With the powerful virtues of patience and conscientious energy, perhaps you will found a collegiate and ethically good major law firm! The question is: do you want to be this sort of lawyer and have you the necessary virtues?

If you have the stamina and interest to apply general morality to legal practice and are willing to found your reputation in the virtues (while taking account of both consequentialism and Kantianism), then you may also benefit from comparing and contrasting your understanding of general morality with a categorisation of legal ethics that describes lawyers' positive functions as 'types', rather than as general moral bases. This framework of four types[66] recognises that lawyers have different but very positive contributions to make to the legal profession. These contributions are all valid ways of looking at aspects of legal practice. They reflect different general moral approaches. You are likely to have a preference for one of more of them:

- the **zealous advocate** (ZA) – is dominant and tends to function within role morality all the time, but ought to confine their zeal to criminal, family and tribunal environments where this type of lawyer is vital. ZA is consequentialist in its focus on achieving the best outcome for clients, Kantian in its concern for fair process and also strongly empowered by the virtues of courage, knowledge, judgment (wisdom) and a desire for justice. Zealous advocates in commercial and transactional cases are often paradoxes and may be psychologically at particular risk because they tend to acquiesce to their clients' demands while remaining reluctant, because of 'commercial reality', to exercise too much of the independence expected of this type;
- the **responsible lawyer** (RL) is often a prosecutor or government lawyer and is generally concerned to ensure that the justice system functions as effectively as possible. The responsible lawyer (sometimes without much humour) gives a Kantian priority to the fairness of the dispute resolution process and other lawyers' duties to courts and benefits from the virtues of courage and justice;
- the **moral activist** (MA) wants social change above all else and is therefore typically consequentialist and uncomfortable with Kantian restrictions. Moral activism strongly identifies with the virtues of courage and justice and such lawyers are well represented in parliaments, legal aid, law reform commissions, community legal centres and broader-based NGOs;[67]
- the '**relationship of care**' (RoC) travels in fellowship with the virtues of compassion and wisdom by nurturing critical relationships (lawyer–client; lawyer–opponent; lawyer–family and friends) above all other goals. RoC resonates strongly for family lawyers and those who practise therapeutic jurisprudence:[68] that is, those who are cautious about conventional notions of just outcomes and of fair process and whose priority is a quest for 'holistic' solutions to legal problems wherever possible.[69] When these comprehensive solutions are unattainable, the RoC lawyer will still try to care for all involved, including opponents.

The connection between these positive descriptions of lawyers and general morality is represented below in Diagram 4.1. Note that virtue and Kantian ethics contribute strongly to all four lawyer types, followed by consequentialism with two types:

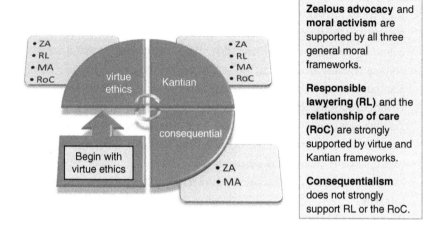

Diagram 4.1 Close encounters of three kinds

Consider and if possible discuss with peers your overall preferences among these types and then work out which of the general moral frameworks associated with your preferred type, appeals to you most.[70] Chapter 9 includes a scale which allows you to work out your preferences among these four types. Ethical awareness in this sense is a preventive tool to counteract laziness, peer pressure and any doubtful firm culture in ethically challenging situations, particularly in large law firms. It may be that sustainable legal professionalism – that is, one that survives – focuses on a respectful dialogue among lawyers who may be zealots, and all other types of lawyers as well, as to what is 'right' as well as what is 'good' in these types.[71]

4.11 Challenging morality: Large law firms as a special case?

The large and global law firm phenomenon[72] sets up a high-stakes environment in which many lawyers wish to work, including good lawyers. There are many good lawyers in large law firms but they face potent challenges. The rewards are large financially and in personal status but entail commensurate risk to physical and mental health, personal relationships and periodically to ethical reputation. The large law firm is perhaps a special case for the good lawyer because these pressures tend to be more acute there than in smaller firms.[73] The larger the firm, the more defined is their business objective and the more concerned they are to ensure that reputation-sensitive legal ethics problem areas are managed carefully. For example, a global firm will give a high priority to running a network of conflict clearing centres.[74] These centres have the job of making sure that when a partner in one part of the globe wants to take on a new client, the firm has no current or past clients anywhere on the planet whose interests may conflict with those of the proposed new client. This business process function is so important to the largest global firms that these centres are separated geographically around the globe in such a way that at least one such centre is open in daylight hours at all times.

Large law firms' ethics are typically opaque to outsiders because dissatisfied clients expect to have their complaints or problems dealt with privately. Consider this example, related to the common problem of backdated documentation, referred to in Chapter 3:

> You are a senior associate in a large corporate law firm. You are worried when you hear that the internal audit committee of your most important client corporation has just learned of what looks like a trail of backdated documents. These documents suggest 'irregularities' in the granting of share options by the CEO to key executives of the corporation two years ago.
>
> None of the options has been exercised yet, so the Board is wondering whether they or you can do something to fix things before the regulators notice anything.
>
> **How will you conduct yourself in the discussion that you know you must soon have with your supervising partner?**

Will you argue (consequentially) to your partner that a cover up is likely to cause as many problems as the original backdating? Or will you say it is unfair to shareholders that they be kept in the dark about their key executives' behaviour? And if your partner looks at you and says you are naïve and you need to 'just fix it', will you take it 'up the line' to your managing partner or the client's Board of Directors?

Very few cases of misconduct from large firms emerge into the public domain, and if large firm lawyers are unhappy or are involved in misconduct in any way, then they are generally on their own – and forced to submit or leave – unless they are willing to become whistleblowers.[75] If you have chosen the right firm, you will be supported and allowed to formally report to the audit committee that the backdating must be brought to the attention of the client's Board. It all depends on the ethical culture of the firm you are a part of. In any law firm, the ethical culture depends on the leadership, but in this highly competitive climate, human psychological capacity for self-deception is strong. The rationalising of bad behaviour as acceptable because of the leakage (really a flood) of role morality into corporate legal practice is well recognised.[76] And firm cultures tend to mould employees' ethics[77] as much as anything else does. In fact, these ethical challenges are so well known that they are often dramatised in novel and film[78] and satirised in cartoons.[79]

Attempts to improve corporate law firm culture have had some success in Australian law firms which choose to incorporate under normal company law provisions. Academic researchers and regulators have combined to introduce a system of ethical audits for such firms[80] and there remains some prospect that all law firms will be so audited in due course.[81] For the moment, however, very large transnational and global firms tend to be so convinced of their business importance that they continue to agitate for separate regulation from smaller firms, particularly where they see it as in their financial interests to represent multiple clients with similar interests. In Australia, this agitation is succeeding.[82]

The thrust of contemporary thinking about life in a large firm reflects Markovits' scepticism about the chances for moral survival.[83] Except for the possibilities of ethical infrastructure audits discussed above,[84] many would conclude that as a good lawyer, you will have little hope of staying good inside such firms. But that is too pessimistic. Individual lawyers of courage and tenacity will always emerge when needed, and it seems important to provide support for their virtues. Moral strengthening comes from your greater ethics awareness. And that awareness complements the 'value-adding' which you, as an independently minded corporate lawyer, can bring to your clients' affairs. So at the risk of appearing naïve, there is actually a business case not just for your moral survival as a corporate lawyer, but for your flourishing. If all that is true, the special circumstances of large law firms may not be so special.[85]

4.12 Conclusion

Connecting character to your roles is an enriching process and offers to you the ability to stay in the game intellectually and emotionally. There is no particular need for more lawyers, but the need for you being a better lawyer will never be satisfied. The essential proposition of this chapter is that better lawyering is best done by good lawyers, and that a lawyer's goodness can be nurtured and developed.

In the following chapters, the capacity for goodness is examined in the context of a number of specific ethical issues, commencing with the primal contest between truth telling and deception, most often in the trial context. As in this chapter, the approach is to reflect on and analyse options in prominent case studies, tabulating the different approaches within general morality.

Notes

1. The International Bar Association appointed a Presidential Taskforce on the Global Financial Crisis, which has attempted to identify a number of factors that led to the crisis. It did not identify lawyers either individually or as a group as at fault in any direct manner. See Peter D. Maynard and Neil Gold (eds), *Poverty, Justice and The Rule of Law*, International Bar Association, London, 2013.
2. 'Flourishing' is also described as *eudaimonia* in Nicomachean Ethics and is best understood as 'human flourishing'. See, generally, Robert C. Bartlett and Susan D. Collins, *Nicomachean Ethics*, University of Chicago Press, Chicago, 2011. Ultimately, the word is derived from the Latin *flos* 'flower': see *The Australian Oxford Dictionary* (2nd edn), Melbourne, 2004, 480.
3. See 'virtue ethics', *The Cambridge Dictionary of Philosophy*, 2nd edn, Robert Audi (ed.), Cambridge University Press, New York, 1999, 960.
4. Kierkegaard coined the term 'earnestness' to describe the attitude necessary in order to switch from mere thinking to doing. See C.S. Evans, 'Søren Aabye Kierkegaard', *The Cambridge Dictionary of Philosophy*, ibid., 468. Reid Mortensen considers that character needs to be exercised and 'muscled up' if it is to flourish (personal communication to author, 2009). See also Tom Wright, *Virtue Reborn*, SPCK Publishing, London, 2010.
5. See, for example, the Myers-Briggs Type Indicator (MBTI). See Isabel Briggs Myers with Peter B. Briggs, *Gifts Differing: Understanding Personality Types* (2nd edn), Davies Black Publishing, Palo Alto CA, 1995. See also Don Peters and Martha M. Peters, 'Maybe that's why I do that: Psychological type theory, the Myers-Briggs type indicator, and learning legal interviewing' (1990) 35 *N. Y. L. Sch. L. Rev.* 169; the Enneagram (www.enneagraminstitute.com/intro.asp).

6. See, for example, Kohlberg's stages of moral development (Lawrence Kohlberg, *The Psychology of Moral Development*, Harper & Row, San Francisco CA, 1984, 636–38); and the Four Component Model of Morality (FCM), developed by James Rest (J. R. Rest, D. Narvaez, M. Bebeau and S. Thoma, *Postconventional Moral Thinking: A Neo-Kohlbergian Approach*, Lawrence Erlbaum Associates, Mahweh NJ, 1999). The FCM uses moral sensitivity, moral judgment, moral motivation (to act) and moral character (to sustain) as its principal subdivisions. US legal educator Clark Cunningham considers that the FCM could be useful for professional adaptation, including for lawyers. See www.teachinglegalethics.org/remediation-program-dentists. See also Moorhead et al., 'Designing ethics indicators for legal services provision'.
7. In the field of medicine, David Seedhouse of Auckland University of Technology has developed an ethics grid for medical practitioners. See D. F. Seedhouse, *Ethics: The Heart of Health Care*, Wiley, Chichester, 1988.
8. Susan Daicoff, 'Lawyer, know thyself: A review of empirical research on attorney attributes bearing on professionalism' (1997) 46 *The American University Law Review* 1337.
9. Ibid., 1394.
10. See Beaton Research and Consulting and beyondblue, Annual Professions Survey 2007, at www.beatonglobal.com/pdfs/Depression_in_the_professions_survey.pdf.
11. See generally Christopher Peterson and Martin E. P. Seligman, *Character Strengths and Virtues: A Handbook and Classification*, Oxford University Press, New York, 2004. This book contains a list of positive human strengths rather than a catalogue of deficits and disorders.
12. See, for example, Jill Stark, 'Are we caught in a happy trap?', *The Sunday Age*, 16 June 2013, 1.
13. Petersen and Seligman, n 11, 130–32. The other three virtues identified by Petersen and Seligman are humanity, temperance and transcendence.
14. See, for example, Barbara Ehrenreich, *Bright-sided: How the relentless promotion of positive thinking has undermined America*, Henry Holt, New York, 2009.
15. See, for example, the Petersen and Seligman *Values-in-Action Inventory of Strengths* (VIA-IS) questionnaire, which is available online (www.authentichappiness.sas.upenn.edu).
16. See S. Cordell, 'Virtuous persons and social roles' (2011) 42 *Journal of Social Philosophy* 254.
17. Countries with common law traditions are generally those colonised at some point by the UK. They tend to share a legal history that emphasises the central role of judges in making the (common) law.
18. The traditional 'cab-rank' rule was designed to ensure that an advocate would accept a case from a poor client. It has been extensively weakened over time and there are now calls in the UK for its abolition. See John A. Flood and Morten Hviid, 'The Cab-rank Rule: Its meaning and purpose in the new legal services market' (22 January 2013). U. of Westminster School of Law Research Paper No. 13–01. Available at SSRN: ssrn.com/abstract=2229235 or http://dx.doi.org/10.2139/ssrn.2229235.
19. See Tomain, 'The legal heresiarchs: Luban's *The Good Lawyer*', 699.

20. See ibid., *Meek v Fleming* [1961] 2 QB 366, and Ch. 3.
21. In formal terms, prosecutors are not permitted as much scope for 'bending the truth' as are defence barristers. The prosecution ought to be concerned to present the case for the state in a fair-minded and non-partisan manner, recognising the reality that the state often has greater resources than a defendant. See Parker and Evans, *Inside Lawyers' Ethics*, Ch. 5.
22. W. Bradley Wendel and Tim Dare are two articulate defenders of role morality and do not see a particular need to confine the concept to criminal, disciplinary or family law fields. See, for example, Wendel, 'Moral judgment and professional legitimation', and Dare, *A Counsel of Rogues*.
23. Justin Oakley, 'Justice, post-retirement shame and the failure of the standard conception of lawyers' roles' (2011) 36 *Austl. J. Leg. Phil.* 177.
24. Ibid., at 180, citing former Supreme Court judge Howard Nathan, quoted in Kerri Elgar, 'A night at the confessional' (1997) 71(11) *LIJ* 14.
25. Shaffer in particular has written about the psychological challenge to lawyers' arising from their moral 'non-accountability' (while in role). See Thomas L. Shaffer, 'On living one way in town and another way at home' (1997) *Val. U. L. Rev.* 879.
26. Justin Oakley and Dean Cocking, *Virtue Ethics and Professional Roles*, Cambridge University Press, New York, 2002, 155.
27. Eshete observes that lawyers typically find it necessary to shield themselves by creating a separate personal self and a 'legal self', so that they can get enough space between the two. See Andreas Eshete, 'Does a lawyer's character matter?', in Joan C. Callahan, *Ethical Issues in Professional Life*, Oxford University Press, New York, 1988, 394–95. See also John Rawls, *A Theory of Justice*, Oxford University Press, Oxford, 1972, 415–16); and Gerard Postema, 'Moral responsibilities in professional ethics' (1980) 55 *N.Y.U.L.Rev.* 63, at 75. See Oakley and Cocking, n 26, at footnote 63.
28. Oakley and Cocking, n 26, 155.
29. Geoff Cockfield and Linda Bortrill, 'Deregulating Australia's wheat trade: From the Australian Wheat Board to AWB Limited' (2007) 2 *Public Policy* 44. See also Parker and Evans, n 21, Case Study 1.3.
30. New South Wales, Special Commission of Inquiry into the Medical Research and Compensation Foundation, *Report*, 2004. A succinct history of the James Hardie affair, up until the appointment of David Jackson QC to investigate the matter, may be viewed in the Australian Parliamentary Library at www.aph.gov.au/library/pubs/rn/2004–05/05rn12.htm; Marcus Priest, 'ASIC seeks bans for Hardie asbestos directors', *Australian Financial Review*, Sydney, 16 February 2007, 1.
31. The major (though still formally denied) case of document destruction in Australia was that associated with the McCabe tobacco litigation (see Camille Cameron, 'Hired guns and smoking guns: *McCabe v British American Tobacco Australia Ltd*' (2002) 25 *University of New South Wales Law Journal* 768), the unsatisfactory result of which led to the creation of the McCabe Centre for Law and Cancer.
32. See, for example, Adele Ferguson, 'Taxing time for tech giants as war is declared', *The Age, Business Day*, 23 November 2012, 1 and 5; Ross Gittins, 'Big companies tax avoidance blatant and shameless', *The Age*, 27 March 2013, 43.
33. See Ch. 2, n 55.

34. See Tomain, n 19; William Simon, 'Ethical discretion in lawyering' (1988) 101(6) *Harvard Law Review* 1083. One author, Daniel Markovits, has produced a major contemporary criticism of role morality and of duty-based ethics. Markovits' view is that (United States) legal ethics – zealous advocacy, by default – is at a dead end because lawyers cannot lead fulfilling lives while they are villainous by necessity (that is, doomed to 'dis-integrity'), since their justified political role is to self-efface and allow the client's case to be maximised in every sense. See Markovits, *A Modern Legal Ethics: Adversary advocacy in a democratic age*. Markovits has been criticised for his claim that distinct lawyer roles are no longer justifiable, particularly by Dare (Tim Dare, 'Can lawyers have integrity?' (2010) 13 *Legal Ethics* 244).
35. Cooper considers that *the* problem of legal ethics is the lack of integrity and too much zeal. See Gregory J. Cooper, '*A Modern Legal Ethics* on the substantive justification of the lawyers' role and its implications for legal practice' (2010) 13 *Legal Ethics* 250. He is supported by Dare and by Woolley (Alice Woolley, 'Truth or truthiness: *A Modern Legal Ethics*' understanding of the lawyer and her community' (2010) 13 *Legal Ethics* 231).
36. Integrity is much discussed in the virtue ethics literature. See van Hooft, *Understanding Virtue Ethics*, 163. Markovits has offered an opinion on the essence of integrity: see Daniel Markovits, 'Reply: Legal ethics rebound' (2010) 13 *Legal Ethics* 261, at 265–66.
37. See justice.gov/civil/cases/tobacco2/amended%20opinion.pdf.
38. See Tomain, n 19, 696. Note in relation to Tomain's reference to a rape cross-examination, that he was describing a common US jurisdictional practice in 1984. Australian criminal law now significantly restricts the zeal with which defence counsel can demean witnesses in sexual assault cases. See, for example, *Criminal Procedure Act 2009* (Vic), s 342. These prohibitions are supported by ASCR 21.8.
39. Van Hooft reminds us that virtues are relative to social and cultural contexts, not to absolute moral standards. Virtue derives from the Latin *virtus*, meaning excellence, capacity or ability. See van Hooft, *Understanding Virtue Ethics*, 1.
40. See Ch. 1, n 27.
41. See Tomain, n 19, 703.
42. Moral philosophers have sought over time to adapt both consequentialism and Kantianism to derive virtue forms of both frameworks. See, generally, van Hooft, *Understanding Virtue Ethics*, Ch. 1 and Robert Audi (general ed.), *The Cambridge Dictionary of Philosophy*, Cambridge University Press, New York, 1999, 'ethics' at p. 284. I do not discount those formulations but for purposes of brevity refer to rather than analyse them here.
43. Amaya, for example, rejects the so-called weak position on virtue ethics and that it can co-exist with duty-based ethics, maintaining there is room only for a strong position. See Amalia Amaya, 'The role of virtue in legal justification', Ch. 3 in Amalia Amaya and Ho Hock Lai, *Law, Virtue and Justice*, Hart Publishing, Oxford, 2013.
44. See ibid., 6–7.
45. Tomain, 'The legal heresiarchs: Luban's *The Good Lawyer*', 700.
46. As recommended by Tomain, ibid., 703.
47. Ibid., 697.

48. Van Hooft, *Understanding Virtue Ethics*, 127–28.
49. See Claudio Michelon, 'Practical wisdom in legal decision-making', Chapter 2 in Amaya and Lai, n 43, 30.
50. See, generally, Evans and King, 'Reflections on the connection of virtue ethics to therapeutic jurisprudence'.
51. See Sherman J. Clark 'Neo-classical public virtues: Towards an aetaric theory of law-making (and law teaching)', in Amaya and Lai, n 43, 81–104.
52. See Ch. 4.
53. See Aristotle, *Nicomachean Ethics, Book Two* (trans. W.D. Ross), University of Adelaide, at ebooks.adelaide.edu.au/a/aristotle/nicomachean.
54. For lawyers in particular, there may also be some special advantages in developing practical wisdom; for example an enhanced capacity to recognise extraneous or fringe factors and appreciate their possibilities for developing the law. Michelon, n 49, 47 and following, mentions Zenon Bankowski as someone who has insisted for some time that *good* legal decision makers develop something akin to a 'legal peripheral conceptual perception'. This capacity consists in 'relentlessly applying the legal categories that frame their perceptual framework to numerous cases', so that when the odd, awkward or misfit case emerges, it will trigger a memo to check the appropriateness of the categories that are normally applied. See, generally, Zenon Bankowski, *Living Lawfully: Love in law and law in love*, Kluwer, Dordrecht, 2001.
55. See Amaya, 'The role of virtue in legal justification', and Dare, *A Counsel of Rogues*.
56. Oakley and Cocking deal in some detail with whether a virtuous character is *enough* to justify actions. See Oakley and Cocking, n 26, 33–37.
57. See Petersen and Seligman, n 11.
58. Discovery is a formal process inside litigation designed to ensure that both parties have access to the documents that support their opponent's position, in the interests of justice, narrowing the issues in dispute and speedy solutions. Discovery compels both parties to disclose all such documents, except those that contain 'confidential communications' made between the lawyer and their client that were made for the dominant purpose of obtaining legal advice, or for use in current or anticipated litigation. The principle case is the High Court's decision in *Esso v Commissioner of Taxation* (2000) 168 ALR 123.
59. Markovits leans carefully towards virtue ethics but resists describing his views as based in virtue ethics. See Markovits, n 34.
60. See Moorhead et al., 'Designing ethics indicators for legal services provision', Chs 4 and 5.
61. Coleman, for example, offers a hybrid ethics framework. See Claire K. Coleman, 'Teaching the Torture Memos: Making decisions under conditions of uncertainty' (2012) 62 *Journal of Legal Education* 81. Recently, a case has been made for the Confucian concept of 'harmony' as a virtue framework for general morality. See Linghao Wang and Lawrence B. Solum, 'Confucian virtue jurisprudence', Ch. 6 in Amaya and Lai, n 43.
62. Markovits' view is that lawyers have no hope of a moral life. See Markovits, n 34, 269.
63. Ibid., 267.

64. Oakley and Cocking, n 26, quoting Nicolo Machiavelli, *The Prince* (trans. George Bull), Penguin, Harmondsworth, 1975, 91–92.
65. For example, Enron Corporation, AWB, James Hardie Industries.
66. A number of writers contributed to developing these stereotypes, but Parker has formulated them recently in an Australian context. See Parker, 'A critical morality for lawyers: Four approaches to lawyers' ethics', 53–56.
67. Farrow thinks Luban articulates this type of lawyer more effectively than most. See Trevor C. W. Farrow, 'Sustainable professionalism' (2008) 46 *Osgoode Hall Law Journal* 51, at 94.
68. Therapeutic jurisprudence (TJ) is a branch of legal philosophy that 'studies the effects of the law on the wellbeing of those affected by it and proposes reforms directed to making the law and its dispute resolution processes psychologically optimal for all concerned'. See Evans and King, n 50.
69. Ibid., 56.
70. While there are examples in medicine of ethics' matrices that permit a doctor to work out many critical questions to ask themselves in order to help resolve difficult ethical problems (for example, Seedhouse, n 7), this diagram is too primitive for that purpose.
71. Farrow, 'The good, the right and the lawyer', 55.
72. See n 80.
73. Large law firms are regularly criticised for taking on new clients with opposing interests (Mitt Regan, *Eat What You Kill*, University of Michigan Press, Ann Arbor, 2004); assisting clients in the commission or cover-up of illegal or unethical behaviour (D. Rhode and P. Paton, 'Lawyers, ethics and Enron', in Nancy B. Rapoport and Bala G. Dharan (eds), *Enron: Corporate Fiascos and Their Implications*, Foundation Press, 2004; S. Koniak, 'Corporate fraud: See, lawyers' (2003) 26 *Harvard Journal of Law & Public Policy* 195; K. Hall and V. Holmes, 'The power of rationalization to influence lawyers decisions to act unethically' (2008) 11 (2) *Legal Ethics* 137); and over-servicing and overcharging (Susan Fortney, 'The billable hours derby: Empirical data on the problems and pressure points' (2005) 33 *Fordham Urban Law Journal* 171). The result is long-term damage to the public confidence in the integrity of the entire justice system (Robert Gordon, 'A new role for lawyers? The corporate counselor after Enron' (2003) 35 *Connecticut Law Review* 1185).
74. See John Flood, 'Megalawyering in the global order: The cultural, social and economic transformation of global legal practice' (1996) 3 *International Journal of the Legal Profession* 169.
75. The major case of an Australian large law firm lawyer who became a whistleblower was that of Christopher Dale, formerly of Clayton Utz. See Ch. 2, n 10.
76. See, for example, Kimberly Kirkland, 'Ethics in large law firms: The principle of pragmatism' (2005) 35(4) *University of Memphis LR* 631; Kath Hall, 'The pathology of corporate law' (2006) 19 *Australian Journal of Corporate Law* 268; Kath Hall, 'Looking beneath the surface: The impact of psychology on corporate decision making' (2007) 49 *Managerial Law* 93; Leslie Levin, 'Bad apples, bad lawyers or bad decisionmaking: Lessons from psychology and from lawyers in the dock' (2009) 22 *Geo. J. Legal Ethics* 1549.

4 Connecting character to lawyers' roles | 113

77. Oakley and Cocking concede that the empirical research of Ross and Nisbett shows that situational factors in the role actually inhabited by the lawyer are better predictiors of their behaviour in different circumstances than are assumptions about underlying dispositions or character traits of particular individuals. See Oakley and Cocking, n 26, 168, referring to Lee Ross and Richard Nisbett, *The Person and the Situation: Perspectives of social psychology*, McGraw-Hill, New York, 1991, especially Chs 4 and 5. This conclusion is broadly supported in Australia by Lillian Corbin. See Lillian Corbin, 'How "firm" are lawyers' perceptions of professionalism?' (2005) 8 *Legal Ethics* 265.
78. See, for example, the novels of John Grisham and the films *Hell Has Harbour Views* (Australia) and *Michael Clayton* (US).
79. See, for example, 'How to stump a corporate lawyer?' in www.gocomics.com/nonsequitur/2006/12/08.
80. See Christine Parker, Adrian Evans, Reid Mortensen and Suzanne LeMire, 'Ethical infrastructure of legal practice in large law firms: Values, policy and behaviour' (2008) 31(1) *UNSW Law Journal* 155–88; Elizabeth Chambliss and David Wilkins, 'Promoting effective ethical infrastructure in large law firms' (2002) 30 *Hofstra L. R.* 69; Christine Parker, Tahlia Gordon and Steve Mark, *Research Report: Assessing the impact of management-based regulation on NSW Incorporated Legal Practices*, Office of the Legal Services Commissioner, Sydney, 2008.
81. The prospects for such audits have improved following recent progress in the development of national legal profession uniform laws. See Ch. 2.
82. See, for example, ASCR 10 and 11, which have effectively been brought into being by the Large Law Firms Group of the Law Council of Australia.
83. Recently, Markovits has conceded that more research is needed as to whether law firms' cultures do subvert individuals' ethical stances over time, though he still insists that in the end lawyers are just too morally weak to resist oppression. See Markovits, n 34, 267–69.
84. See n 80.
85. Farrow agrees. See Farrow, n 71, 81.

Chapter 5

TRUTH AND DECEPTION

5.1 Introduction: Tools for analysis

Truth and deception are close companions for lawyers. Our everyday moral challenge is to increase our truth telling and reduce our deception. Nowhere is this more difficult than in adversarial tribunals and the courts. Here we assume a judge or jury (or both) can pick up on what is most likely to be the true position in any disputed version of reality and save us from worrying too much about what we have said or done. In Chapter 4 the reasons for this necessary 'buck passing' were justified. To assist us and the court, we have constructed the idea of the zealous advocate; someone who is allowed to be almost outrageous and certainly provocative in order to test the motives and circumstances of others' behaviour. And unless there is some inexpensive, wholly reliable discovery around the corner in the neuroscience of identifying truthfulness, then it is hard to identify a better system than what we have.

Zealous advocacy is a positive approach to being a lawyer in certain types of legal practice providing it is underpinned by goodness in the sense explored in prior discussion; but there are still limits to its practice. In this chapter, these limits are discussed not in terms of any direct comparison with other legal ethics types such as responsible lawyering, but in the context of general morality and the rules of conduct. This comparative framework is suited to questioning and justifying the limits to zealous advocacy because general morality (that is, virtue ethics, consequentialism and Kantianism) provides moral scrutiny. Zealous advocacy, responsible lawyering, moral activism and the relationship of care are not analytical tools; they provide us with positive, descriptive names for the preferences that we share in different degrees and are valuable for our understanding of our functional priorities as lawyers. But they do not help us analyse what is good and what is not *within* any of these types.

Diagram 5.1 (below) sets out the formal hierarchy of lawyers' duties: that is, the list of Kantian and consequentialist obligations that the courts

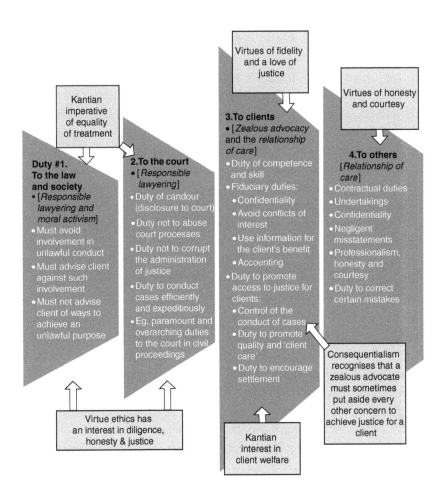

Diagram 5.1 The formal hierarchy of lawyers' duties

116   The Good Lawyer

repeatedly say we must use to prioritise our responsibilities.[1] This list also connects the four lawyer types to some of these duties and makes explicit some of the concerns of general morality. Note that the duty to clients is not first, as the concept of zealous advocacy might suggest, but third on the list.

Legal ethics would be under very little pressure if this hierarchy was always adhered to. In practice, however, the duty to clients tends to dominate. The various statutory conduct rules, for example, the *Australian Solicitors' Conduct Rules* (ASCR) reflect many of these duties and are formally binding on us as lawyers. Subject to the common law, their breach can amount to misconduct,[2] but they are not always observed. The relationship between conduct rules, general morality and actual cases is therefore complicated – and best set out by exploring some of these cases.

The following tables explore particular issues of truth and deception which arise from too much zealous advocacy.[3] These tables – and those in Chapters 6, 7 and 8 – generally consist of case studies of lawyers' inappropriate behaviour. It would be better to give examples of good lawyering and to analyse such behaviours according to general morality, but those examples are known only anecdotally, do not come with sufficient detail and tend to come to public attention only through lawyer trade magazine 'awards', which have law firm marketing importance and can lack credibility.

The case studies in these tables usually come to attention because of judicial or disciplinary analyses. Their details are therefore forensically accessible and provide a strong focus for general moral analysis. While at first sight they communicate more gloom than optimism about lawyers' moral consciousness, the intention in the analysis of each situation is to offer an antidote to such pessimism. Analysis of these decisions and rules in terms of general morality helps to clarify whether the limits set by case law and conduct rules are appropriate. As explained in Chapter 4, those who take the time to go through the process of comparative moral analysis will be strengthened in their capacity to engage with moral complexity. And as it grows, that strength delivers optimism about the potential for good lawyering and the rejection of dubious behaviour.

Table 5.1 deals with active and passive deceit, 5.2 with destroying documents, 5.3 with abuse of process, 5.4 with 'knowing too much' and 5.5 with evading tax. Over time, these issues have generally resulted in judicial decisions and more and more conduct rules designed to set limits on what is often perceived to be hyper-zealous behaviour.

5 Truth and deception 117

Table 5.1 The apparent distinction between active and passive deceit

It is no surprise to state that as lawyers we cannot deceive a court in an effort to get some extra advantage for our client. But sometimes real problems arise when, instead of telling a lie in an active sense, a lawyer passively allows a lie to emerge or be communicated to another party or to a tribunal in an effort to gain that advantage. Three cases illustrate this temptation:

1. *Meek v Fleming* [1961] 2 QB 366. The plaintiff alleged that the defendant had assaulted him. At the time of the alleged assault, the defendant was a chief inspector. Prior to the court hearing the defendant was demoted to sergeant for deceiving another court in the course of his duty in another case. The defendant's barrister decided not to make the demotion known to the court. Plaintiff's counsel and the judge frequently addressed the defendant as 'Chief Inspector' and nothing was done to correct the misapprehension.

Later, the English Court of Appeal said that the concealment misled the judge and jury on an important matter, namely the defendant's credibility. As a consequence the 'not guilty' verdict of the court below was set aside.

2. *Legal Services Commissioner v Mullins* [2006] LPT 012. A Queensland barrister, Mullins, represented a 48-year-old former builder who became a quadriplegic from a car accident. In a 2003 mediation, Mullins allowed the insurer on the other side to assume that his client had a normal lifespan, and the insurer settled for more than $1 million. In fact, Mullins knew his client had lung cancer and that the cancer had spread to other sites in his body. When prosecuted for his actions, Mullins claimed that he was entitled to remain silent (and not violate any rules relating to candour) as long as he did not positively mislead the insurer as to life expectancy. The Queensland Legal Profession Tribunal disagreed and fined him $20,000 for a 'fraudulent deception'.

3. *James Hardie Industries.*[4] James Hardie Industries (JH) made building products from asbestos for decades (for example, 'Hardiplank' wall cladding), knowing that its workers and consumers were likely to contract fatal lung diseases from even minor exposure. The company was financially very successful. When JH became aware that it faced up to $2 billion in compensation payments to those who were dying or would die from the diseases, its strategy was to set up a minimally funded compensation fund in Australia in order to give the impression that it had provided sufficient funds for asbestosis compensation and then relocate its corporate headquarters to the Netherlands, where it believed it would be effectively immune from civil action.

JH's head in-house lawyer and company secretary, Peter Shafron, asked the then large firm Allens Arthur Robinson (now the leading transnational firm Allens Linklaters) to help the company relocate to the Netherlands. However, JH reckoned without the determination of government to shame them at a political level. When JH were challenged by the Federal and NSW governments, they were forced to restructure and accept full financial liability to the many thousands who had suffered and died (or would suffer and die). When Allens were later asked why they had not stood back and asked themselves what they should be advising their client to do, they responded to the effect that they were advising their client on 'the letter of the law, no more and no less'.[5] What would you have done if you were the responsible Allens' partner?[6]

***

These cases illustrate that if you know that the effect of your silence as a lawyer – even if you have said nothing incorrect – is to allow an opposing party, a tribunal or even the public at large to treat as fact something you know to be wrong, you will be crossing the bright line between an acceptable silence and an active fraud or deception. But these issues get harder still.

In criminal practice, there is a long-standing conduct rule which allows an advocate to be silent when they know or suspect that the prosecution is unaware of their client's prior convictions.[7] Tribunals are very much in need of accurate information about a defendant's past record in order to determine an appropriate sentence for a current offence. But in effect, this rule endorses a deception on courts because of another general principle that defendants need not incriminate themselves. In other words, if the prosecution does not, for whatever reason, tell a court about something they need to know, then defence advocates are off the disclosure hook. You might think that advocates' silence in relation to a past record is entirely justified before a defendant is found to have committed an offence, but dangerous thereafter. You will be disappointed and certainly perplexed that this is not so. Is the competing justification for a defence silence (the right not to self-incriminate), strong enough in terms of general morality to support this deception of the court?

118   The Good Lawyer

Table 5.1 (cont.)

Now consider this fact situation, taken from *Legal Services Commissioner v Stirling (Legal Practice)* [2012] VCAT 347: A barrister entered pleas of guilty to charges of professional misconduct and unsatisfactory professional conduct. He had failed to lodge returns for income tax for 8 years, failed to lodge business activity statements for 5 years and had not paid any tax for 9 years. There were no extenuating circumstances whatsoever and he lodged returns only after the Deputy Commissioner of Taxation prosecuted him for failure to do so.

He was charged with misconduct, and the Legal Practice division of the Victorian Civil and Administrative Tribunal had to assess the penalty. Stirling elected not to give personal evidence on his own behalf (exercising the right not to self-incriminate) but still argued that he should not be suspended. He acknowledged that while he had had a lavish lifestyle, he was now reformed. He also sought to impress the tribunal with the fact that he was well liked in the profession, submitting character evidence from a judge and senior barristers. Arguing that he had substantially repaid his original tax debt, he appealed to the Court of Appeal in Victoria against a reprimand and a 3-year suspension of his Practising Certificate. On appeal, the Court reduced the period of his suspension to 6 months, subject to a number of conditions.[8] A lawyer who claims to be rehabilitated but refuses to give personal evidence or allow himself to be cross-examined, having pleaded guilty to serious charges, is asking a lot from a disciplinary tribunal in relation to his credibility and their credulity. It is difficult to see how the Court of Appeal, which had also not heard from the appellant personally, could wind back the tribunal's decision. Stirling's retreat into silence was lawful but not ethical. There appears no reason why he was allowed to, in effect, tell the court that he was not willing to be cross-examined as to the true extent of his claimed reformation.

In each of these cases, role morality was invoked in order to support a silence which effectively kept a tribunal, another party or the community as a whole in the dark as to the reality of the underlying situation.

Analysis from a virtue ethics perspective (the relevant virtues are italicised)

The virtues of *honesty* and a love of *justice* are important in ensuring that a court, tribunal or opposing party to a negotiation are aware of all material information that will affect a decision. *Prudence* is also called for, since a decision or determination that is based on misinformation or passive deceit may be unstable and unsustainable, as occurred in Mullins' case and James Hardie Industries. If a case decision unravels, there may be a financial claim against the lawyer responsible for any passive deceit on the basis that the decision to remain silent was negligent or amounted to misconduct. The prudent lawyer will wish to avoid deceit that could lead to subsequent decision reversal, claims for damages or loss of their own reputation.

Advocates' not surprising desire to assert their 'right' to acceptable silence wherever possible (exploiting zealous advocacy at the cost of responsible lawyering), lacks *courage*. Their decision also lacks the *foresight* to recognise that the wider rule of law is damaged in the eyes of the community when, as lawyers, we try to take advantage of other principles in order to restrict tribunals' or public access to full information.

Consequentialism

The consequences of silence (as passive deceit) depend on the calculus of possible gain and possible loss. On the one hand, if the deceit is effective in the sense that the lawyer's client is advantaged and either gains a financial return or avoids a negative finding as to conduct, then the calculation of gain justifies the silence (and reflects a zealous advocacy). But if the loss in community regard for the rule of law is greater (denying the responsible lawyer), as it may be if a passive deceit is exposed, then there will be a negative impact on the confidence of the community in dispute resolution that outweighs the positive gain of the single advantaged client. Losses to insurers may also be a factor where passive deceit contributes to unjust insurance claims. The consequentialist will ask which result is more likely, but will have difficulty predicting and comparing the outcomes. They might not therefore be in a position to do more than list potential losses to wider groups as compared to the gain for a single individual.

Kantian ethics

A Kantian will be strongly influenced by the sense of unfairness that accompanies passive deceit or by individual or corporate unwillingness to be exposed to scrutiny when seeking a benefit and will be inclined to judge silence in negative terms. In this decision, they will also reflect a relationship of care for their client.

Table 5.1 (cont.)

Applicable law and conduct rules

Case law has often examined deceit[9] and there are many conduct rules which attempt to spell out the twists and turns of acceptable silence. ASCR 19–21 set out these restrictions in great detail.[10]

In civil proceedings, legislation in several jurisdictions has also introduced a set of 'overarching obligations' which lawyers and their clients must abide by. These obligations channel the virtues fairly closely in requiring the lawyer to act honestly, to proceed on a proper basis (that is not frivolous, vexatious or an abuse of process), to only take steps to resolve or determine the dispute, to cooperate in the conduct of the civil proceeding, not to mislead or deceive, to use reasonable endeavours to resolve the dispute, to narrow the issues in dispute, to ensure costs are reasonable and proportionate, to minimise delay and to disclose the existence of documents.[11] It is not the duty to the client, but the lawyers' overriding duty to the court that dominates in all these decisions.[12]

Conclusion in relation to the quest for an 'acceptable silence'.

General morality in the form of both virtue ethics and Kantian approaches is intolerant of 'acceptable' silences when legal relationships are in dispute or in negotiation and there is the potential for silence to allow one party to oppress another or treat them unfairly. Relationships of care and responsible lawyering are evident here. Consequentialism is potentially critical as well, but it may also be comfortable with a zealous advocate's desire to achieve clients' outcomes no matter what hurdles exist, providing those outcomes are not too disproportionate to the means.

The conduct rules are finely tuned to allow us to remain silent as much as possible. They would not pass any test that might be applied by a moral activist, since to achieve any balance in a court or tribunal, they depend on the equal resourcing of both parties to a dispute, which is a matter of increasing doubt. We do not know the extent to which these rules actually balance litigation processes to achieve a degree of fairness.

Increasingly, the governing law (in the form of civil procedure obligations) offers a negative opinion of the types of silence permitted by the conduct rules. Overarching disclosure obligations do not apply to criminal law, but moral activism would find it difficult to say why, for example, it is still acceptable that a court remains in the dark as to a defendant's prior convictions when at least one of the advocates before it is aware of the facts. Both advocates are officers of the same court and their highest priority responsibilities lie with that court.

5.2 Key issues in truth and deception: Active and passive deceit

One way in which lawyers can, if they choose, rationalise a decision to deceive someone is to avoid telling a lie (which would be an active deceit) by saying nothing when their silence allows a false or misleading state of affairs to continue. In these cases, the real question is whether such silence amounts to a passive deceit. Answering that question requires another to be asked: 'Am I obliged to speak?' In the ASCR and according to role morality, the issue of obligation is interpreted narrowly, so that we are permitted to remain silent more often than would be acceptable according to general morality. Table 5.1 shows how much can be at stake in this simple distinction.

120   The Good Lawyer

5.3 Hiding embarrassing documents

A second type of deceit, of a far more active nature, involves hiding – and in some cases disposing of – incriminating documents.

Table 5.2 Producing or destroying documents

When something has to be proved to be true, lawyers can put forward witnesses to give oral evidence or produce documents to support what their client says. Lawyers' use of oral evidence has limitations because of memory lapse, distinguishing fact from opinion and judging honesty. You may therefore think that proving truth from documents is easier, because what they 'say' is in writing and not subject to a person's memory or willingness to speak. But documents have their own problems. Whether they are on paper or recorded on video, disc or flash drive, documents can record lies as well as truths. They can be forged or altered and can go 'missing' as effectively as any human memory.

Another problem with documents is that they are not all available to a court. In general terms, documents created just for the legal process can be classed as 'privileged' and may be kept secret by a party. Client privilege is discussed in Chapter 6. For present purposes, we are concerned with documents that are not privileged but are still unavailable because they have gone missing for some reason. If documents are genuinely lost, that is one thing. But documents are also destroyed to keep secrets. Even this destruction remains a secret because the existence of the documents was itself a secret. When that sort of destruction occurs in close connection with the court process, it generally means that laws are being broken.[13] But sometimes, destruction of relevant documents is characterised by some lawyers as innocent and therefore as legitimate. This is a very murky area for those who seek to unravel the truth.

In Chapter 4 the comments of Judge Kessler of the US District Court were included to show that tobacco industry lawyers were involved in destroying documents in order to delay and frustrate court processes in that country. In Australia, we have also had a major case.

McCabe v British American Tobacco Australia Services [2002] VSC 73

The McCabe case is among the most important in the last 30 years on the issues of truth and deception. This extract sums up the story:

> Rolah McCabe, a terminally ill victim of lung cancer, had sued British American Tobacco Australia Services (BATAS) alleging that her cancer was a result of her childhood addiction to nicotine acquired from smoking and that BATAS was responsible because it had known of the toxic and addictive qualities of tobacco at the time they were marketing their cigarettes to her as a child. Mrs McCabe succeeded in persuading Justice Geoffrey Eames at first instance that the defendant, knowing that litigation was imminent by someone addicted to nicotine and suffering from lung cancer, had destroyed its own historical documents; documents which presumably showed that it knew of the toxicity of nicotine at the time of its cigarette marketing. BATAS's defence was struck out by Justice Eames on the basis that a fair trial had been denied to the plaintiff when the defendant (having destroyed its records) failed to provide sufficient discovery.
>
> More particularly for the present purpose, His Honour found that BATAS was assisted by Clayton Utz in developing a 'document retention policy', which was in fact designed to systematically destroy incriminating documents, noting that they had 'advised Wills [BATAS] on the wording of the policy, [ensuring] that words were inserted into the written policy document to which reference could be made in order to assert innocent intention and to disguise the true purpose of the policy'.
>
> The court made other findings as to the effect of later variations in the policy which included holding documents off-shore and in the custody of Clayton Utz, to make it easier to deny discovery to any future plaintiff. The general import of the whole judgment was to suggest that commercial pressures on Clayton Utz to support the client were suffocating its primary duty to the court to see that a fair trial occurred and justice was done.

5 Truth and deception   121

Table 5.2 (cont.)

Clayton Utz vigorously defended its actions and its reputation. In December 2002, the Victorian Court of Appeal comprehensively reversed the judgment of Justice Eames and exonerated the firm, asserting that destroying documents was not unlawful unless it amounted to an attempt to pervert the course of justice or was a contempt of court. The appeal court effectively affirmed Clayton Utz's behaviour, but the damage had been done. Despite the reversal, public distrust of the profession was again boosted when Melbourne newspaper *The Age* published a critical commentary on the appeal court decision and its implications for document destruction.[14] The case at this point seemed to set up in the public consciousness a stereotypical 'bad' firm representing a 'bad' and wealthy corporate client. The stereotype was highly overstated, but more was to come.

In July 2003, a whistleblower emerged from the tobacco industry and reignited the flames. In an affidavit, a former executive of BATAS asserted that it was in fact the company's practice to destroy documents that might have been embarrassing. Clayton Utz responded quickly by asserting that the NSW and Victorian regulators had withdrawn investigations into any alleged wrongdoing by the firm in relation to the 'document retention policy'. An appeal to the Australian High Court was unsuccessful but the case had by then made an even larger impact. The State of Victoria enacted new criminal and civil penalties for individuals and corporations who destroyed documents 'reasonably likely' to be used in cases already underway or likely to begin. In October 2006, an internal draft report by Clayton Utz on its own behaviour was leaked to the press by another former partner and appeared to confirm, despite the firm's own previous denials, that a small number of its partners and staff were involved in deceiving the Supreme Court. There were counter allegations against that former partner of mixed motives, but the leak was in the public domain. Subsequently, those involved all left the firm. Although the exact circumstances of their departure were not made public, it is fair to say that the remainder of the partnership was appalled and in due course went to Herculean efforts to persuade the public that the firm was honourable and the actions of the few were not representative of the remainder. Nevertheless, the possibility that the court process had been subverted by these few lawyers' unethical behaviour was plain for all to see.

Clayton Utz have since done much to restore their reputation and have been partially successful. Initial concerns for the loyalty of their client base did not reduce their long-term profitability. The firm announced, in the interim between the initial finding of Justice Eames in April 2002 and the appeal court reversal in December 2002, that it would cease acting for tobacco companies and that it had appointed former High Court Chief Justice Sir Anthony Mason to head a 'professional excellence committee'.[15] [footnotes omitted]

Virtue ethics

If some lawyers lose sight of the duties to the law and to the court then their duty to their clients can dominate. The virtue of *wisdom* tells us as lawyers that our proper first priority is to the court when a client asks for or encourages us to find a way to hide the past in the past. Particularly if we love *justice* and regardless of any rules of procedure, would we not wish to see non-privileged documents that will assist a court disclosed? And if we have *compassion* for parties to litigation who have suffered (exhibiting a relationship of care), our desire for *justice* may give us the *courage* to say to our client 'this document must be disclosed'. In doing so, we may also be showing *prudence* in our client's interests, since document destruction is now often criminalised, as well as offensive to virtue ethics.

Consequentialism

As a consequentialist lawyer confronted with proposed document destruction, you might reason with your client that the 'greatest good for the greatest number' rules out such destruction where the benefits of disclosure are greater for the opposing party (and others of that class) than for your defendant client. The fact that your client might then seek to fire you, or ask your firm to fire you, might not be a bad thing in the long run, since the consequences of continuing to represent such a client are likely to be adverse to you.

122 The Good Lawyer

Table 5.2 (cont.)

Kantian ethics

As a Kantian it will be very difficult for you to shake the reality that the fair judicial process requires document disclosure to work fairly. This is responsible lawyering. Of course, your firm culture might only superficially agree with this and your partner or senior associate may pressure you subtly not to get in the way of your client's instructions. Your firm's zealous approach may be reminiscent of that identified by Judge Rakoff in Chapter 2, and it may characterise the proposed document destruction as 'arguably legal', on the basis that the contents are insufficiently material to the issues in dispute or are in fact irrelevant to those issues or that litigation is not objectively likely.

If your client or firm also argues that the document destruction process is merely good file housekeeping and is intended to ensure that the client's records are not too voluminous or inaccessible, you ought to be wary. The process of converting corporate paper-based records to digital formats is now well advanced and the unit cost of converting and storing a single record is minute. Conversion need not involve *any* destruction for cost reasons or to 'tidy up' corporate archives. In fact, the individual identification of documents for purposes of such possible destruction is likely to cost significantly more than simply storing all digital records.

The fact that your services are required at all means that someone has identified a potential litigation problem. As a Kantian, you will need to be on guard and identify this sort of pressure for what it may be – an effort to subvert fairness and your responsibilities to the court.

Applicable law and conduct rules

The *Crimes (Document Destruction) Act 2006* (Vic) and similar legislation in other jurisdictions, together with the rules of civil procedure (for example, the *Supreme Court (General Civil Procedure) Rules* 2005) make clear what is required of us as lawyers in relation to the production of documents that may be needed in current or likely litigation. ASCR 14.2 supports these provisions so far as lawyers' storage of client documents is concerned by stating that the usual seven-year period for retaining such documents is subject to extension under contrary legislation.

Conclusion in relation to the retention of corporate documents

The limits set by case law and conduct rules are appropriate having regard to general morality. None of virtue ethics, consequentialism or Kantian ethics are sympathetic to the destruction of material documents and Kantianism in particular would be on guard against document destruction that is described as necessary for cost saving or for administrative simplicity. In this commercial context, responsible lawyering is appropriate and zealous advocacy has no legitimate role.

5.4 Hiding the true purpose of a legal action

Disposing of relevant documents is bad and damaging to the rule of law; there are other forms of deceit which have a similar effect. Deceiving a court as to the true purpose of a legal action is one of these.

Table 5.3 Duty not to abuse process

A central principle behind all dispute resolution is the concern that the parties use the dispute resolution process to solve exactly what they say is in dispute and nothing more. When lawyers are acting for clients who have differences with each other, they are concerned to try to identify the core of the disagreement between their clients. Most lawyers quickly realise that they will do a better, less expensive job for their client (and perhaps be

5 Truth and deception   123

Table 5.3 (cont.)

paid earlier) if they try to get to the bottom of an argument and settle it without going to court. If they are good at resolving problems because they do cut to the chase and focus on central rather than peripheral issues, they develop reputations for being cost efficient. These are successful people because they are so efficient. This is why effective negotiators and mediators ask their clients about underlying tensions, about wider issues and about business strategies before they attempt a negotiation or mediation. This principled or interest-based approach[16] can go into what might really be behind a dispute and solve it before courts or tribunals need to be involved.

But when a party or their lawyer is not prepared to genuinely expose what lies beneath and is concerned to use a court argument as a smokescreen for an underlying and usually illegal purpose, then the truth is obscured and in effect, a deception is practised on the court. There are several varieties of abuse here: they include making baseless allegations for political purposes or to assist an improper purpose such as revenge, to pursue a truly hopeless case[17] or simply to waste the time, money[18] and energy of the other party for commercial reasons.

Courts struggle to identify such abuse for two reasons. First and foremost, they depend on us as lawyers to inform them about what is going on in a case. If we choose not to let a judge know about what is really happening, they may never actually know how to decide the case or instruct a jury properly. If they do get an inkling of an underlying problem by listening to witnesses, they may not be certain about what to do about it if they think we, as lawyers, are misleading them and may go on doing so. Courts must decide between competing viewpoints as to what are presumed to be genuine legal claims and need advocates to put forward evidence as to what is really at stake in such claims. Such evidence will be irrelevant or inherently unreliable if it is proposed in support of objectives that are illegal or at best immoral. When a judge has to deal with this type of abuse and cannot rely on us, their own experience and judgment is all that they have available, and some will inevitably misjudge the situation.

Second, court time is very expensive. The salaries of judges, associates and many administrators, not to mention the time and fees of the party who is being deceived, will typically run into hundreds of thousands of dollars. If a case is delayed or even fails entirely because there are attempts by one party or their lawyer to use it for some immoral purpose, a great deal of money is thrown away. Abuse of process undermines the capacity of governments to pay for the court system.

A well-known case illustrates what is meant by an underlying dodgy purpose. In this case, a judge could only discover the truth about a prior case because certain documents unexpectedly came to light. In the second, a judge was provided with plenty of information about what was really going on and became quite convinced, if not angry, about what was being attempted.

1.*White Industries v Flower and Hart* (1998) 156 ALR 169

Flower and Hart was a well-established Brisbane law firm with a number of commercial clients. This extract summarises their ultimately notorious abuse of process.

> [Flower and Hart] . . . acted for a property developer in financial trouble and who needed to buy time in the hope of avoiding payment on a [legitimate] multimillion dollar debt . . . [T]hey devised an immoral strategy to gain time for the company by frustrating a major creditor, a construction company that had built a shopping mall for the developer and wanted to be paid. This strategy involved the developer corporation suing the construction company for fraud on grounds which both the advocate and the instructing solicitors (attorneys) knew were totally unsustainable. Justice Goldberg of the Federal Court of Australia found that the fraud proceedings had no real prospects of success and, since they were designed only to cause delay, were an abuse of process. The judge considered the activities of the two lawyers [the partner Meadows and the QC, Ian Callinan] to be reprehensible, basing his decision on a paper trail which included the written advice from Callinan to Meadows . . . in which Callinan had warned Meadows that the proposed action lacked credibility, but suggested they proceed in any event.
> The trial judge was affirmed on appeal to the Full Federal Court, but there was no reaction by the then conservative Australian Government, which had in the meantime appointed Callinan to the . . . High Court of Australia and wanted no scrutiny of the propriety of its decision . . . To this day there has been no formal attempt to review the impact of these lawyers' conduct upon community confidence in the justice system.[19] [footnotes omitted]

124   The Good Lawyer

Table 5.3 (cont.)

Virtue ethics

The duty of a lawyer not to abuse the process of dispute resolution is based on the virtues of *honesty* and *transparency*. To the extent that we seek out the truth in the judicial process, we are seeking *knowledge* of the real purposes of litigation. Accurate information is needed to make a judgment based on legal principles rather than on ulterior purposes. If transparency is lacking and courts are used to help avoid legitimate obligations through false assertions, or even to settle scores or gain political advantages through true assertions, then *justice* fades away.

Consequentialism

Lawyers who know that a commercial claim is legally weak or hopeless but pursue it within the umbrella of role morality to the point of false allegations, must either be lacking in any moral purpose or be very clear in their own minds that the desired outcome is morally worthwhile. But they cannot in conscience invoke zealous advocacy to this civil environment in support of the abuse. In the end they must be willing to provide an acceptable justification. It is hard to see how consequentialism justifies such allegations in the world of commerce.

Consequentialism, moral activism and responsible lawyering are in closest alignment when this issue of the public interest is present, though who is defining the public interest is often important. For example, a refugee lawyer may be quite clear that it is acceptable for them to commence delaying administrative law proceedings to prevent an imminent deportation of a politically active Tamil family to Sri Lanka, even though they know the merits of the case are legally hopeless and the action is designed only to give time for media pressure to be brought on the Minister for Immigration. Are such proceedings brought for an improper purpose?

Kantian ethics

Kantian views in relation to the purpose of litigation can lead a lawyer in several directions depending on the understanding of fairness adopted. On the one hand, a Kantian (only somewhat tongue in cheek) might consider that every case should first be mediated or would otherwise benefit from alternative dispute resolution, in the interests of everyone's equal right to avoid the judicial process. But if litigation is inevitable, they are likely to condemn any proceedings which hide their real purpose, particularly purely commercial purposes, since these proceedings will not be fair to those who seek to defend themselves. The right to a fair trial, so stated, will be at the top of a Kantian list.

Occasionally, however, when a defendant is perceived as undeserving, then Kantian approaches may give way to consequentialist calculations as to who among the litigants is more worthy. Kantian insistence on fair process no matter who is involved is an admirable reminder to lawyers that one of our critical roles is to guarantee fairness for undesirable clients, regardless. It is this quality of Kant that captures lawyers' hearts more firmly and more commonly than does consequentialism, even if few use this terminology.

Applicable law and conduct rules

Flower and Hart[20] and *Clyne v NSW Bar Association*[21] are authority for the proposition that the merit of a civil case is subject to the condition that the parties' motives are proper and focused only on the truth or otherwise of the facts and the applicability of the law to those facts. *Clyne* is also authority for the proposition that a lawyer must not argue a particular defence for an ulterior purpose.

The casting of baseless 'aspersions', that is, allegations that imply a deficient character without any foundation, is also on the prohibited list. In support, see, for example, ASCR 21, BR 31–35; *Civil Procedure Act* 2010 (Vic) ss 18, 42 and *Rees v Bailey Aluminium Products* [2008] VSCA 244.

ASCR 3.1 supports all these principles by affirming the paramount duty of lawyers to support the administration of justice,[22] regardless of any other duty, and ASCR 8.1 requires a lawyer to follow only the lawful, proper and competent instructions of their client.

5 Truth and deception   125

Table 5.3 (cont.)

Conclusion in relation to abusive civil proceedings

Abuse of process is abusive of the trust a court places in its lawyers and undermines their integrity in the eyes of the community. A cynical consequentialism drives them, though some consequentialists draw on noble virtues of compassion and of a great desire for justice.

The consequentialist nature of abuse of process is clearer in the case of purely corporate and commercial disputes, but abusive proceedings undertaken for political purposes are no different in principle. Lawyers who are willing to use the courts in this way are deceiving and belittling them as a means to achieve what may well in some cases be a greater end, but even if driven virtuously, such lawyers need to know that they may be sacrificing some of another virtue – their integrity – in the process.

5.5 Criminal lawyers who 'know too much'

Criminal legal practice also harbours difficult ethical issues about deceit, though for the most part, the difficulty arises because of a misunderstanding about the role of criminal defence lawyers.

Table 5.4 On knowing too much – acting for apparently 'guilty' clients

---

It is a source of constant amazement to non-lawyers that as lawyers we can with a clear conscience go in to bat for defendants who 'are guilty'. The gap between public understandings of guilt and innocence and the reality of a criminal trial is still wide, possibly due to the numerous courtroom dramas which attempt – and fail – to accurately describe the process in popular media.[23] It takes some effort to persuade citizen interrogators that they are assuming quite a lot about the issue of guilt, but then admit that we also can fall into the same traps.

If you decide to become a criminal defence advocate or barrister, the issue of your clients' guilt or otherwise is not something you should immediately address, let alone answer to your own satisfaction. With the armour of role morality you can be determined to resist premature conclusions about your client or their culpability and be intent on running a robust defence, but you will still be tempted to reach some of those conclusions before you ought to. Never mind that you have been given the brief because the solicitor thinks you will be good to handle a 'not guilty' plea. This is something on which you must make your own mind up, and before you do that there is much to consider. In preparing for a trial, there will be many claims on your attention: you will be trying to fill holes in the brief you have received from your instructing solicitor, juggling procedural obligations in relation to admissible evidence, teasing out inconsistencies in witnesses' statements and trying to understand the limitations of forensic evidence.

All of this takes time, and to be truly zealous in your client's interests, all these factors need to be addressed before you ask your client too many questions. If, when you are ready, you do ask those questions and your client gives answers that are not inconsistent with a plea of 'not guilty', then it is your zealous duty to proceed on that basis.

You will anticipate that you will go home that night and will perhaps be challenged by 'what did you do today?' questions. So because you are emotionally integrated and understand the claims of general morality on your wider life, you will have considered whether your client is mentally coherent enough to have committed an offence, and be well enough to stand trial; you will also have considered whether substance abuse has had an effect on their intentions; and you will also have taken into account any cultural factors that could have influenced

126 The Good Lawyer

Table 5.4 (cont.)

your client's understanding of what they were doing; but most of all, because you have self-respect, you will be able to say two things honestly to yourself:

- you have not prevented your client from giving you self-incriminating information;[24] and
- you are not putting someone forward on a 'not guilty' plea if you are certain that they are guilty of the offence as charged.[25]

Fortunately (or not), being 'certain' about guilt is not that easy. By the time of trial, any confession should have been thoroughly tested and either accepted (leading to advice to plead 'guilty') or rejected, often on the basis of mental illness, which has taken away intent to commit a crime even if the act itself occurred. And yet there are still situations where you can be caught out. What if, in the middle of the trial, something goes really wrong? The following case is one of the most famous in Australian legal history, for many reasons, as this extract makes clear:

Tuckiar v the King (1934) 52 CLR 335[26]

[A]n Aboriginal elder was charged with the murder of a policeman in Arnhem Land. Tuckiar, or Dhakiyarr as he was and is now known in his community, had come upon the policeman as he (the policeman) was taking Dhakiyarr's wife away in chains during a search for other Indigenous people who were suspected of killing some Japanese fishermen. According to tribal law, the action of the policeman was probably a 'taking' and therefore Dhakiyarr's intervention was justified. Dhakiyarr speared the victim, narrowly missing his wife and young child in the process.

He was captured and tried in Darwin. However, it was only during his trial that Dhakiyarr communicated to his counsel, through an interpreter, enough of the circumstances of the spearing to produce a hasty and uninformed reaction in the lawyer. The now infamous advocate immediately got to his feet in front of the jury and stated that he was in 'the worst predicament he had encountered in all his legal career' (code for 'my client did it') and needed to speak to the judge.

Counsel did not argue any defence on Dhakiyarr's behalf throughout the case and his client was subsequently convicted. On appeal to the High Court, there was a unanimous decision that advocates are bound to keep silent in such circumstances and continue with fully testing the prosecution case, although they must avoid putting their clients in the witness box to give affirmative evidence of innocence. Dhakiyarr won his appeal on the basis that his advocate's statement to the court had produced a substantial miscarriage of justice (not that Dhakiyarr's actions were, by the standards of the day, acceptable). He was released, never to be seen again. As a result of the appeal, however, it is clear that the duty of confidentiality binds advocates' actions providing no active misleading of the court occurs. In other words, fairness does dominate. The irony of Dhakiyarr's case, apart from the tragedy of the clash of two uncomprehending cultures, is that his own evidence, had he been allowed to give it, might have caused a modern jury to think he was not guilty, though this result was probably most unlikely before a jury in 1930s Darwin.[27] [footnotes omitted]

Dhakiyarr's lawyer was rebuked by the High Court for disclosing a privileged communication of his client.[28] The High Court said that he had a plain duty to the client and to the court to press such rational considerations as the evidence gave rise to in favour of a complete acquittal, or conviction of manslaughter only and that this obligation did not change simply because his client appeared to be saying something new.

Virtue ethics

Virtue is tested by the mid-trial 'confession' because your first instinct would be to 'fess up' to the court, driven by *honesty* and a desire for what you might think to be *justice*. But *wisdom* ought to assert itself as well, since such confessions, coming at the time they do, point to deeper issues that may mean the 'confession' is false and must be explored privately. *Prudence* requires your immediate silence and reflection. And even if your client has had a change of heart and decides genuinely to confess, your *judgment* ought to persuade you to test the prosecution case regardless, since your client might be sacrificing themselves for other reasons. It will take *courage* to cross-examine prosecution witnesses despite what your client has just told you, but that courage is called for. This is an appropriate example of zealous advocacy.

However, to decline to ask your client before trial about 'what really happened' is to deny the virtues of *truth*, of *integrity* and perhaps of a love of *justice*.

5 Truth and deception   127

Table 5.4 (cont.)

Consequentialism

If you decide to protect your client in the interests of achieving an acquittal even though you have received a confession, you may do nothing about it and continue on as planned, calculating that your client, if acquitted, will be grateful and will not reoffend or cause further harm. You may even place your client in the witness box if you believe that their confession was false or flippant and they are once again clear that they are innocent. But if your calculation is that you cannot be sure as to the truth of the confession and or that the victim(s) of the crime as charged will suffer more as a result of an acquittal (aided by your silence), you may determine to adopt the course required by the ASCR, reasoning that better consequences are likely if those conduct rules are observed.

Kantian ethics

The Kantian perspective is straightforward in relation to the mid-trial confession. Fairness as between your client and the justice system means that you will seek the middle course required by the ASCR and do only so much from that point onwards as is consistent with pressuring the prosecution to prove its case.

But in relation to pre-trial questioning, much more is at stake, and here the role morality of zealous advocacy would be inferior to general morality. If you decide not to ask 'what really happened?', you may try to justify your approach by saying that your client is entitled to a fair trial – that is, to the presumption of innocence – and it is your (zealous) role not to pre-judge anything, but rather to make the state prove its case. This is the time-honoured, conventional and dominant view as to what is 'fair'. However, if at the minimum, your intuition (which is finely honed as a result of your experience) is that your client is not being honest with you, then it cannot be unfair to all of those individuals affected by this alleged crime (that is, the defendant themselves, victims and the relatives and friends of both), to exhibit an ethic of care and ask the critical question. After all, Kantian ethics is clear that the categorical imperative (see Chapter 3) requires fairness towards all those affected by our actions.

Applicable law and conduct rules

There is no judicial decision and there are no conduct rules which compel a lawyer to ask their client whether they committed an offence or not. Similarly, no law requires us to refrain from asking about such an issue.

In itself, *Tuckiar*'s case provides a foundational template for a lawyer's behaviour when confronted by a mid-trial 'confession'. ASCR 20 is generally an effective guide to behaviour in the Dhakiyarr situation. This rule properly allows such an advocate to continue to act providing they confine themselves to testing the prosecution's evidence (ASCR 20.2.2(iii–v)) and avoid leading affirmative evidence of innocence by anyone, including their client (ASCR 20.2.2(i– ii) and 20.2.3)). BR 161–2 similarly affirms a duty upon an advocate to 'act honourably', while ASCR 20.2.1 permits a lawyer to withdraw if there is time before the trial to do so and if their client consents.

During a hearing, it is only when a client insists on giving false evidence or requires their lawyer to assert a false innocence on their behalf that that lawyer may withdraw (ASCR 20.2.3). In practice, a client who is informed early on by their lawyer that they will withdraw in these circumstances and that such action will be protected by ASCR 20.2.3 or BR 161–2 will not insist on such evidence being led or such assertions being made. A 'noisy withdrawal' of this nature would have a big impact on a court and increase the chances of conviction even though a prosecutor could not comment adversely on the withdrawal in the presence of the jury.

Conclusions in relation to knowing too much

Advocates tend to seek implicit justification from (zealous) role morality for their silence when, before a trial or hearing, they decline to ask questions of their clients about 'what happened'. But there is no compulsion to be silent arising from any of role morality, consequentialism or Kantian ethics and no legal authority that compels them to be silent in these circumstances. If they are so silent, that silence offers comfort with likely deception, at the cost of their integrity.

On the other hand, consequentialism and Kantian ethics would concur that an advocate's proper, zealous course when confronted by an apparent confession during a trial or hearing is to observe the ASCR and BR provisions. Virtue ethics would agree but go even further in the pre-hearing situation, encouraging you to 'ask the question'.

128   The Good Lawyer

5.6 Evading tax

The last of the major issues affecting deceit in legal practice concerns taxation. Taxation presents a strange face to the community and even to lawyers. Most people regard paying tax, whether personal income tax or company tax, as a civil issue. That is, tax is something we pay to government in the same way as we pay for utilities such as electricity, gas or water, or to local councils in municipal rates. But tax is much more than this. Many think that evading tax is reasonable because government cannot be trusted to use tax well. Perhaps that is why government has always regarded non-payment of tax not just as a civil matter, but as criminal.

The problem is: some lawyers, though sworn to uphold the law and serve the administration of justice, regard truthfulness and openness in relation to paying tax as quasi-optional, in the same way as do many other taxpayers.

Table 5.5 How much tax avoidance is morally acceptable?

Taxation is always a challenge for lawyers because many clients want to pay as little tax as possible. And more often than not, we find ourselves in agreement with them. Even those of us who believe taxation is a social good that supports many critical government services will also be happy to take advantage of whatever allowances, deductions and rebates are available to 'legitimately' reduce our tax liability. So when we can help our clients to pay less tax, we start from the proposition that that objective is as legitimate for them as it is for ourselves.

But this is where paying enough tax but no more than one has to becomes more difficult and the temptation to deceive becomes seductive. As discussed in Chapter 3, the distinction between evasion of tax and avoidance of tax allows us to structure our financial affairs in such a manner as to legally avoid paying some tax.[29] Most income earners cannot take advantage of this rule except in their use of the everyday allowances, deductions and rebates referred to above.[30] Some earn enough to make it worthwhile to use slightly more complex mechanisms such as family trusts. But higher income earners and particularly the highest 5% of income earners are able to access all sorts of schemes to pay less tax – and sometimes, almost no tax. A typical strategy is to use a tax haven such as Luxembourg, Vanuatu or Cyprus (before it imploded financially in April 2013) in order to park money or shares where they can earn high interest or corporate dividends but pay next to nothing in tax.

These schemes can be legal if they can fit within increasingly restrictive anti-evasion provisions and be classed only as avoidance, or they can be illegitimate (and illegal) if they are considered 'artificial', contrived and evasive.[31] The tax opinion case which helped to bring down the large Chicago law firm Jenkens and Gilchrist (Chapter 2), is an example of the latter.

But when it is not clear which category a scheme sits in, then it is up to the client's adviser, who is frequently a lawyer, to determine the position. And here there is great potential for circularity of argument. When law (which asks 'what is evasion?') entirely replaces ethics (which only asks 'what is moral?') but achieves no certainty in the process, there is a disconnect that destroys respect for both. Ultimately, tax lawyers who struggle to determine what is artificial or contrived without reference to what is moral – that is, without reference to general morality – are struggling because they ignore the very tools that determine artificiality and contrivance.

Table 5.5 (cont.)

Virtue ethics

If as a tax scheme promoter you are a lawyer of *integrity* and obviously seek to minimise tax with *transparency* by publishing to the tax office complete documentation that clearly shows money flows, the ultimate beneficial owners of all assets and the location of those assets, then these virtues will be evident to that office, to your peers and to your potential clients. You will miss out only on those clients who want transactional secrecy. These clients are also of a class whose businesses are likely to bring you personally to the attention of the tax office.

Consequentialism

All clients' desired outcome is to pay a lot less tax. This 'greatest good' seems entrenched in many societies as morally good as well as legally appropriate (see below under the applicable law), but secrecy is the means to this outcome for tax advisers and clients alike. As a means to an end, secrecy must arouse some moral concern where taxation is concerned.

Tax lawyers can, if they wish, marry a narrow consequentialist perspective with role morality and in so doing be unable to see that the wider consequences of too much tax avoidance lead eventually to degradation in social infrastructure. A traditional consequentialist perspective values wider social stability above individuals' desire to artificially structure their affairs to pay less tax.

Kantian ethics

Kantians are also initially sensitive to the dominant social view that tax is at best a necessary evil. They will naturally be attuned to the notion that it is completely 'fair' for an individual to pay as little tax as possible. But they will also accept that fairness as between all individuals involves a degree of income redistribution and that the tax system is the central means by which that process is made possible.

Applicable law and conduct rules

In the *Westraders*[32] case Barwick CJ (a 'pro-taxpayer') emphasised the duty of Parliament to specify what was legal or not, and Deane J concurred, equating any effort by a court to plug loopholes as offensive to the rule of law.

In distinguishing between tax evasion and tax planning (avoidance), the ambivalence of the courts is illustrated by the statements of Viscount Simon LC in *Latilla v Inland Revenue Commissioner* [1943] AC 377 at 381 and Lord Macnaughton in *Commissioner of Stamp Duties v Byrnes* [1911] AC 386 at 392. Referring to what today we would call tax planning, Viscount Simon took a determined consequentialist view and said:

> There is . . . no doubt that they are within their legal rights, but that is no reason why their efforts . . . should be regarded as a commendable exercise of ingenuity . . . On the contrary, one result of such a method . . . is . . . to increase . . . the load of tax on the shoulder of the great body of good citizens who do not . . . adopt these manoeuvres.[33]

By contrast Lord Macnaughton said that 'none is bound to leave his property at the mercy of the revenue authority if he can legally escape its grasp'. The broader issues of morality raised by Lord Simon may be rationalised by placing responsibility not on the lawyer, but on the regulators. The practitioner's role as 'amoral technician' is thus rendered acceptable. Sir Anthony Mason once expressed the view extra-judicially that the morality of tax avoidance (as distinct from evasion) is a matter for the individual taxpayer and the tax lawyer should be as free from criticism as lawyers in other fields.

The summary is therefore: while it is competent and necessary for us as lawyers (as a part of the fiduciary duty to care about clients' financial affairs) to advise them of legitimate tax minimisation opportunities, do not advise them to engage in tax avoidance arrangements of an artificial character, for they then become tax evasion.

Conclusion in relation to how much tax is enough

General morality supports tax lawyers' efforts to openly assist their clients to pay less tax within the opportunities provided by legislation. In this activity, the key indicator of their moral sensitivity is the degree of transparency they bring to their activities.

130   The Good Lawyer

5.7 Conclusion: The possible consequences if caught 'lying'

Though it may seem gratuitous to conclude this chapter by mentioning penalties for crossing the lines into deceit, they ought to be stated. If before you seek admission to practice, you have hidden some plagiarism or a serious criminal history, you may be denied admission.[34] The consequences of misbehaviour which occurs after admission to practice can also be very severe: that is, 'striking off the Roll' or disbarment so that you cannot practise law again. Striking off is, however, reserved for the most serious misconduct and is something which can follow on from disciplinary proceedings commenced by a Legal Services Commissioner.[35] In some states and territories, law societies and bar associations can also commence proceedings. The regulatory tribunals which hear discipline cases can also cancel and suspend practising certificates for varying periods, or fine or reprimand, as the case requires. Legal costs amounting to many thousands of dollars will also be awarded against you if you are disciplined by the local regulatory tribunal.[36]

Other extreme consequences open to a court which will seriously dampen your reputation are punishment for the criminal offence of contempt of court, or being the recipient of an injunction which prevents you from representing your client. Occasionally, the result of a successful case can even be reversed.[37]

However, none of these cases or predicaments need impact on you. Staying inside the bounds of truthfulness by reference not just to the cases and conduct rules, but also to general morality,[38] offers many benefits. Your long-term reputation for integrity is more important than anything else, but so also is the ability to defend yourself to yourself, so that you are able to do good not just in the glare of court or opponent scrutiny, but also in private, when no one is looking.

In the following chapter, the challenges posed by this last issue – what to do with clients' secrets? – are examined using the same criteria as have been applied here to truth and deception.

Notes

1. See, for example, *Giannarelli v Wraith* [1988] HCA 52 at 555–56, per Mason CJ.
2. The ASCR is binding in those jurisdictions that have adopted it. See Ch. 2, n 72 and accompanying pages in main text.

5 Truth and deception   131

3. For a full list of all issues arising in relation to truth telling and deception, see Dal Pont, *Lawyers' Professional Responsibility* (5th edn), Chs 4.70, 10, 17 and 19.

4. See Chris Merritt, 'Options canvassed for Hardie law changes', *Australian Financial Review*, 12 November 2004, 59. A succinct history of the Hardie affair, up until the appointment of David Jackson QC to investigate the matter, may be viewed in the Australian Parliamentary Library at www.aph.gov.au/parliamentary_business/bills_legislation/bd/bd0405/05bd074. See also the Jackson Inquiry (Report of the Special Commission of Inquiry into the Medical Research and Compensation Foundation, 21 September 2004, NSW Cabinet Office at www.pandora.nla.gov.au/tep/45031), commissioned by the NSW Government in an attempt to discover who was responsible for the under-funding of the asbestosis compensation process.

5. See Richard Ackland, 'Irresistible charms', *Business Review Weekly*, 30 September 2004, 48.

6. The High Court has held that seven of the directors of JH had breached their duties by approving the company's release of a misleading statement to the stock exchange indicating that their asbestos compensation scheme was 'fully funded'. See www.smh.com.au/business/hardie-directors-breached-duties-high-court-20120503-1y0cu.html#ixzz2QawhaOQD. Contrast the Allens' approach with the views of former Blakes' (Ashurst) partner Tony Greenwood, in 'Ethics and Avoidance Advice' (1991) 65 *LIJ* 724.

7. See, for example, ASCR 19.10, which allows a solicitor to remain silent about their client's prior convictions where they know or suspect that the prosecution is unaware of them. See also BR 157–59, which emphasise that although there is no obligation to correct an omission, an advocate cannot mislead the court either.

8. *Stirling v Legal Services Commissioner* [2013] VSCA 374.

9. See also, for example, *Vernon v Bosley (No. 2)* [1997] 3 WLR 683; *Jenkins v Liversey* [1985] 1 CA 424 per Lord Brandon of Oakbrook; *Clarkson v Clarkson* [1972] 19 FLR 112.

10. See ASCR 19–21. These duties include obligations not to knowingly mislead the court on any matter (ASCR 19.1; BR 19, 50); not to present false or misleading evidence or conceal material facts; not to knowingly submit a false document (*Rajasooria* [1955] 1 WLR 405 and *Kyle v LPCC* (1999) 21 WAR 56); not to knowingly make misleading statements about law or legal processes (BR 19; *R v S(F)* (2000) 144 CCC (3d) 466; to inform court of authorities that go against their client, even if their client instructs them otherwise (ASCR 17.2.3; BR 24); to correct misleading misstatements (ASCR 19.2; BR 20 and *Re Foster* (1950) 50 SR (NSW) 149); and to provide a great deal of potentially damaging information to a court when seeking an order *ex parte* (in the absence of the other party) (ASCR 19.4–19.9). Prosecutors are also bound by a range of duties designed to ensure that they in their role exhibit fairness and act impartially. See *Whitehorn v R* (1983) 152 CLR 657; *MG v R* [2007] NSWCCA 57; ASCR 29 and BR 134–48.

11. See, for example, *Civil Procedure Act 2010* (Vic), ss 17–26 respectively.

12. *Civil Procedure Act 2010* (Vic), ss 15.

13. The civil litigation process contains a set of procedures collectively termed *discovery of documents*. Discovery requires each party to identify several classes of documents. See *Supreme Court (General Civil Procedure) Rules* 2005, Rule 29.01.01(3). See also

132 The Good Lawyer

David Bailey and John Arthur, *Civil Procedure Victoria*, LexisNexis, 1986 [I 29.01.205].

14. Jonathan Liberman, 'Do judges now admire corporate connivance?', *The Age*, Melbourne, 11 December 2002, 17.

15. Adrian Evans, *Assessing Lawyers' Ethics*, Cambridge University Press, Melbourne, 2007, 9.

16. See, generally, Michael King, Arie Freiberg, Becky Batagol and Ross Hyams, *Non-Adversarial Justice*, Federation Press, Sydney, 2009.

17. Lawyers still need to distinguish 'hopeless' from 'weak but arguable' cases. This is frequently difficult to do, particularly if the culture of their employment or the weight of the law firm partnership behind them has a bias towards regarding all matters as arguable in the sense identified by Judge Rakoff (see Ch. 3). Strictly understood, if a case is hopeless (that is, has no chance of success), you must advise your client not to proceed.

18. See *Giannarelli v Wraith* (1988) 165 CLR 543; *A Team Diamond Headquarters Pty Ltd v Main Road* [2009] VSCA 208; *Saragas v Martinis* [1976] 1 NSWLR 172; BR 17; *Civil Procedure Act 2010* (Vic) ss 7, 18–20, 22–5.

19. See Evans, n 15, 27.

20. *White Industries v Flower and Hart* (1998) 156 ALR 169.

21. *Clyne v NSW Bar Association* (1960) 104 CLR 186.

22. Supporting the administration of justice involves a number of responsibilities, including resisting perjury (ASCR 24.1), counsel against disobedience of court orders (ASCR 20.3) and ensuring the integrity of evidence given (ASCR 24).

23. The UK television series *Garrow's Law* is a significant exception. See Ch 1, n 16.

24. Some lawyers think it is consistent with their zealous advocate role not to ask their client questions that might produce answers that would then compel advice to plead 'guilty'. But the virtuous and zealous advocate will be repulsed by this. Note that, once such questions are asked and answers are received, it is an offence to connive at improper conduct. An example is a Canadian case where a lawyer advised their client to be forgetful and evasive in answering police questions about his connections with a criminal gang. See *R v Sweezy* (1988) 39 CCC 182.

25. *Tuckiar v the King* (1934) 52 CLR 335 makes it clear that a lawyer must never assert as true what they know to be false, or be a party to fraud.

26. A more recent example of a similar dilemma is *R v Nerbas* [2011] QCA 199, referred to in Ch. 3.

27. See Parker and Evans, *Inside Lawyers' Ethics*, and Ch. 5.

28. See Ch. 6.

29. *Commissioner of Taxation v Westraders* (1980) 144 CLR 55.

30. Many lawyers seem to have a personally unsophisticated approach when it comes to their own tax affairs, but there are also more than a few QCs who have themselves simply ignored the obligation to lodge tax returns – hardly a concealed effort at tax evasion. Stirling's case (n 8, at para 96) provides a contemporary list of transgressing barristers.

31. See Barkoczy, *Foundations of Taxation Law* (5th edn).

32. (1980) 144 CLR 55.

33. [1943] 1 All ER 265 at 266.

34. See Ch. 1.11.
35. See, for example, *Legal Services Commissioner v Piva (Legal Practice)* [2009] VCAT 1200.
36. See, for example, *Baulch v LyndockWarnambool Inc.* [2010] VSCA 30.
37. For example, *Meek v Fleming* [1961] 2 QB 366; *Rees v Bailey Aluminium Products* [2008] VSCA 244.
38. See Tomain, 'The legal heresiarchs: Luban's *The Good Lawyer*', 703.

Chapter 6

PROFESSIONAL SECRETS

6.1 Introduction: The shrinking world of secrets

Consider this situation:

> You are a large law firm leader. You have just been told by another senior partner that s/he has been having an affair with the Chief Legal Officer of one of the firm's major clients. Both your partner and the CLO are currently married, but not to each other. To your knowledge, no one at the client company knows of the affair as yet.
>
> **What will you do?**

This particular secret is about to become less secret anyway, since office romances are inevitably known to someone, despite best efforts at discretion. But will the client company be keen for this relationship to come out, so to speak? Do you – or does your firm – owe that client any duty of confidentiality here? Does your colleague understand what a conflict of interest is? And what will the client company consider to be at stake, quite apart from whether your colleague wants everything to stay quiet? When it all goes 'pear-shaped', will your firm be blamed if you do nothing while you have the chance?

Lawyers are full of secrets, just like everyone else. But some secrets we hold as lawyers are a bit different. When we learn something from a client in the course of our job as a lawyer, we are usually required to keep that information secret. Non-lawyers can generally disclose 'secrets' without any particular

134

legal consequences, but we can be disciplined and sometimes sued if we breach our client's confidentiality. In the case above, it is not impossible that the client corporation would agree that while you do not owe it a formal duty of confidentiality in relation to this affair, once you became aware of the situation you should tell them about it, so that all concerned can discuss the considerable implications for the client. And if this meant your own colleague would avoid you, that might be the price of a loyalty to client. Fortunately, most commercial lawyers realise that sexual relationships with officers of their corporate clients are full of this sort of risk, but that does not mean that they or anyone else in the legal profession can afford to be casual about secrecy. This chapter explores the world of lawyers' secrets: the principles and the exceptions and the situations that challenge lawyers in behaving ethically.

The first challenge lawyers have is working out what constitutes a secret these days. Not much, perhaps. In an age of WikiLeaks, of increasing surveillance of email[1] and of a long list of technological devices and software which record, disseminate and correlate the many individual pieces of information, conversations and images that were previously private, why must we get overly anxious about secrecy when the rest of the community is disclosing as much as possible? These are just a few of the known mechanisms by which privacy is unravelling:

- GoogleMaps' ability to picture where marijuana is being grown is limited at present by the low refresh rate, that is, the infrequency of repeat aerial photographs. With time, GoogleMaps will be satellite-based and will refresh its global surveillance images every day;
- Google Street View, which photographs the physical environment of many private houses;
- apps embedded in mobile smart phones that record and transmit GPS coordinates of users' movements to their internet service providers, often on a default basis;
- the ease with which online credit card payments are hacked and their owners' identities appropriated for overseas fraud purposes;
- local government and private corporations' CCTV surveillance of many public spaces;
- public transport smart cards, for example the Melbourne Myki, under which about 1 million public transport users so far, have registered their name, address, transaction records, fare type, direct debit or credit card

136   The Good Lawyer

details with police, transport authorities and an international private contractor, Keane International Incorporated;

- supermarket and retailer loyalty cards (personal information, product, location, date and time): 6.5 million Woolworths and 5 million Coles customers have shared this info with data centres, analysts, mailing houses and printers;
- the very porous 'cloud', where everyone, including lawyers, stores their information, even though cloud storage is quite transparent to anyone determined to obtain access; and
- most significant of all – the increasingly integrated efforts of government departments in many countries (national security agencies, securities' regulators, tax offices, social security and legal aid) to combine their separate databases in an effort to build up comprehensive, searchable profiles of everyone in the country.

As lawyers, our efforts to keep our clients' secrets secret may be no more effective than those of anyone else. For example, very few typically encrypt their email, even though unencrypted email in an age of constant surveillance is borderline negligent for practising lawyers. Our lives and any 'secrets' committed to text are likely to be exposed. We will not even need an identity card.

Surveillance, not privacy, is increasingly the modern reality, including inside a law firm.[2] And many of the above monitoring mechanisms are operated through smart phones and their ubiquitous apps,[3] devices and software which lawyers have adopted as quickly as anyone.

However important personal privacy is, we do need to consider if the deep moat around the confidentiality of all lawyering is real, especially as lawyers themselves are increasingly dependent on everything connected to the internet. Is it not better to recognise that the idea of a 'secret' is increasingly a hope rather than a reality?

Ethical disasters such as *McCabe* (Ch. 2), *James Hardie* (Ch. 5) or *Flower and Hart* (Ch. 5) may be less likely in future because of the changing nature of record-keeping. In *McCabe*, Clayton Utz attempted to solve the problem of embarrassing documents which recorded damaging information by physically shredding them or arranging for them to be warehoused outside the jurisdiction. The now collapsed international accounting firm Arthur Anderson tried unsuccessfully and at the last minute to use industrial shredders to get rid of the records of Enron Corporation's massive debt to try to prevent its disclosure or their involvement in hiding it all. In future, such records are likely to be routinely moved to the cloud, where 'documents' could be a lot less secure and might never in fact be able to benefit from privilege, because they will have 'leaked' long ago. Cloud storage is porous for the following reasons:[4]

- Data containing client confidences is still commonly sent by lawyers to the cloud through unencrypted email, and as such, is normally available to both the cloud provider and its outsourcing contractors. Unencrypted email is likely to be scrutinised and stored by computer algorithms for key word associations as a matter of course. These associations are important for security services the world over in their efforts to limit terrorism and monitor political figures, organised crime and global financial movements. Many of these individuals have information stored by lawyers. Arguably, unencrypted cloud storage *per se* means disclosure and waiver of client privilege, even if lawyers use local, on-the-ground data backups to guard against data destruction or corruption;
- Even when client data is encrypted both for transmission and cloud storage, it is protected for only as long as the integrity of the encryption and the pace of computing innovation allow. As quantum computing initialises and expands over the next few years, it will massively increase processing power, to the point that stable encryption (that is, confidentiality) may become increasingly illusory;
- The cloud provider will routinely subcontract cloud control, perhaps to a jurisdiction with a deserved reputation for corruption and bribery;
- Cloud providers and their subcontractors, often located in corruption-prone economies, must screen their employees for past breaches of security. This process is technically difficult, easy for employees to subvert and expensive to operate on an ongoing basis. Employee screening is therefore likely to be very porous;
- The initiating lawyer is completely reliant on their head contract with the cloud provider. They have no privity of contract with the sub-contractors who actually operate the cloud and hence only indirect access to those contractors when problems occur. Discovery processes are difficult to guarantee in the cloud;

138   The Good Lawyer

- There is a risk of extra-jurisdictional legislation (for example, the UK *Bribery Act 2010* or the US *Patriot Act 2001*) and foreign security services rendering cloud provider contracts redundant;
- Because lawyers' cloud storages are well known to contain information that is likely to be commercially valuable, their servers are 'high risk' hacking targets. As such, clients need to be fully informed of the firm's cloud provider details and the reality of their lawyer's actual supervision of their head contractor; and finally,
- Since cloud servers are by definition controlled outside the firm and from time to time administered and segmented by 'uncontrolled' individuals, a proportion of any cloud-based information barriers that might be kept intact if controlled directly by the firm will inevitably disintegrate.

6.2 Professional secrecy remains important: Confidentiality and client privilege

Acknowledging that much information is not at all secret, we still need to make a careful case to our clients to trust us with their information. Otherwise, it is very difficult for mutual respect to be developed or for any thorough legal advice to be given. There clearly are some good secrets – secrets that are still important – and clients need to know that we understand this. This means encouraging full and frank disclosure as the basis of our representation, and more generally, to foster trust in lawyers and legal system. And however difficult or naïve this may appear, we need at the minimum to let our clients know that we will not talk about what they tell us, providing the secrecy is not harmful to others and does not damage important public interests.[5]

Confidentiality is the label we try to attach to the positive, socially just dimensions of trying to keep secrets, even though the wider community and the media may have different standards.

The principles of confidentiality and client privilege and the relevant professional conduct rules try to strike a balance between what is properly secret and what ought to be disclosed. Client confidentiality and client privilege sit together as a practical expression of the duty to clients (third on the list of lawyers' duties, see Diagram 5.1). Privileged information is a subset of the wider category of all confidential information. This diagram explains their relationship:

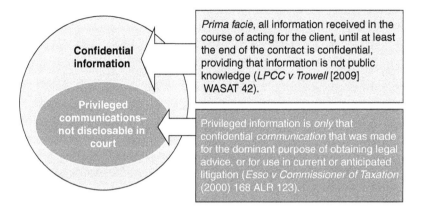

Diagram 6.1 Confidentiality distinguished from privilege

A communication might be confidential but not privileged: for example, if a current client sees you at the football or a nightclub and, in the course of the conversation, mentions the identity of an inside trader in their internal audit office. You may not disclose this information to others because the confidence arose as an incidence of your retainer, but it is *not* prima facie privileged because it does not fit the *Esso* test (that is, communicated for the dominant purpose of obtaining legal advice). You may therefore be compelled by a court to disclose it.

6.2.1 Confidentiality

Your obligations in relation to confidentiality are summed up in ASCR 9. Note the major exceptions highlighted in **bold**:

> ASCR 9.1 A solicitor must not disclose any information which is confidential to a client and acquired by the solicitor during the client's engagement to any person who is not:
> - 9.1.1 a solicitor who is a partner, principal, director, or employee of the solicitor's law practice; or
> - 9.1.2 a barrister or an employee of, or person otherwise engaged by, the solicitor's law practice or by an associated entity for the purposes of delivering or administering legal services in relation to the client,

> **EXCEPT as permitted in Rule 9.2.**
> **9.2** A solicitor **may** disclose confidential client information if:
> - 9.2.1 the client expressly or **impliedly authorises** disclosure;
> - 9.2.2 the solicitor is permitted or is compelled by law to disclose;
> - 9.2.3 the solicitor discloses the information in a confidential setting, for the sole purpose of obtaining advice in connection with the solicitor's legal or ethical obligations;
> - 9.2.4 the solicitor discloses the information for the sole purpose of **avoiding the probable commission of a serious criminal offence;**
> - 9.2.5 the solicitor discloses the information for the purpose of **preventing imminent serious physical harm** to the client or to another person; or
> - 9.2.6 the information is disclosed to the insurer of the solicitor, law practice or associated entity.

Very personal as well as large-scale corporate legal problems arise in relation to confidentiality. An example of the former involves the increasingly common situation where isolated elderly or otherwise disabled clients begin to lose their mental capacity to make decisions or care for themselves. Such clients are often fiercely independent and indeed are entitled to the dignity that any of us deserve, no matter our circumstances. Put yourself in the shoes of your client.

We may insist that our lawyer does nothing to intervene, while at the same time we may know deep down that we are increasingly failing in our capacity to self-care. Are you, the client, entitled to insist on your confidentiality? Ought your complaint to a legal regulator be upheld and your (former) lawyer disciplined when they effectively blow the whistle and seek a court order appointing an administrator over your affairs? A lot depends on your perspective. If you are the lawyer, analyse your options according to general morality in the manner set out in these chapters, but remember that ASCR 9.2.5 (above) does not provide a clear-cut exception for you. As a good lawyer, what do you do? Where is the greater compassion or the greater dignity? Check your proposed decision against how your client is likely to see things: the client will be fairly confident of having that interfering and patronising lawyer – you, in this example – done over properly for having the impudence to threaten their independence.

6 Professional secrets   141

The rules take us so far and no further. It is worth emphasising, in the light of these previous discussions about diminishing privacy, that ASCR 9 governs what happens with confidential information. Information that has never been private or is no longer confidential because it is public knowledge or has been leaked and is in the public domain (that is, the purpose served by confidentiality no longer exists), is not protected by the ASCR or any other law.[6]

Later in this chapter, an example of a corporation and its in-house corporate lawyers is used to illustrate the transactional cases where it seems that lawyers leave their own virtue undeveloped and over-identify with the interests of their client corporation by remaining silent in the face of immoral activity on a large scale. These lawyers identified themselves so closely with their particular client that it was hard for them to see themselves as independent of or separate from their client, who was also their sole employer. It did not register with them that one of the essential bases of legal professionalism is the concept of separation of the lawyer from the client. This separation, which is also referred to as the autonomy of both lawyer and client in their dealings with each other, is what was so dangerous about the office affair in the vignette at the start of this chapter. Lawyers need the virtue of self-respect. Lawyers who cannot see themselves as separate from their clients, or clients who see their lawyers as required to do everything demanded of them, may not always understand this principle. In such cases, appropriate confidentiality can be subverted and used as a crutch to support what can be thought of as passive deception.

When an in-house lawyer stays quiet while their client behaves unconscionably or illegally, they often seem to stand shoulder to shoulder with their clients – and they often 'go down' with them. Rarely do they later say, 'We were wrong.' A sense of personal shame, contrition or penitence on the part of the in-house lawyer is not often a part of the post-mortem in cases such as this.[7] This misguided confidentiality might be seen as appropriate loyalty on the part of those lawyers, who also suffered, but if the corporation in question behaves badly, that loyalty might be seen as misplaced.

In many of these situations, confidentiality was the overarching ethical concept in play, but it was not the main focus of attention. Running beneath the surface and reinforcing the stance of all lawyers concerned to maintain clients' confidences, is the derivative concept of client privilege, which is, if anything, more powerful. Client privilege has a greater impact in maintaining secrecy, because, subject to very few exceptions (discussed below), lawyers are able to refuse to provide information or answer questions in court when they can reasonably assert that a 'communication' is privileged. It is the protection in court that is most valuable, and many of the judicial arguments about confidentiality are conducted in the context of client privilege.

Together, confidentiality and client privilege generally support the Australian justice system and the consensus of most lawyers is likely to be that they work reasonably well, because they generally encourage clients to trust their lawyers. Without that trust, nothing in the current system would function on merit and the process would revert to a corrupt, 'who you know' mechanism, beset by the bribery and favour-based exchanges that dominate many 'justice' systems worldwide. But inappropriate silence of the lawyer 'lions' and hence their apparent complicity in the periodic misdeeds of the corporations or private individuals they work for is not an insignificant issue.

6.2.2 Client privilege

Just as information that is in the public domain is not confidential, it cannot by definition be privileged, though the communication which contains the information is protected. As explained in Diagram 6.1, client privilege seeks to protect the privacy of communications (which contain information) that are intended in some way to support the litigation process or to help someone obtain legal advice.[8] For example, your client may be known to be a paedophile in the sense that he has a conviction for rape of a child. That information is not confidential. But if he tells you, in order to obtain your advice about new charges that he faces, that a person related to his previous conviction is connected to the current charges (for example, that the victim of the offence for which he was convicted in the past is willing to give him an alibi for these latest charges), then that 'telling' is *prima facie* privileged, even if part of the information relates to an offence that is already known to the public at large.

This narrow category of confidential information is defended by the courts as essential to lawyers' roles, because no client such as the one in the example above would take the risk of disclosing a continuing and secret connection with a previous victim of their abuse if they thought that the information could be forced out of their lawyer. But the uses to which privilege has sometimes been put have been criticised by some judges and governments, despite its role as a 'pure' protector of legal advice and an aid to lawyers' complete understanding of a case. These critics increasingly regard privilege as a major commercial litigation tactic designed to hide both individuals' and corporations' crimes. The *McCabe* case (see Chapter 2) is an example where the use of privilege was seriously criticised.[9] Over time, therefore, several restrictions on the use of privilege have been developed. These restrictions disallow a claim of privilege where there is an illegal or criminal purpose,[10] or where:

- it is directed against the public interest;[11]
- legislation has specifically removed the privileged status of those communications,[12] for example where the Commonwealth Parliament considers there is a risk that some lawyers will connive at setting up tax evasion schemes;[13]
- your client has acted inconsistently (even on a single occasion) with the exercise of that privilege;[14]
- your client knowingly and voluntarily disclosed the substance of the communication;
- the communication is disclosed with the express or implied consent of your client; or
- your client has acted in a way that would make it unfair to then claim privilege.[15]

Ethical lawyers need a strong sense of when to keep silent and when to speak – to walk the line between privacy and public interest. In developing that judgment, the specific situations discussed in the tables below try to come to grips with what is really important about confidentiality and privilege, having regard to general morality and ASCR 9. These tables are as follows: Table 6.1 – Keeping past crimes secret; Table 6.2 – Using privilege to cover up corruption; and Table 6.3 – Using confidentiality and privilege to evade prosecution.

144 The Good Lawyer

6.3 Keeping quiet – murder

Table 6.1 Keeping the past in the past – the Lake Pleasant bodies

This case has an element of 'only in America' and 'only on American television', but Australia has had similar extreme examples. And the processes of ethical reasoning of the lawyers involved is still as fresh and real today as it was in the early 1970s.

In 1973 in northern New York state, two criminal defence lawyers were engaged by legal aid to represent an accused murderer, Robert Garrow. Garrow was mentally very ill. He had been mistreated by his parents, and had had a truly shocking upbringing after that. He left home and lived separately on a neighbouring farm for many of his teenage years, during which time (it was later accepted) he drank animal blood and had sex with farm animals.

On the surface, he was a married man with children and had a good job as a mechanic at a bakery. But underneath, he was in the habit of kidnapping, raping and murdering teenage girls, and sometimes killing their boyfriends as well.

Garrow was charged with the murder of one of those boys, and although suspected of murdering others, no other bodies could be located. Under hypnosis administered in an amateur manner by one of the lawyers (without supervision or, it would seem, any possibility of informed consent), Garrow confessed to other murders and described where the bodies of two girls lay, at the bottom of a mine shaft. The lawyers were dumbfounded, but one of these girls had been missing for only 3 weeks, so there was a very slim chance that, if Garrow was lying, she might still be alive. So the lawyers, bound by the then rule about confidentiality, kept quiet, although they went to search the mine shaft, near Lake Pleasant. They found the bodies of the girls, and took photos of the remains. But they were then in even more ethical trouble and even more frightened. Should they tell the relatives of the dead girls, who were all grieving and hoping for a miracle? Or would that disclosure, once made public, prejudice their efforts to get the prosecution to agree to accept a plea of 'not guilty due to insanity' on the current charge in exchange for the lawyers giving up the location of the dead girls?

They decided that they could not reveal the information they had because the confidentiality rule (as in the Alton Logan case[16]) prevented them from disclosing confidential information obtained in the course of legal representation. That rule is the same as in Australia and binds us to silence except where there is a risk of commission of a serious crime (see ASCR 9.2.4) or serious physical harm (ASCR 9.2.5). But it makes us stay silent when the crime is in the past. Later on, when all these events came out, the mother of one of the lawyers confronted her son about his silence and he complained that 'a lawyer is like a priest'. But she would have none of that and told him he was not a priest. But the challenge for him and his colleague was not over.

Ultimately, the case is famous because it raises very acutely the question of whether we as lawyers, by reason of our special role, are exempt from general morality. Luban says not and he is correct, at least to the extent that both general morality and professional roles must be weighed in the balance. Both lawyers initially ignored general morality and prioritised their zealous roles. But as the case went on, they revised their view. This extract from an interview of an American law teacher explains what happened next:

> Garrow was sent to prison and he actually pretended that he was paralysed and was stuck in a wheelchair, so although he was in a maximum security prison, they didn't watch him all that carefully, and eventually he scaled a wall and escaped from prison. And when they searched his prison cell they found a hit list in his cell that included the names of both of his lawyers. And [beforehand, during the murder trial, the lawyer Frank's] daughter Dorina had come into the courtroom, and Garrow – who had never met her – turned to her and said, 'Nice to see you again, Dorina.' And that led Frank to believe that his client had actually been stalking his daughter.
>
> So at the point at which Garrow escaped from prison, the lawyer decided, and when he learned that he was on a hit list that had been made by his client, he decided that enough was enough, and he told the police what he knew about where Garrow might be hiding, and then the police went to search that location, found Garrow and in the course of apprehending him, killed him. And I asked Frank how did it feel to have revealed a confidence in a way that resulted in the death of his client, and he said, 'I'm not a hero, my feet are of clay. I was relieved.'[17]

6 Professional secrets **145**

Table 6.1 (cont.)

Virtue ethics

It was not weak of Garrow's lawyer to eventually own up to the call of general morality because he felt his family was threatened. His zeal was replaced by his relationship of care. Even if we might not succumb to a threat to ourselves, most of us would speak when our families are involved. His courage in denying information to the grieving parents (since that silence was the only way he might have succeeded in negotiating a plea with the prosecutors) was replaced by the need to protect his own daughter. Virtue recognises the need to protect in the exercise of *judgment*.

But the lawyers never had it easy. They felt *compassion* for the parents of the murdered girls and anguished over their silence for many years later. They searched for but could not discover a basis for immediately disclosing that they had found the bodies, so that past harm had to remain in the past.

If this or a similar case should happen again, the lawyers involved may be assisted by this ethicist's reflection on what a lawyer seeking virtue might argue: '[H]arm may be taken to be future harm only. All wrongful . . . harm done in the past may in a sense be reduced to future and present experiences of wrongful harm. [In this sense] all harm is present and future harm.'[18] *Benevolence* may be the virtue that is central to the virtuous lawyer's preference to disclose secret past harm.

Kaptein also makes this quirky plea for more virtue in relation to lawyers' secrecy about past harm: '[P]rofessionally and humanely virtuous lawyers will always ask themselves what more or less rightful means may lead to rightful results, given the truth of the matter as far as is available. Virtues are not just of jurisprudence, but also of practical wisdom in a wider sense or 'moresprudence', [and] are rather more important than observing legal rules.'[19]

Consequentialism

The consequentialist perspective seemed clear-cut. The desired outcome according to role morality was a plea bargain, but this was impossible without something to 'trade'. So the means were to be justified by the ends. But as is possible in consequentialist thinking, accurately predicting what will happen was problematic. When the hit list was disclosed, it became clear that the zealous 'rules' of silence could not just be obeyed absolutely and the limitations of duty based on consequences became very clear. It was not a responsible lawyering concern for justice that overtook the lawyer, but fear.

Kantian ethics

Deciding between competing claims to fairness in the Lake Pleasant case depends on where and when one stands. An analysis eventually accepted by many was that the lawyers could not initially be fair in the zealous sense to Garrow unless they were silent. But the same analysis accepted that once the hit list was discovered, disclosure of Garrow's location (and later of the bodies' resting place) was fair and it was not a breach of confidentiality of the sort that could damage Garrow any further.

Fairness to the grieving parents was seen as a lesser obligation, but not perhaps if you were those parents. Though it would be open in an Australian setting for lawyers to allow their client to plead not guilty, the relatives' later perspective was that the lawyers would always have known, once they found the bodies, that they could not allow Garrow to put forward a simple plea of not guilty. So from their point of view there could be no objective loss to Garrow from revealing what they knew a lot earlier than they did. The difficulty with Kantianism here is that there was no way to simultaneously satisfy all claims to fairness. A judge or jury in a rural community which knew of Garrow's murderous past and proven confessions would be hard pressed to fairly decide the appropriate sentence for him in relation to another murder.

Applicable law and conduct rules

The silence which even now is permitted by ASCR 9.2.4 and 9.2.5 does not extend to revealing past crimes. When Garrow escaped and there were grounds to believe he was threatening future crimes, all bets were off. But that development could hardly be anticipated.

When this sort of case occurs locally, disclosing the past means going outside what the ASCR permits and the ASCR exceptions will provide no protection for lawyers who consider that they cannot keep silent. And in cases which involve no physical harm, for example the revealing of past or proposed financial crimes, there is even less protection for lawyers if they decide to reveal what they know. Past financial crimes do enormous physical harm to many people of only modest income. General morality is needed here to guide actions, subject to the law of privilege, which does not protect communications made for criminal purposes.

146   The Good Lawyer

Table 6.1 (cont.)

Conclusion in relation to buried bodies

A very few laws do require disclosure of past crimes, for example the tax law. The criminal law of conspiracy deals with anticipated or planned crimes. But while the ASCR allows disclosure in some circumstances, these rules never require it.

It is almost always up to an individual lawyer what they disclose where information is not privileged but does fall within one of the permissible ASCR exceptions. Many of these decisions will require the virtue of judgment after considering the other claims of general morality. The important question will then recur: do you have, or do you wish to develop, that necessary sense of judgment?

6.4 Keeping quiet – corruption

Judgment is also called for when the scene shifts from the insane murderer to the seriously disturbed corporation. As we saw with James Hardie Industries in Chapter 5, the most prestigious of corporations is only as solid as the integrity of its leading executives and managers. The in-house lawyers of Australian wheat exporter AWB needed such judgment badly.

Table 6.2 Privilege as a cover up for corruption and bribery – AWB in Iraq

In an effort to sell more wheat to Iraq in the period before the fall of the dictator Saddam Hussein, the monopoly Australian wheat exporter AWB agreed to pay significant bribes to Iraq, disguised as 'trucking fees'. These fees were supposedly for land transport of the wheat after it arrived at a grain terminal by ship. But the fees went straight back to Hussein's government and amounted to many millions of dollars over several years, until allegations of bribery first surfaced publicly in 2003.

Canadian wheat exporters became suspicious when they noticed the large volumes of Australian wheat coming in to Iraq and pressured the United Nations to begin an enquiry. The UN enquiry found that the bribes were particularly obnoxious to the international community and designed to subvert very specific UN sanctions applying to Iraq. They provided much needed finances to Saddam Hussein at a time when Iraq was regarded as the key member of the then US President George W. Bush's 'axis of evil' (that is, Iraq, Iran and North Korea).

AWB was formerly the well-respected Australian Wheat Board and the company used that residual public respect to support its denials that it had done anything wrong. Eventually however, these were too hard to believe and the Australian government (an active member of the coalition forces opposed to Iraq) was forced to set up an enquiry: the Cole Commission.[20] Meantime, AWB got busy on a strategy to delay and frustrate its critics. This extract explains:

[AWB] set up an internal investigation into the allegations, code named 'Project Rose', under the control of their in-house lawyer. He in turn called in three external law firms and two barristers to review emails and documents and to advise on whether AWB had paid illegal bribes. At the Australian government's commission of inquiry in 2006, the AWB Board then claimed privilege over all the legal advice they had received, and also all internal minutes and records that related in any way to the advice received from external lawyers. AWB's in-house lawyer also claimed privilege to prevent him from answering any questions about his own opinion about any of the documents the external lawyers had been asked to advise on since, he said, even his own opinion would be based in part on the outside advice, which was privileged. Since hundreds of emails and other documents had been handed over to the external lawyers, this left very little that the in-house lawyer could be questioned about. Other AWB Board members and staff also refused to answer questions on the basis of similar claims of privilege.

AWB also tried (unsuccessfully) to claim privilege over a document accidentally given to the commission which recorded a draft 'statement of contrition' prepared in a teleconference with external

6 Professional secrets | 147

Table 6.2 (cont.)

lawyers and a corporate image and crisis management consultant. This consultant had advised that AWB should apologise 'sooner rather than later', and an apology had been drafted. But AWB decided it did not want to admit that level of responsibility. Some of the statements made by the AWB chief executive in the draft apology were inconsistent with what he later told the commission about AWB senior management's awareness of, and responsibility for, bribery.[21]

Virtue ethics

An in-house lawyer of known integrity would clearly have resisted the initial bribery, but it is doubtful if any organised program of bribery would be 'run past' such an in-house lawyer when the company was furtively engaged in establishing that program. More likely, the bribery would be brought to the lawyer later on, when its existence was about to become a problem and the company had to find a way to rationalise its corruption. At that point, the lawyer would have a choice: use the principles of client confidentiality to subvert any possible investigation for as long as possible, or counsel the CEO to take the realistic course and come clean as soon as possible. The latter course of action is *wise*, *prudent* and an example of responsible lawyering. In the history of corporate scandals, considerable damage is done to many reputations by covering up past crimes.

Consequentialism

The question of consequences would have loomed large in the mind of the in-house lawyer once they became aware of the scale of the bribery. Do we push internally for full disclosure, or do we blow the whistle if the CEO will not come clean, or do we try to 'manage' the problem by using privilege to delay long enough for some other scandal to claim public attention? Or do we simply resign now in an effort to get out before everything blows up? Deciding between these from a consequentialist perspective depends on having a sense of duty to seek right outcomes, rather than simply avoid bad behaviour.

Consequentialism is an ethical approach: it is not a value-free calculation where someone assesses which consequences are least damaging, but is about which course of action, among a discouraging set of choices, is likely to promote the greatest good. The consequentialist in-house lawyer will be weighing up the risk of job losses for lots of AWB employees if and when the scandal breaks and comparing that to the chances of protecting wheat growers' short-term interests by riding out the criticism through a resort to privilege. There is even a risk of harm to public confidence in capitalism. If the greatest good is the criterion, then the responsible lawyering priority is to strengthen the reputation of AWB as soon as possible. Insisting on the CEO's early and complete disclosure of the bribery is responsible, morally active and as rationally defensible as is holding out under the umbrella of privilege.

Kantian ethics

A concern for fairness to individuals involved in the scandal (and by extension, to the corporate entity of AWB) could be used by the AWB in-house lawyer as a justification for invoking privilege. If privilege is a legitimate mechanism to allow clients to obtain legal advice that stays private when they know they are in trouble, why is the claim of that privilege not also fair?

Commissioner Cole referred to exactly this point in his report when he commented that even if they are entitled to claim privilege, corporations always have a choice as to whether they should do so.[22] A responsible lawyering concern to be fair to the wider public interest could mean that the right to assert privilege is not exercised.

Applicable law and conduct rules

Sooner or later, the strength and legitimacy of determined efforts to assert privilege will be scrutinised by a court, tribunal or commission of enquiry. That scrutiny may be easier in future than it was with AWB because the records that are so important to uncovering bribery are increasingly likely to be stored by default in the cloud. Cloud storage is insecure and some if not all of these records are likely to be accessible to investigators. When that scrutiny occurs, judges or commissioners will pronounce on the legality of the underlying effort to keep secrets. If that effort is found to be illegal or criminal, a claim of privilege will not be sustainable.

Similarly, a judicial finding that a claim of privilege is directed against the public interest is enough to knock it over. A moral activist might run with this, but such findings require opposing litigants with deep pockets prepared for months of litigation. Those asserting dubious claims to privilege will often only be seeking the tactical advantages of delay, hoping that their opponents give up for cost reasons.

148   The Good Lawyer

Table 6.2 (cont.)

Conclusion in relation to dubious claims to privilege

General morality is easily capable of undermining the efforts of those who make unworthy claims of privilege and supporting those who confine it to its legitimate purpose: that is, to genuinely assist in obtaining legal advice. Beyond that, the corporate officers who are generally responsible for the misuse of privilege will be able to resist that temptation using any and all of these approaches.

AWB went to a lot of trouble to deny any bribery and then to hide the evidence. The key to proving what the corporation and its officers knew about the 'trucking fees' was contained in the corporation's records. 'Discovery of documents'[23] is the name of the process of obtaining access to them, and arguing claims of privilege is the way in which that access is disputed. In the past, the actual records were simply copious amounts of paper. In the future, the vast bulk of records will be in the cloud, and although the law of privilege will remain very important, access may improve because of the nature of that storage.

As a virtuous in-house lawyer you will want to tell your corporate CEO about the implications for privilege if corporate information, including communications between you as the in-house lawyer and the CEO, is to be stored in the cloud. And although that discussion may be difficult, the insecurity of the cloud may also assist you to exercise some moral and protective influence on the corporation's activities. Who knows, you may prevent another AWB yourself!

6.5 Hit-run-hide

In this final example of (un)professional secrecy, a still 'unhealed' South Australian case of a sudden and innocent death on the roads in 2003 has emerged as one of the most devious and unfortunate illustrations of the need for a comprehensive general morality in legal ethics. In the 2007 film *Michael Clayton*, the anti-hero lawyer played by George Clooney takes a late night phone call and is asked (or required) to attend the home of a prominent client. The problem: 'Fix it so that the hit run killing I just did goes away.' Michael Clayton is expected to fix it, and the rest of the film chronicles his attempts to get free of his reputation for dodgy lawyering. By the end he has redeemed himself, but it's not really clear what will eventually happen to the lawyers in this non-fiction equivalent.

6 Professional secrets **149**

Table 6.3 Leaving the scene – Eugene McGee

A well-known criminal defence lawyer, Eugene McGee, attended a leisurely lunch with wine at an Adelaide suburban hotel in late 2003. McGee finished and left the hotel in his car, driving alone down Kapunda Road and knocking over and killing a cyclist, Ian Humphrey. McGee left the scene without stopping or rendering assistance.[24] But he called his lawyer several times within a matter of minutes. We do not know what was said despite the establishment of a South Australian Royal Commission dedicated solely to finding out what happened and why.[25] The problem is, the lawyer who 'did it' (McGee) and his lawyer (David Edwardson) are not saying what they discussed. And the communication is *prima facie* privileged.

Significantly, McGee was not interviewed by police until the following day and not breath tested. His brother had driven him safely – and undetected – through a police roadblock set up to stop McGee's own car, which he had parked at his mother's place. By the time Edwardson ultimately contacted police, it was near midnight and over 6 hours since the actual hit-run had occurred, which was well past the normal 3 hour window for an effective breath test. Many years of protracted prosecutions ensued, but the lack of a breath test, of any admissions by McGee and of any direct evidence of drunkenness were all enough to allow McGee and his lawyer to resist, if both were able to stay focused. The eventual formal criminal law outcome for McGee was a minor conviction for driving without due care and a fine of $3100.

Despite much public agitation and political brawling inside the SA government and between the government and opposition,[26] McGee received no significant professional penalty. A prosecution of McGee and his brother for conspiracy to pervert the course of justice failed. The SA Legal Practitioners Conduct Board, which was a disciplinary body set up under the exclusive control of the SA legal profession, found that he was not guilty of 'infamous' conduct in November 2011 and could continue practising.[27] Since then, repeated efforts by politicians to reopen the case in some way have come to nothing, because the sort of evidence that would allow more serious action, if it exists, is hidden behind the legal wall of silence known as privilege.

And the larger issue remains: that the South Australian public thinks that a 'fix' has been put in. The Conduct Board found that McGee 'was suffering from post-traumatic stress disorder when he left the scene of the accident, and it ruled that it could only consider his actions in the first few seconds after the crash and couldn't consider some of the actions that had happened subsequently, such as the calls to his legal adviser or his actions to avoid police'.[28] The wider political and public perception, fair or not, is not only that McGee escaped justice, but that the organised community of lawyers in that state is to blame; through allowing Caesar to judge Caesar, that is, by lawyers protecting lawyers.[29]

Virtue ethics

There are two lawyers involved here. A virtuous lawyer in McGee's position might wish to show his *compassion* for the widow and children of the man he killed and tell her what happened. The ongoing misery of Humphrey's widow and children has been shown on television in the years since the killing. His silence to date acknowledges no relationship of care and has compounded their suffering. He might even seek her forgiveness.

McGee's lawyer, Edwardson, is in a slightly different position. He knows a lot about what happened, but is secure behind the secrecy allowed by role morality. There is no doubt that he has acted zealously and appropriately because this is a criminal law environment, but he has the opportunity, if he is compassionate, to go privately to his client and plead now for McGee to have *courage* and bring some finality to the suffering of those affected by his actions.

Consequentialism

Consequences are hard to predict. At the time he first advised McGee, Edwardson could not have predicted that his advice would reflect not just on how his client would be perceived ten years afterwards, but also on himself and on the whole of the SA legal profession, however irrational some of that perception may be. With hindsight, Edwardson might have suggested to McGee that the price of silence might be too high. He might also have argued that the loss to community support for lawyers in South Australia was so substantial that that consequence tipped the scales against McGee's interests.

But Edwardson cannot defend himself and we cannot know what he said to his client at the time. His likely objective as a zealous advocate was to keep his client out of prison. He has succeeded in that narrow but legitimate objective.

150   The Good Lawyer

Table 6.3 (cont.)

Kantian ethics

Fairness is sorely tested by the McGee case. There appears little balance between the interests of the deceased cyclist's family and the protection of the rights of a criminal lawyer, who knows how important it is to manage the period immediately after a road killing. A Kantian could conclude that that balance has been lost and ask, without much hope, for specific legislative intervention. But that is now unlikely and a Kantian will remain unsatisfied.

Applicable law and conduct rules

Taken as a whole, there is unlikely to be a satisfactory legal solution to Humphrey's hit-run death. The law of privilege entitles McGee to require Edwardson to maintain his silence in relation to the communications between the two.

Some of the exceptions to the protection of privilege discussed above could apply, in theory. For example, actions directed 'against the public interest': specifically, Edwardson's possible knowledge of McGee's alleged efforts to conspire with his brother to avoid the police immediately after the killing. But there would need to be a judicial finding that privilege was not available for a reason such as this, before Edwardson could be required to say what he knows.

ASCR 9.2.4 allows a solicitor to disclose 'information for the sole purpose of avoiding the probable commission of a serious criminal offence', but such rules are permissive rather than mandatory and could not compel Edwardson to say anything about his then knowledge of his client's efforts to avoid the police, and in any event, this rule cannot override the protection of privilege.

SA law has changed as a result of this case. While the Law Society of South Australia was compromised, a public sense of moral activism has produced change. The definition of misconduct has been widened so that it includes 'a substantial or consistent failure to reach or maintain a reasonable standard of competence and diligence, and it will be able to look at conduct inside and outside the practice of law that would justify a finding that the practitioner is not a fit and proper person'[30] to practise law. But this change is prospective, not retrospective, and will not affect McGee.

Conclusion in relation to McGee

General morality condemns the whole of the McGee case as a failure of justice. The traditional protection given to accused persons, that they not be compelled to incriminate themselves, is one thing. But his lawyer's silence is another thing entirely. McGee's claim of privilege over what he told Edwardson is objectively highly suspect and could fail a public interest test, if that exception were squarely raised. The considerable public interest in knowing the truth about the efforts of McGee to evade the police immediately after the killing, is likely to have been subverted.

Edwardson could display considerable virtue in determining now that the public interest exception to privilege has been established in the light of a decade of community dismay about the case in South Australia. He could show courage, taking the reasonable chance that neither McGee, the Law Society of South Australia or the Attorney General would now seek to challenge him.

6.6 Conclusion

If the *McGee* case confirms anything, it is that general morality and lawyers' understanding of what is fair can be kilometres apart. A lot of the difference in perspective arises from community ambivalence about secrecy, especially in the digital age, as compared to lawyers' ingrained preference for privacy even when crimes are underway. But if wider society is progressively giving up on its insistence on individuals' rights to privacy and is frustrated by cases such as *McGee*, for how much longer will it be reasonable for lawyers to rely on the concept? If confidentiality is on the way out in wider society how can zealous advocacy, which depends so much on secrecy, avoid coming up against even greater public distrust? The three cases highlighted in this chapter – the missing bodies, the corrupt corporation and the hit-run – are all hard cases that most lawyers hope never to see. But they signal the limits to role morality at which the wider community will require general morality to have a say. If we as lawyers default to role morality in every case, rather than show courage and routinely include general morality as a contributor to all decisions, extreme criminal and civil cases will continue to undermine the public's view of lawyers' roles rather than justify them.

In the majority of cases, however, it seems increasingly necessary to re-legitimise lawyers' support for secrecy, not as a means of hiding their clients' dubious practices (perhaps, as unconscious zealous advocates), but because lawyers' ability to keep confidences is still important to the administration of justice. Responsible lawyering and the ethic of care do support the notion of 'good' secrets: the normal privacy that we all need.

In most cases confidentiality is important because clients will not trust you with full information about their problems if they think that you will talk. And if you are inclined to the view that there seem to be so many exceptions to the principle of confidentiality that clients ought to be warned about them before they spill the beans, then that is appropriate client care. In appropriate cases you can also remind them that our modern surveillance society is increasingly intrusive. Since everyone's confidentiality means less and less as technology advances, there are other very pragmatic incentives for clients to work within general morality rather than try to evade it.

Ultimately, deciding to keep a secret for good reasons can be a moral act. When you keep client secrets for 'good' reasons, and not in order to evade tax or support other criminal activity, you are upholding the important part of confidentiality, even in the face of technology which might lead to disclosure at a later date. Use your knowledge of general morality (from Chapters 3 and 4) and of the ASCR, as well as your preference for lawyer types, to wisely decide when it is important to keep a client's secrets, having regard to both the public and private interests involved.

152   The Good Lawyer

In the following chapter, another demanding issue of lawyers' ethics is analysed: conflicts of loyalty and interest. 'Conflicts' have led to many disappointments for law firms, particularly larger firms. In the financially lucrative areas of transactional law, conflicts present a challenge to morality because they test our loyalty. Chapter 7 asks the fundamental moral question: to whom are we loyal?

Notes

1. Security services engage in massive online monitoring of telephony and data, as a reaction to 9/11, but this surveillance is increasingly normalised in an effort to deal with corporate and sovereign state 'cyber-attacks' on corporate and government data bases. For example, in April 2012 the United Kingdom government proposed a comprehensive electronic strategy to limit threats to security from another global financial crisis, from organised crime and from terrorism, by eavesdropping on email traffic. See www.bbc.co.uk/news/uk-politics-17576745.
2. While there is a formal exception to confidentiality in respect of *intra*-firm disclosure, the true position is less comfortable. Law firm risk manager *IntApp* has reported as a result of a survey of 30 large Australian law firms that 66% of respondents indicated that client information is completely accessible to all staff in the firm. See Justin Whealing, 'Client not-so confidential', *Lawyers Weekly*, 9 November 2012, 1.
3. Vince Chadwick, 'Mobile apps allow analysts to view private information', *The Age*, 19 September 2012, 3.
4. These reasons were published in a less developed form in Parker and Evans, *Inside Lawyers' Ethics*, Ch. 4. They were derived from points made by Michael Park (Partner, Norton Rose) and Ka-Chi Cheung (Snr Associate, Norton Rose) in a presentation on 'The ethics of cloud computing' to the Law Institute of Victoria, May 2012.
5. In Ch. 5, I discuss the specific challenges for criminal lawyers who tend not to ask if a client committed an offence in case the answer prevents them from allowing a client to plead not guilty to that offence.
6. See, for example, *Legal Services Commissioner v Tampoe* [2009] LPT 14; *Legal Profession Complaints Committee v Trowell* [2009] WASAT 42. However, an attempt by a well-known lawyer to argue that the mistaken disclosure of confidential (and privileged) documents during the court discovery process was sufficient to waive privilege in those documents was recently rejected by the High Court. See *Expense Reduction Analysts Group Pty Ltd v Armstrong Strategic Management and Marketing Pty Ltd* [2013] HCA 46.
7. See Oakley and Cocking, *Virtue Ethics and Professional Roles*, 155 onwards.

8. For a full discussion of confidentiality and privilege, see Dal Pont, *Lawyers' Professional Responsibility* (5th edn), Parts 10–12.
9. See, for example, Matthew Harvey and Suzanne Le Mire, 'Playing for keeps? Tobacco litigation, document retention, corporate culture and legal ethics' (2008) 34(1) *Monash University Law Review* 163.
10. This extract is from Parker and Evans, *Inside Lawyers' Ethics*, Ch. 4.
11. See *Evidence Act 2008* (Vic) s 125.
12. Examples are in legislation designed to limit tax evasion or the use of corporate cartels to restrict competition. There must be a clear, unambiguous statutory intention to remove the exception. See *Daniels Corporation v ACCC* [2002] HCA 49.
13. For a useful discussion of these issues, see Barkoczy, *Foundations of Taxation Law* (5th edn).
14. See, for example, *Evidence Act 2008* (Vic) s 122.
15. See Dal Pont, n 9, 275–81. Note that it is an *abuse of process* (see Ch. 5) to claim privilege without reasonable grounds, as a delaying tactic in litigation (Cole Commission and ALRC Report 107: Privilege in Perspective: Client Legal Privilege in Federal Investigations www.alrc.gov.au/report-107).
16. See Chapter 3.
17. Transcript of interview of Lisa Lerman, Catholic University of America, by Alan Saunders. The transcript is from 'The Philosophers Zone – The Ethics of Keeping Your Mouth Shut', ABC Radio National, 20 September 2008, available at www.abc. net.au/rn/philosopherszone/stories/2008/2366647.htm#transcript.
18. Hendrik Kaptein, in Amaya and Lai, *Law, Virtue and Justice*, 229.
19. Ibid., 237.
20. Inquiry into Certain Australian Companies in Relation to the UN Oil-For-Food Programme (The Cole Commission), *Report*, 2006, Vol. 1 [7.42] Legal Professional Privilege; Vol. 4 [31] Findings: AWB and Associated Persons.
21. Extract from Parker and Evans, n 11, Ch. 4.
22. Statement in a hearing for the Inquiry into Certain Australian Companies in Relation to the UN Oil-For-Food Program, Sydney, 6 March 2006, 4042 (T.R.H. Cole, Commissioner) www.oilforfoodinquiry.gov.au/agd/WWW/rwpattach.nsf/VAP/(2A296B295C1E058B328FED2164E40B7D)_OFI060306.PDF/%24file/OFI060306.PDF.
23. See Parker and Evans, n 11, Ch. 6.
24. Government of South Australia, Report of the *Kapunda Road Royal Commission*, Ch. 2, at www.sa.gov.au/upload/franchise/Crime,%20justice%20and%20the%20law/KRRC/krrc_report_2.pdf.
25. Ibid., Ch. 2, 27.
26. Andrew Dowdell, 'New push to have hit-run driver, lawyer Eugene McGee, punished', *The Advertiser*, 21 February 2013. See www.adelaidenow.com.au/news/south-australia/new-push-to-have-hit-run-driver-lawyer-eugene-mcgee-punished/story-e6frea83-1226582712265.
27. See 'Lawyers Act to be reviewed after hit-run', *The Age*, 9 December 2011, www. theage.com.au/national/lawyers-act-to-be-reviewed-after-hitrun-20111208-1olce. html.

154   The Good Lawyer

28. Suzanne Le Mire, *The Law Report*, Radio National, 16 April 2013, www.abc.net.au/radionational/programs/lawreport/sa-legal-profession-laws/4629776.
29. Ibid.
30. Ibid. This more expansive definition is also contained in the *Legal Profession Uniform Law Application Act 2014* (Vic), Sch 1, s 297.

Chapter 7

CONFLICTS OF LOYALTY AND INTEREST

7.1 Introduction: What is a conflict of interest and why are conflicts so difficult?

Consider this vignette, which is constructed from a number of decided cases.

Documents, faxes, emails and drinks

You are working in a merger team on the 4th floor of a large transnational law firm. Your client is Emirates Airways, which has proposed a merger with QANTAS, now that their code share alliance is succeeding.

On the 3rd floor, another team from your firm is working for QANTAS on the same issue. QANTAS is struggling financially, but both airlines have developed some confidence in each other and think they can save some legal costs by using just the one law firm – yours.

The firm's email system blocks the access of either team to emails from the other team, so that both teams can work independently of each other. But early one morning an email is copied to you from someone you think you remember meeting the previous evening at the firm's cocktails event, which was held to celebrate the merger deal. You do not have any clear memory of the evening or what was said, but the email contains vague references to a financial problem in QANTAS, which seems to have debts that you know Emirates is not aware of. The author of the mail is proposing a 3rd floor meeting to discuss how this debt issue will be handled. You are immediately concerned.

What should you do with the email?

155

156   The Good Lawyer

A conflict of interest is a significant problem for all professionals, but especially for a lawyer. We must act only in the interests of those who entrust us with their secrets. The general idea is that we act for only one client at a time, so that we avoid a conflict of interest. So what happens when the law firm as a whole has two clients trying to negotiate a corporate get-together and one lawyer in one team – yourself – suddenly learns something private about one of those clients that could derail the whole deal?

We should get out quickly, and most of us do, ending the problem. But you can't remember much about what happened the night before. Maybe you were told about these debts at the cocktails event and whoever told you wants you to know? Why else would you have been copied into the email? And if you go to your supervisor now, you might be in trouble yourself because you are supposed to be maintaining confidentiality about Emirates' affairs and have nothing to do with the QANTAS team?

Some large firms try to 'finesse' these situations and pretend everything is all sweetness and light. They do not want to see any evidence that one team has had any contact with another team, however brief or inadvertent. This pretence is generally expensive and stretches credibility. When a firm is attempting to act for both sides at once and knows too much about them, there can be a temptation to try to persuade both clients that somehow, half the firm can keep one secret and the other half will keep the other secret and no one need doubt the firm's integrity. An enormous body of case law and literature has been built up by lawyers seeking to argue for and against such toleration, both sides seeking legitimacy according to law, though not always justice. This chapter is not concerned to explore every nuance of these cases, since there is already much that is available.[1] Rather, this discussion proceeds as other chapters have done and concentrates on the moral sense that ought to underlie our understanding of conflicts.

The dominant approach to legal ethics (role morality) requires us as lawyers to avoid situations where our own interests conflict with those of our clients and always seek to prioritise their interests when a conflict cannot be entirely avoided. The same approach generally applies when two or more clients turn out to have opposing interests, as in the above vignette. This duty of avoidance also arises from the law of fiduciary responsibility[2] and is called loyalty. Loyalty is a highly desirable virtue of good lawyering and for most of us, is not a contentious issue.

Conflicts of interest become a problem when as lawyers we step outside role morality, general morality and even the requirements of the administration of justice. We can forget that loyalty is a human quality and that human loyalty is by nature indivisible: that is, it cannot be apportioned between different interests or different clients. In the QANTAS–Emirates vignette, we cannot be a little bit loyal to one client and a little bit loyal to another when both of them are negotiating, through us, to maximise their own position within the merger. When a firm sets an artificial wall inside itself so that one lawyer can be totally loyal to one client and another lawyer totally loyal to the other, there is still the problem that both lawyers report to a single human, the law firm CEO, and that CEO cannot be 100% loyal to both airlines' CEOs when information leaks in the manner described above. Each airline CEO will eventually consider him or herself deserving of 100% loyalty.

Conflicts are usually more straightforward for those of us who practise in criminal law and family law;[3] they are complicated when the conflict occurs in large commercial and corporate law environments where transactional law is practised. Transactional law provides a reasonably steady income stream for the largest firms because contracts, mergers, acquisitions, insolvencies and similar retainers follow more predictable courses than does litigation and, unlike litigation, the legal fees received are generally not subject to external scrutiny or review. A law firm that can act for both sides at once can earn almost as much as would two separate firms.

In these commercial areas of legal practice, the main practical argument of those who want to keep two or more opposing clients and two or more sets of fees is that as lawyers we are rarely sole practitioners any more. We tend to work in partnerships or incorporated legal practices, so it is argued that one partner or employee lawyer can keep the secrets of one transactional client and another partner/lawyer can keep other opposing secrets of the other client(s). And even though both clients are to varying degrees sceptical about the situation, it will be alright because each partner can be trusted to set up and comply with so-called information barriers inside their firm to keep respective clients' confidential information confidential. If a merger between Emirates and QANTAS were ever to be proposed, these barriers would be set up by a large law firm (LLF) seeking to get the joint business. We are told that these very expensive barriers (paid for by both clients) will keep both of these highly competitive partners and their various staff teams away from each other's information and loyal only to their

158   The Good Lawyer

designated client; meanwhile, in these LLFs, both lawyer groups must work to maximise their fees from their own client.

Put more boldly, both partner teams retain a financial interest in a case strategy that will maximise the advantages for their own client (undermining loyalty and other fiduciary responsibilities) while also seeking ways and means to secure slight advantages over their opposing partner. As a generalisation, the larger the firm, the more intense is the pressure on lawyers in a conflict situation, despite the risk to reputation if the house of cards should collapse. We ought not to forget that the contractual negotiations of transactional lawyering can be as competitive as any court argument. Opposing partners may not choose to exploit gaps in the information barriers, but clients' interests – and the interests of the lawyers in each partner team – are ultimately in conflict, whether such barriers are breached or not.

A lot of effort, described below, has been put into devising highly complex rules inside the ASCR to make the fiction of professionalism more or less plausible in joint transactional representation. The particular rules have been in development for several years, at the request of the Large Law Firms Group (LLFG) of the Law Council of Australia. Certain 'sophisticated' commercial and corporate clients are permitted to agree to accept less than 100% loyalty, so that they and any opposing clients, who must also be sophisticated users of legal services, can both be represented by just one law firm. Is this regime credible? Certainly it is to those who designed it. We are told by the LLFG that their clients need and want this system: we are also told that there are so few really skilled lawyers in each specialised corporate area that clients are prepared to accept less than 100% loyalty if that means they can get access to this specialised expertise. Finally, we are told that the fact that the LLFs involved can, as a result of this system, charge each client for advising them on how to get the best deal from the other client, is not the point.

In modern family law there is a relatively new approach known as collaborative law (see Chapter 2) which allows both litigants to agree to each of their lawyers having full access to all their confidential information, so that they can collaborate in an effort to resolve a dispute to the mutual satisfaction of both partners. Collaborative family law does not breach any duty of loyalty or confidentiality because the parties must agree to firing their current lawyers and retaining entirely new lawyers if their efforts to resolve their dispute fail and they must then go to trial. But the lesson from collaborative family lawyers has not been taken up by the transactional lawyers.

Rarely are the LLFs prepared to detach themselves from both of their clients if they fail to resolve something and find they can no longer subdivide their loyalty in the way the ASCR has been designed to operate.

The essential problem with our conflicts of interest remains unwillingness by some large firms to face the fact that the idea of loyalty means there is an obligation to avoid conflicts, not to create them, or try to manage them once they occur, so that they can keep the fees from two clients rather than just one. This unpleasant truth is behind this warning from former judge Philip Cummins:

> What bedevils the prohibition of a conflict of interest is a confusion of purposes. The purpose of prohibition of conflict of interest is not to remedy an offence or a failure. The purpose of prohibition of conflict of interest is to prevent an offence or a failure. Prohibition of conflict operates up stream of offence or failure. It is preventative. It is prophylactic. Thus it is no answer to breach of conflict to say that in fact no harm occurred, that the client was not harmed. If harm, a loss, a failure, an offence occurred, you would be dealt with for a consequential matter. Prohibition of conflict is an antecedent matter. That also is why the phrase 'potential conflict of interest' is tautologous.[4]

An uncomfortable reality about conflicts is that they can be hard to identify if we are at the centre of them.[5] Some years ago a prominent criminal defence lawyer was confronted in court by a police prosecutor who alleged that he (the defence lawyer) had a conflict of interest because he was acting for a defendant charged with a sexual assault at the same time as one of his partners was acting for the alleged victim of that assault.[6] There was no information barrier inside the lawyer's firm but he found it difficult to believe that anyone could think that his client might, through him, have obtained access to information on the file of the alleged victim that would assist his defence. This lawyer was and is well regarded and he was highly resistant to the notion that any conflict of interest existed – his view was that he and his partner simply did not exchange information on their respective clients. That sense of disbelief is not uncommon. If we are doing our own job conscientiously, the idea that anyone would think there is a possibility of wrongdoing is offensive, but that is not the point. Preventing conflicts is an essential objective of the good lawyer; trying to clean up after them is not.

In this chapter, various types of conflicts are discussed in the light of general morality, the common law and the ASCR. As in prior chapters, several case studies are presented in table form to explain the specific problems in detail and to suggest the approaches that flow if we have regard to virtue, Kantian and consequentialist ethics, as well as to the different lawyering types and the ASCR.

The first issue, of lawyer–client conflicts, has a number of dimensions, but the focus here is on our own fees and costs. We are conflicted because we want to be paid as much as possible while at the same time delivering a service to our clients at the lowest possible – but still competitive – price. This conflict is unavoidable for all professionals, but is particularly potent for lawyers because we have additional fiduciary responsibilities to our clients – responsibilities that are intended to prioritise our obligation to them above our own financial interests. There are many legislative provisions designed to reduce the impact of this conflict by ensuring that we disclose our likely fees to clients. Over the years, many cases of gross overcharging have demonstrated that as a profession, we often fall victim to this 'conflict'. General morality has a critical role to play here in re-equipping us to prioritise clients' interests.

7.2 An overview of lawyer–client conflicts

Conflicts of interest fall into two broad classes – those between lawyers and their clients and those between two or more clients. Diagram 7.1 below sets

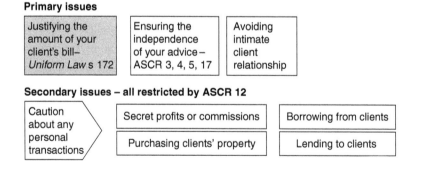

Diagram 7.1 Types of lawyer–client conflict

out the various ways in which the first category of conflicts – between lawyer and client – can arise.

It is important to avoid an intimate personal relationship with a current client for many reasons, but particularly because of the risk to your ability to give independent legal advice, as in the Chapter 6 vignette.[7] There is also potential for infringing your independence when the quality or appropriateness of your past advice is questioned by your client. Would you be able to continue to act autonomously and without rancour for a client who has challenged your competence? At the very least, a frank but respectful discussion between the two of you would be needed before either of you continues with the retainer. And if only one is then satisfied, there is only pain ahead if you go on. Similar concerns for independence apply in relation to personal financial transactions with your client. These areas of conflict are controlled by case law and the ASCR,[8] and they are avoidable. But it is much harder to avoid conflicts in relation to your own fees.

Most lawyer–client disputes arise in relation to costs, which uniquely represent for us both a conflict of interest and a legitimate interest. Our way through the dilemma is to submit a valid, fair bill. Every zealous, responsible and relationship of care lawyer believes in this principle, but we need several virtues to make it happen. When we do submit fair bills we are usually paid more easily than if the bill can be legitimately challenged, but that likelihood does not seem to reduce the number of arguments about bills. Wisdom is needed to achieve fairness and requires an appreciation of many factors: the complexity of the work, our client's original and current expectations, their agreement with us as to the amount of costs, our own efficiency as a practitioner and any costs scales that are applicable to the job. Applying our considered judgment to all of these is the only way to achieve the necessary balance.

There are different acceptable approaches to charging for services, depending on the type of legal work involved.[9] In a pragmatic sense, much of the potential for disagreement with your client about costs can be minimised if you pay careful attention to the cost disclosure rules, from the very beginning of the retainer. These rules are concrete expressions of the virtue of transparency, in the interests of fairness and an effort to ensure that the desired outcome – payment for services rendered – is achieved with maximum goodwill. Diagram 7.2 sets out how the costs disclosure rules can minimise the impact of this area of lawyer–client conflict.[10]

162 The Good Lawyer

Begin by carefully estimating ...

- the **basis on which the legal costs will be calculated** (including whether a costs determination or scale of costs applies to any of the legal costs; **avoid time-based billing**. Instead, discuss the value of the work with your client in advance.
- If the matter is a litigious matter, provide an estimate of the range of costs and disbursements (including barristers' fees) that may be recovered if your client is successful in the litigation; and the range of costs they may be ordered to pay if unsuccessful.

...provide an estimate of the total legal costs, if practical; or

- If it is not reasonably practicable to estimate the total legal costs, provide a **range of estimates** of the total legal costs and an explanation of the major variables that will affect the calculation of those costs.
- Ensure that the client is notified of any substantial changes to the matters disclosed.
- **See your client in person**, explain costs carefully and **give all this information in writing**. Make sure they understand that an **estimate is not a quote.**

...discuss billing and

- Explain the client's right to request and receive **progress reports** (*Uniform Law* s 190); to receive a bill; and to **request an itemised bill within 30 days after receipt of a lump sum bill** (*Uniform Law* s 187).
- Give details of the intervals (if any) at which your client will be billed – **interim billing is the best practice.**
- Specify the rate of interest (if any) that you will charge on overdue bills.

...what your client can do if they wish to discuss or dispute costs

Verbal progress reports, even when nothing has happened, are the only way to demonstrate integrity, compassion and an ethic of care. And they will maximise the chance of early bill payment.

- First, give details of how your client may **contact you to discuss the bill.**
- In the event of a dispute in relation to legal costs, organise a **costs assessment** under *Uniform Law* Div 7, s 197.
- Your client may seek to set aside a costs agreement if it is not fair and reasonable (*Uniform Law* Div 2, s 175 and following).

Diagram 7.2 Communicating wisely about costs

7.3 Client–client (concurrent) conflict

As indicated in the introduction to this chapter, client–client conflict, especially inside the larger commercial firms, is at the centre of the challenges presented to general morality by modern lawyering.

7 Conflicts of loyalty and interest   163

Table 7.1 Costing your clients too much – Keddies Lawyers[11]

When a lawyer sets out to 'define the culture' of his or her firm, the result can be dramatic. 'Wholly client focused', 'delivering excellence' and 'specialised and effective' are common epithets on firm websites and most firms strive to achieve these promises because excellence in client service is at the heart of financial success and important to work satisfaction. But occasionally the morality of the key lawyer involved pushes the firm in the opposite direction and the result is systematic client exploitation.

In 2008 Keddies Lawyers was the largest personal injury firm in NSW and a significant competitor to the national leader in this sector, Slater & Gordon. In that year, however, Keddies' secret began to emerge: the firm leader, Russell Keddie, had presided over a system designed to fleece personal accident clients by relying on their relative ignorance of the legal process.

Literally hundreds of clients were overcharged significant sums. For example, in the Liu case the claim was settled for $140,000, but the client herself received less than $50,000. $90,000, or nearly twice as much as the client actually finally received in compensation for her claim, was siphoned off in false legal fees.

For example, three-line letters were billed for 12 minutes of time at a senior litigation lawyer rate of $435 an hour, a charge of $87. Perusal of a five-line letter was charged at $184 – a time charge for 24 minutes. Junior staff and paralegals were being billed out at partners' rates of $460 an hour for 'perusing and considering' two-line letters. Clients were never sent bills but were sued, charged for work that was not done, and grossly overcharged for other work.

Many former clients complained to the Legal Services Commissioner and others sued independently. The three former Keddies' partners (Keddie, Scott Roulstone and Tony Barakat) were ordered to repay around $4 million to 30 clients, but only a fraction of that amount has been paid. It is reported that two other firms each represent about 100 former clients of Keddies and are in the process of suing the former partners.

In 2011, Keddie and his two former partners sold their firm to Slater & Gordon, reportedly for $32 million. Keddie declared himself bankrupt in June 2012 and accordingly may not have to comply with court orders to repay former clients. Before he declared himself bankrupt, he tried to limit his exposure to his former clients. His reported strategies include selling, in July 2011, his half of his five-bedroom family home in Double Bay to his wife for the sum of $1 and, also for $1 and to his wife, his share of their multimillion-dollar beach house, which overlooks Bungan Beach. It is reportedly rented for $1500 a week. And land title records show that Mrs Keddie's company, of which Keddie is a shareholder, sold half its rural holdings for $4.6 million during 2012. Exactly where the remainder of his money is may remain hidden. Some or all of these manoeuvres may be reversible by his trustee in bankruptcy, but there is no certainty in that. The former partners are reported to be likely to owe up to $11 million when all costs are totalled.

The NSW Administrative Decisions Tribunal ordered that Keddie be removed from the Roll of Practitioners on 4 June 2012.[12] In fact, he handed in his practising certificate and retired, so the order was more or less redundant. Charges brought by the Legal Services Commissioner against Roulstone and Barakat were dropped after Keddie agreed to take the blame for the firm's bad behaviour. Roulstone, a former vice-president of the NSW Law Society, is now a partner at Slater & Gordon. Barakat has opened his own firm, Barton Lawyers. He denies that there was systematic overcharging in his former firm.

Virtue ethics

All the opposites of virtue are present in the Keddies case. Where costs disclosure was practised, it was a smokescreen so that gullible clients would feel reassured and drop their guard. As acknowledged in Machiavelli's quotation (see Ch. 3), there is little advantage and great risk in practising virtue if all around you there is only deceit and disguised contempt. So it will be that some lawyers lacking honesty will use costs disclosure as a device. But many others will see such disclosure as an opportunity to earn respect from clients, knowing that their reputation for transparency will steadily build returning clientele who trust them.

Consequentialism

A consequentialist would surely conclude that any process of systematic client exploitation will eventually fail, unless there is no proper application of consequentialism at all and the strategy is to factor in eventual failure, transferring funds to hard-to-locate places in the manner used by Keddie before his bankruptcy. True consequentialism would never countenance Keddie's behaviour.

164   The Good Lawyer

Table 7.1 (cont.)

Kantian ethics

Kantian ethics is also astounded at the Keddies' tragedy, not the least because its affects have played a comprehensive role in undermining Queensland community faith in all lawyers' sense of fairness.

Applicable law and conduct rules

Professional misconduct is the finding when gross overcharging occurs, but there is no provision in the legislation to reimburse clients when their money is effectively stolen by lawyers' overcharging. Clients must pursue civil remedies and hope there is still money to recover through a court order which binds any trustee in bankruptcy. They must take the chance that the trustee can 'trace' money that has been transferred away just before bankruptcy is declared.

Conclusion in relation to recovering your costs

A satisfactory Kantian approach would be to change the existing law which covers so-called fidelity or client compensation.[13] Under these provisions, lawyers are obliged to pay annual levies into central fidelity funds which are used to compensate clients when their lawyers steal from them by raiding their trust account balances. These laws could be expanded to compensate clients who cannot recover overcharged fees because their lawyer is insolvent.

    Gross overcharging is little different from direct stealing. The amount of damage that is done to professional trust when lawyers such as Keddie systematically fleece hundreds of clients requires a moral activist perspective and a change in the law. General morality suggests that fidelity levies be applied to provide protection in these circumstances for clients and good lawyers alike. If this proposal were to come from the Law Council of Australia, the demonstration of an overarching fidelity would be tangible evidence not just of good lawyers, but of a good profession.

Client–client conflicts show the following broad typology. In criminal and family law contexts, role morality is strong and dictates in nearly all situations[14] that there must be a separate lawyer for each client.[15] So we rarely see client–client conflicts of interest emerging in these areas. In the much larger commercial and corporate practice areas, however, client–client conflict is more common.

Sometimes, such conflicts are described as merely 'commercial', and as not as important as 'legal' or prohibited conflicts. 'Commercial' conflicts are allowable in legal terms, though they are morally unwise, and can be contrasted with prohibited conflicts – those which offend the case law and ASCR 10 and 11. These rules try to walk the narrow plank of role morality while balancing zealous advocacy with responsible lawyering. In so doing they again demonstrate how role morality is inferior in a commercial transactional environment and ought to be subservient to general morality. Table 7.2 below explains the differences between 'commercial' and prohibited conflicts:

7 Conflicts of loyalty and interest   165

Table 7.2 Differences between 'commercial' and prohibited conflicts of interest

Commercial (legally allowable) conflicts and prohibited conflicts of interest

'Commercial' client–client conflicts	Legally prohibited client–client conflicts

A commercial conflict is one that is not strictly a conflict because it is outside the prohibitions of the common law or ASCR 10 and 11. For example, your law firm acts for two IT companies in relation to completely separate or unrelated matters, but the two companies compete with each other for market share.
 	
This is still a commercial problem for your firm even if it is not a 'legal' problem, because neither client is entirely sure that their corporate information is secure from the partner or team representing the other client.
 	
At the centre of the commercial conflict is the issue of loyalty, and particularly, the perception of loyalty.
 	
For example, you are the managing partner of a large law firm (LLF) which is dominant in the mining industry. You have two major miners on your books with many partners working for each miner on opposite sides of an information barrier. [Information barriers are covered in more detail below.]
 	
You think the information barrier is effective and neither client is able to fault the barrier in any objective way, but one of the miners eventually says to you that they are anxious nevertheless about a possible leak in the barrier at some point in the future, given the ultra-competitive nature of the mining sector and the developing perceptions of its major institutional shareholders about the importance of good corporate governance.
 	
You protest that the barrier is solid, but ultimately decide you cannot risk losing both miners as clients, which could happen if the partners on the other side of the information barrier learn of their rival partners' problems with their client, but say nothing to their own client. At that point a commercial conflict would become a prohibited conflict.
 	
So you decide you must try to ditch the less important miner of the two although you are not acting in contravention of the current conflicts rules. When you discard the less important client, you may be challenged by that client on the basis that its confidential information will be put at risk if there is only a legacy information barrier remaining in place inside the firm.
 	
The critical factor in a commercial conflict is not therefore the legality of the situation, but the perception of impropriety as seen through a general morality lens.
	This is the suite of conflicts that are likely to be prohibited by the common law and ASCR 10 and 11. In these areas, the affront to loyalty is seen as 'just too hot' and has led to their prohibition. They include:
	
	• when you or your firm seeks to act for two or more current clients (concurrent conflict) in contentious (litigious) cases about the same or a related matter.[16] Even if the case is not initially contentious (that is, transactional) it can become contentious, and the prohibition will then apply.[17]
	
	• acting for two or more parties in a transactional case, where there is an ineffective information barrier.[18] [Information barriers are covered in more detail below.]
	
	• acting on behalf of a current client against a former client (successive conflict), where there is an ineffective information barrier and where:
	  • your former client provided confidential information to you at the time and
	  • your former client does not consent to your firm acting against them.[19]
	     A key question posed by general morality here is whether, as a former client, you would be comfortable if your former lawyer asked you if they could now rely on an effective information barrier to represent a competitor against you, in litigation, or if you found out later that your consent was not sought and your former firm sought to rely only on the barrier.
	
	• acting against a former client where a court would consider that you have breached an obligation of loyalty to that client or where the administration of justice could be said to be compromised.[20]

When client–client conflict is thought by a current or former client to be unacceptable, they will go to court if they cannot get your firm to cease acting. Sometimes, such action will be taken whether or not your alleged conflict is in the prohibited zone, because even so-called sophisticated clients (usually large corporations), tend to see these matters as issues of general morality, that is, of loyalty. When that happens, they will try to assert one or more of the following bases for court intervention, to prevent what they see as either a concurrent or a successive conflict:

- your fiduciary responsibility to protect confidential information (derived from both general and role morality);
- your duty to protect the administration of justice through your supervision as an officer of the court (zealous advocacy conceding dominance to responsible lawyering); and finally
- an obligation of loyalty you owe to them as a former client (derived from general morality and the equitable principle of fiduciary responsibility).

Clients who are unhappy about an LLF's decision to keep acting for an opposing client will first say that the confidentiality of their information is threatened, because that issue is a frequently litigated and well-recognised concern of the law. They will then argue that the administration of justice is threatened, because that worries judges' larger sense of the authority of the courts, and lastly they will assert a breach of loyalty. Clients will put loyalty last on the list not because they think it unimportant (to the contrary), but because loyalty comes from general morality, is open-ended and unpredictable as a concept and (in the case of successive conflict), there is still some disagreement over whether a duty of loyalty survives the end of the lawyer–client relationship.[21]

Historically, the principal worry for clients has been – and remains – the leakage of their confidential information to the other client. LLFs have therefore been active in developing information barriers in an effort to prevent such communication in both concurrent and successive conflict situations, even though the barriers are no answer to concerns about the administration of justice and any duty of loyalty. Diagram 7.3 sets out the features and limitations of the more credible information barriers.

7 Conflicts of loyalty and interest   167

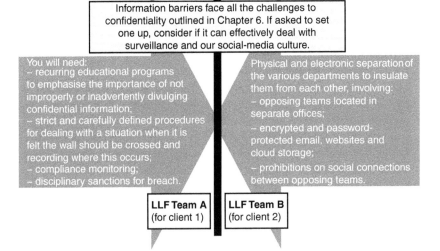

Diagram 7.3 Realities of information barriers

You might face a conflicts situation and wander into this mix of confusing loyalties, dubious barriers and the pressure to maximise fees. You may even have some hope that the ASCR will provide a solution. That is not the case. ASCR 11, set out below, tries and fails to deal with concurrent client conflict with the following provisions. The areas of contradiction or imprecision are in bold:

> ASCR 11.1 A solicitor ... must avoid conflicts between the duties owed to two or more current clients, **except where permitted by this Rule**.
>
> 11.2 If a solicitor or a law practice seeks to act for two or more clients in the **same or related matters** where the **clients' interests are adverse** and **there is a conflict or potential conflict** of the duties to act in the best interests of each client, the solicitor or law practice must not act, except where permitted by Rule 11.3.

168 The Good Lawyer

> 11.3 Where a solicitor . . . seeks to act in the circumstances specified in Rule 11.2 the solicitor may, subject always to each solicitor discharging their duty to act in the best interests of their client, only act if each client:
>
> - 11.3.1 is **aware** that the solicitor or law practice is also acting for another client; and
> - 11.3.2 has given **informed consent** to the solicitor or law practice so acting.
>
> 11.4 In addition to the requirements of Rule 11.3, where a solicitor . . . is in possession of confidential information of a client . . . which **might reasonably be concluded to be material** to another client's matter and **detrimental to the interests** of the first client if disclosed, there is a conflict of duties and the solicitor . . . **must not act except** as follows:
>
> - 11.4.1 [in respect of confidential information] . . . where each client has given **informed consent** to the solicitor acting for another client;
> - 11.4.2 [in respect of confidential information] . . . where an **effective** information barrier has been established.

Judgment must be used to decide the meaning of terms such as 'material', 'detriment' and 'effective'. And what is material or detrimental or effective is entirely dependent on the particular circumstances of a case. Having abandoned principles, the ASCR has no use for general morality and the virtues of knowledge, prudence, wisdom and judgment, even though they remain indispensable to any decision.

ASCR 11.3 attempts to cure conflicts acknowledged as real by ASCR 11.2 by declaring that a client can give informed consent to the ongoing conflict. But many clients, even corporate clients with experience, will consent to what you tell them is in their interests. Why else are they paying your significant fees? The rule seems to deny the human reality that our own judgment as to what is a conflict and what is in our client's interests can be effectively overshadowed by our own interest, which is to retain both clients for as long as possible.

The slippery concept of 'informed consent' illustrates this conflict well. Put yourself back in the job as a managing partner of an LLF. In transactional matters where informed consent is apparently obtained from both clients under ASCR 11.4.1, for how many clients will the partner responsible first take them through, in detail, all the clauses of the proposed contract? For how many clients will that partner explain where the agreement could be slanted in their favour rather than in the favour of the other party (which is also your client), and in the expectation that the firm, as the lawyer for both clients, is giving the opposite analysis to the other party?

How could either party realistically rely on your integrity as their shared law firm when sooner or later your firm must make a decision, even in minor ways, to prefer the interests of one party over the other? Inside a large and highly competitive firm, would we really put the true nature of this process to each of our clients before asking them to consent – that is, in an informed manner – to our joint representation?

ASCR 11.4.2 takes the absurdity even further. It requires an effective information barrier to be set up in advance of the proposed conflict in order to protect against disclosure of 'detrimental' information. The effectiveness of the barrier is a condition that must be established before the joint representation commences, but can never be satisfied until it is tested by the existence of the joint representation. In this context, effectiveness is a terminological nonsense.

If you are confronted by the contrived and contradictory nature of ASCR 11, the only significant safeguard you have will be to revert to general morality and ask yourself: what are the virtues I need to display in determining this conflict?; what is the fair thing to do here?; and what action will achieve the greatest good for the greatest number?; and then to judge accordingly. This will never be easy because rapidly merging and de-merging LLFs acquire and lose corporate clients with some frequency. Even with the assistance of a conflicts clearing house,[22] it can be difficult to keep track of which clients have interests that are opposed and which partners know things about those clients and must therefore be kept apart, if possible.

Table 7.3 below illustrates the complexity of a concurrent conflict and shows the judgment one LLF made about the proper course of action to maintain confidences and a sense of propriety. The integrity of that judgment according to general morality is also explored and compared to the conduct rules as they now are.

7.4 Acting against former clients – successive conflicts

When your firm has a client who is in dispute with a former client, there is a successive conflict. The issues that arise are similar to those that are relevant in concurrent conflicts. Your former client will nearly always consider that your firm ought not to be acting against them. They may consider you are

170 The Good Lawyer

Table 7.3 The instability of concurrent, opposed clients – Allens and Big Pharma[23]

The Melbourne branch of major national law firm, Allens Arthur Robinson (now Allens Linklaters), found itself acting for three drug companies with potentially conflicting interests.

Two companies, Pfizer and GlaxoSmithKline, were 'originators': that is, they were and are major multinational pharmaceutical companies that invent, develop and manufacture new drugs. They had been Allens' clients for many years, and Allens acted for them on many issues.

The third client was a 'generic' manufacturer, Mayne. Generic drug companies do not develop their own drugs, but manufacture drugs developed by other companies by waiting until originator companies' patents expire, or by successfully challenging originators' patents. Generic and originator drug manufacturers are strong commercial competitors, and also routinely engage in disputes and litigation over intellectual property rights. The Allens partner who acted for Mayne had previously acted for them from time to time when he had had his own small firm. That firm, and its practice, was then acquired by Allens.

For several years Allens maintained both Mayne and its originator clients on its books. Allens judged that this was appropriate, as they considered there was no 'actual' conflict of interest between the clients – that is, the firm held no specific confidential information on the operations of each client that was of relevance to the matters they handled for other clients. But there was always potential for conflict, so Allens also put in place information barriers to make sure that any confidential information that did exist would not pass between the lawyers acting for the different clients.

[Note that at the time of these arrangements, conflicts of interest were considered as arising principally in relation to possible breaches of confidence. Factors such as the proper administration of justice and loyalty to clients were not seen as particularly significant in comparison.]

However, five years after the partner representing Mayne had joined Allens, 'it became increasingly clear [that] there was a real potential for conflict'.[24] By this stage, Allens had already been acting for both GlaxoSmithKline and Mayne in relation to the same transaction (with the consent of both). Now, after five years, the other longstanding client, Pfizer, was likely to sue Mayne in relation to a patent dispute, and was not happy that Allens also acted for Mayne.

Allens considered it necessary to 'let go' one client – Mayne – in an attempt to keep the other more significant clients. But Mayne was piqued and took action against Allens for breach of retainer, alleging, among other things, a conflict in Allens' continued representation of Pfizer. The Mayne action was settled on undisclosed terms with Pfizer remaining an Allens' client.[25] The partner and his team who had represented Mayne, however, left Allens and joined another firm where, presumably, they could continue to act for Mayne.

Allens believed that the context and history of their relationship with both sets of clients made their decision to dispense just with Mayne appropriate. Mayne were recent clients, brought into the Allens fold only as a result of a firm merger. Further, Allens' representation of Mayne was sufficiently limited so that a degree of consensual separation akin to an information barrier had been constructed for the specific purpose of enabling that representation to occur. The originators, GlaxoSmithKline and Pfizer, were clients of much longer standing and had been represented by Allens in litigation as well as in a wide range of transactional matters. Allens did not refer to 'loyalty' in any public sense when explaining itself, but it apparently believed that they owed less of it to Mayne than to their other clients.

Virtue ethics

As a *prudent* LLF managing partner, you will not just be wary of acting for two or more clients who are major players in the same industry. You will be determined to demonstrate the virtue of loyalty by actively preventing mergers with other law firms or partner imports that bring with them new clients in the same sector. If you are pressured by the executive team inside your firm to be more accommodating or 'commercially realistic', your response will be to argue that longer term *loyalty* to existing clients is more important to overall reputation, that prevention of conflict rather than its accommodation will reduce the huge transactional costs in maintaining an information barrier and, with the *courage* of your convictions, you will suggest that you are prepared to step aside (and resign as managing partner) if that approach is unacceptable to the firm.

7 Conflicts of loyalty and interest   171

Table 7.3 (cont.)

Consequentialism

With an eye to outcomes as an LLF managing partner, you will be weighing up the greater good in supporting or rejecting prospective new clients who compete commercially with existing clients. You may consider that your firm's representation of both clients is really in their best interests, because no other firm is as expert as your own. But you will be very cautious about choosing, as Allens did, only to take action when forced to do so by imminent litigation between your clients, because the firm will by then have acquired much information on both clients and litigation has the potential to bring into the public spotlight the strengths and weaknesses of the internal barriers used to keep that information separate.

Reputation loss will be a factor for you. If other unrelated clients see the firm's procedures examined in court they may start to be anxious about the security of their own secrets. If you decide that the greater good amounts to protecting the firm's reputation and all other clients' equanimity, as well as the privacy of long-standing clients and their information, you will not be prepared to accept mergers or new partners where they bring clients who compete in the same sector as existing clients.

If you decide to acquire such new concurrent clients on a *bona fide* consequentialist basis, that decision must be because you are completely confident (on a zealous basis), that the financial benefits to both clients are far greater than what you consider to be an insignificant risk (the failure of the information barrier separating their confidential information). Your own receipt of two sets of fees can play no role at all in your decision.

Kantian ethics

Kant's emphasis on fairness derives from his concept of the 'categorical imperative', that every individual as a free agent is an end in themselves and therefore has an equal and irreducible right to the same treatment as any other individual. In that sense, your decision to take on new clients who compete with existing clients must involve a decision to treat them equally in all respects. This attitude demonstrates an active relationship of care. That will mean that information barriers will be strictly and indefinitely maintained and that neither client will be preferred to the other, despite any disproportion in their financial significance to the firm.

If either client decides, for whatever reason, that they are unhappy with continued joint representation, or if litigation between them is imminent, fairness will dictate that you cease acting for both clients rather than just the client who is unhappy. Ceasing to act for both clients prevents any possibility that the legacy information barrier will degrade over time and leak the information of the departed client.

Applicable law and conduct rules

The ASCR does not see any insurmountable problems with confidentiality arising from joint representation of clients who are in commercially competitive positions *vis-à-vis* each other. Under ASCR 11.4.2, any problem is cured by an 'effective' information barrier, regardless of consent.

But ASCR 11.5 asserts that your continued representation of one client after an 'actual' conflict is identified is only possible if the confidentiality of the departing client's information is preserved and that client gives their informed consent.

Conclusion in relation to concurrent conflicts

Everything depends on the strength of information barriers when joint representation is involved. These barriers have been proved to be thin in the largest firms,[26] and when they fail, they leak not just information but a firm's reputation for competence and integrity.

When one client, even a sophisticated client, wakes up to the fact that it is simply not possible for you as a managing partner to maximise their interests behind an inherently porous information barrier, while simultaneously maximising the interests of another opposed client, litigation can easily occur. Any litigation impacting upon your firm's reputation will have unpredictable and likely adverse consequences for your other clients. The ASCR formula is inadequate to protect your reputation or the confidences of your clients. Your proper initial judgment should be to avoid commercial conflicts at their inception, so that they do not develop into prohibited conflicts.

172   The Good Lawyer

bound to them because of a vague sense that you were their confidant in past matters and you should still have a sense of loyalty to them, even though your contract of retainer is in the past.

But if a sense of loyalty is the issue, your firm certainly owes that loyalty to your current client, unless your current client is removed from the scene by a court order – as a result of an injunction sought by your old client. As discussed earlier, loyalty is indivisible. You and your firm cannot share it between a current client and a former client. Your former client may assert not just that the loyalty they consider they are owed is under threat, but first of all, that their confidential information is threatened: that while you were acting for them, you acquired important confidential information and that that information will assist your firm's new client in the current dispute. Confidentiality definitely survives the end of the prior relationship, where loyalty may not. It is therefore in the area of confidentiality that the ASCR strives, without any pretence of moral worthiness, to make it possible for you to act against your former client in the face of their objections. Consider how the ASCR first says 'no conflicts', but then says, 'go ahead':

> ASCR 10.1 A solicitor and law practice must avoid conflicts between the duties owed to current and former clients, except as permitted by Rule 10.2.
>
> 10.2 A solicitor or law practice who or which is in possession of confidential information of a former client where that information might reasonably be concluded to be material to the matter of another client and detrimental to the interests of the former client if disclosed, must not act for the current client in that matter UNLESS:
>
> - 10.2.1 the former client has given informed written consent to the solicitor or law practice so acting; **or**
> - 10.2.2 an effective information barrier has been established.

In most cases, a court will be focused on the extent to which you or your firm has in your possession confidential information that will damage your former client if your firm now acts against them. If they determine that you did receive confidential information at the time, the court will next want to consider whether any information barrier that your firm sets up will be effective. As the use of the word 'or' at the end of ASCR 10.2.1 (above, in bold) makes clear, the LLFG is very determined to allow your firm to act against your former client even if they are asked for and refuse to give their consent. The LLFG has limited use for loyalty, but does value expediency. All that is needed is the 'effective' barrier.

These current–former client barriers can also present a special problem for you if you happen to be the partner who acted for them previously. The barrier can only be effective if you and all your files, emails and other records relevant to your former client, are quarantined or cocooned inside an information tent, so that everything you may know about your former client is kept away from the lawyers who will now act for the new client. The cost of this cocoon cannot be shared by the former client, unlike the position with conflicts between two current clients (as expressed in the QANTAS–Emirates vignette above), as the former client no longer provides any revenue to the firm. And you are not to have anything to do with these lawyers, even though you may know them well and socialise with them. All the issues of leakage that are raised by information barriers for concurrent conflicts are also relevant here, with one possible additional factor: to some degree, you may be regarded as a costly inconvenience. You will certainly be exposed to some monitoring, because your silence is essential to the revenue generated from the new client. If you are not delivering sufficient billable hours and if your former client was your major client, your continued presence in the firm could be under review.

If a judge cannot find in your particular case that confidential information is at risk of disclosure, they may still stop your firm acting for its new client and grant an injunction on the basis of a breach of an obligation of loyalty[27] or because in the particular dispute between your current and former clients the court has inherent jurisdiction to determine which of its officers may be allowed to represent parties to argue cases before it. As a concurrent conflict, that concern is for the proper administration of justice.[28]

A timely concluding example of the complexity and fine judgments that must be made in relation to conflicts of interest has recently arisen in relation to another aftermath of the *McCabe* case.[29] In Chapter 2, reference was made to a former whistleblowing partner of Clayton Utz who provided information to the press in 2006 that suggested that earlier on, there had in fact been a small number of Clayton Utz partners and staff whose job had included hiding or destroying the incriminating documents of tobacco companies. That partner, Christopher Dale (the 2004 President of the

Law Institute of Victoria) had earlier been dismissed by Clayton Utz for what was described as an unrelated matter concerning a breach of the firm's *pro bono* policy, but he did not take his dismissal lying down. In 2011 Dale issued proceedings claiming that his expulsion from the partnership was unlawful. Clayton Utz filed a defence that was signed by Alan Myers QC, a senior barrister who had also, over the years, acted for tobacco companies. This meant that Myers would be representing Clayton Utz in court and cross-examining Dale once his case commenced. Dale was unhappy that Myers was involved because he claimed he had himself consulted Myers in 2004 and 2005, before his expulsion by Clayton Utz, in relation to the problems he was having at the firm.

Dale challenged Clayton Utz's decision to retain Myers to act for them and asserted that Myers was in a successive conflict situation and could not act for Clayton Utz against his former client (Dale). Dale alleged breach of duties of loyalty and of confidentiality and asserted the need to protect the administration of justice. It is important to note that Myers denied any recollection of providing advice to Dale and did not believe he had acted for Dale at all. Diagram 7.4 below sets out the timeline:

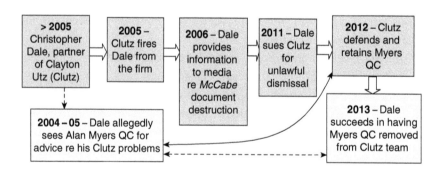

Diagram 7.4 Successive conflict connected to *McCabe*

Dale was able to persuade the court that confidential information might have been provided to Myers and that both that fact and the need to protect the administration of justice required that Myers be restrained from acting for Clayton Utz and against himself. The court made several references to the fact that Myers' statement that he had no recollection of the relevant discussions, while accepted, did not mean that they had not occurred.[30]

7.5 Conclusion

The sense of general morality that ought to underlie all our activities as lawyers is put under much pressure when conflicts of interest are allowed to arise or to continue, once identified. The ASCR is not a satisfactory guide to preventing conflicts, but the courts are at least willing to champion partial solutions when they protect confidentiality as an issue of fairness. In their reassertion of the importance of loyalty and the protection of the administration of justice as a part of modern lawyering, Australian courts are also saying to the whole of the profession that the 'fit and proper' person test administered prior to admission is not just an empty formula, but a concrete expression of a great many virtues needed to prevent conflicts of interest wherever possible.

The following chapter tackles the final significant issue for good lawyers – the extent of our competence. Competence is normally understood narrowly as the technical capacity to perform a legal task efficiently and 'correctly'. This definition is accurate but begs its own question, since the meaning of correct or competent performance involves both technical proficiency and moral judgment. The chapter connects general morality to the notion of competence in the interests of a more holistic understanding of competent lawyering.

Notes

1. A detailed treatment of conflicts can be found in Dal Pont, *Lawyers' Professional Responsibility* (5th edn), Chs 6–8 and Parker and Evans, *Inside Lawyers' Ethics*, Ch. 8.
2. Fiduciary responsibilities or duties are grounded in virtue and Kantian ethics as developed by equity and are an important part of the lawyer–client relationship. A 'fiduciary' owes to the principal (client) a higher level of proper conduct than is required by the law of tort or contract. The central duty of a fiduciary is one of loyalty. See generally Dal Pont, n 1, para 4.40.
3. This statement seems wrong because criminal and family law practice is anything but easy. However, criminal and family lawyers have developed a more sharply defined priority for Kantian 'fairness'. See in particular Dal Pont, n 1, para 8.135, 8.140 and para 8.85, and *In the Marriage of McMillan* (2000) 26 *Fam LR* 653.
4. Justice P.D. Cummins, 'An ethical profession: Dealing with ethical dilemmas' (speech delivered at a Law Institute of Victoria Continuing Legal Education seminar, Melbourne, 28 February 2002). Original on file with author.

5. This is noticeable when we offer to or are pressured to act for members of family or close friends and even sexual partners.

6. *Legal Ombudsman v Woods* [2000] VLPT 27.

7. See Ch. 6.

8. See Dal Pont, n 1, and ASCR 12.

9. For a detailed explanation of billing approaches, see Parker and Evans, n 1, Ch. 9.

10. Extracted from Parker and Evans, ibid.

11. I acknowledge with thanks the above salient points in relation to the *Keddies* matter, which were provided by Christine Parker. A transcript and audio recording of the background of the case can be found at the ABC Radio National *Background Briefing* website: www.abc.net.au/radionational/programs/backgroundbriefing/2012-07-22/4139052#transcript.

12. See *Legal Services Commissioner v Keddie* [2012] NSWADT 106.

13. See *Legal Profession Uniform Law Application Act 2014* (Vic), Sch 1, Part 4.5.

14. The exceptions being collaborative family law and the joint representation of criminal co-accused where both clients plead guilty and both clients have the same level of culpability for the offences as charged.

15. In both the family and criminal law jurisdictions, there is a greater emphasis on justice being done and the perception that it is being done, and on the preservation of confidence in the administration of justice.

16. See *Prince Jefri Bolkiah v KPMG* [1999] 2 WLR 215. Contentious work means actual litigation or other cases where issues are in contention (there is a real dispute) between the parties involved.

17. While at first sight no conflict is likely to arise in transactional matters (and subject to the ASCR it is permissible to act for more than one party in such matters) the practice of doing so has been criticised by the courts in cases where there is the slightest possibility of conflict arising. Arguably, a lawyer concerned never to give the impression of partiality will avoid any transactional conflicts, by not acting.

18. Information barriers are also known as Chinese Walls, or disparagingly, as 'Dutch Dykes' or 'Dingo Fences'. All of these terms refer to their porous history. In two-party transactional (non-contentious) representation information barriers are becoming far more common as large firms try to persuade both clients that they can and will keep separate their handling of both clients' affairs. The constant mergers and acquisitions occurring between upper-tier firms place partners in conflict with each other on a regular basis. The *Optus Networks* case – *Asia Pacific Telecommunications Limited v Optus Networks Pty Limited* [2007] NSWSC 350 – provides a recent example of a failed information barrier involving Clayton Utz. In that case, Bergin J described the barrier as 'paper thin', which was a euphemism for deficient.

19. Remember, consent can always be retracted, so it is, in practice, dangerous to rely on such consent as a business strategy.

20. The principal case here is *Spincode Pty Ltd v Look Software Pty Ltd* [2001] VSCA 248. *Spincode* is a Victorian case has not been completely accepted throughout the country, but it has been influential. In that case, McPherson and Kelley (an outer-suburban Melbourne firm with a strong commercial client base) changed sides in the middle of litigation by seeking to act against their former client in the same

7 Conflicts of loyalty and interest   177

matter. Brooking JA described an 'abiding negative obligation [derived from the fiduciary obligation of loyalty] not to act against the former client in the same matter'. An information barrier would be irrelevant to this situation, not simply because of the need to protect confidential information, but also because, in Brooking JA's view, a breach of loyalty occurs whether or not there is confidential information at stake.

21. The opinions of Brooking JA in *Spincode Pty Ltd v Look Software Pty Ltd* [2001] VSCA 248 suggests the duty does survive and that sense is gradually increasing around the country. But it is not a solid principle of law, as NSW courts in particular do not appear to support the concept of a duty of loyalty. The issue awaits High Court authority. See, generally, Dal Pont, n 1, paras 8.35–8.40.

22. See further Ch. 2.

23. This modified extract of the Allens–Mayne dispute is taken from Parker and Evans, n 1.

24. Quotation from an Allens spokesperson reported in 'Mallesons prospers from Allens IP conflict', *Lawyers Weekly* (Sydney), 11 September 2003.

25. Christopher Webb, 'Dramatic exile on Mayne Street', *Strictly Private, The Age* (Melbourne), 18 June 2003, 4.

26. See the *Optus Networks* case, n 369. Bergin J was deciding on this issue inside Clayton Utz after having previously warned the firm, in prior proceedings, that its information barrier was under scrutiny.

27. This is particularly the case in Victoria. See *Spincode Pty Ltd v Look Software Pty Ltd* [2001] VSCA 248, affirmed in *Adam 12 Holdings Pty Ltd v Eat and Drink Holdings Pty Ltd* [2006] VSC 152; *Pinnacle Living Pty Ltd v Elusive Image Pty Ltd*, [2006] VSC 202; *Commonwealth Bank v Kyriackou* [2008] VSC 146.

28. *Kallinicos v Hunt* [2005] NSWSC 1181.

29. See *McCabe v British American Tobacco Australia Services* [2002] VSC 73 and Ch. 5.3.

30. See *Dale v Clayton Utz (No. 2)* [2013] VSC 54. The judgment of Hollingworth J goes into considerable detail concerning the connections of this matter to the *McCabe* litigation and its aftermath.

Chapter 8

THE MORALITY OF COMPETENCE

8.1 Introduction: Competence requires morality

Most clients think of good lawyers as people who are skilled and therefore effective in achieving outcomes. These ideas reflect the common notion that technical 'competency' is an important quality which lawyers ought to have. This has to be correct, as far as it goes, but it's really the combination of intelligence, technical skill and ethics that is important.[1] Previous chapters have concentrated on the many dimensions of moral goodness because these are under-appreciated in modern lawyering. But you will not be surprised that even competence requires applied morality: that is, the exercise of judgment. The simplest of illustrations makes this clear:

> Are you known for getting things done comfortably on time, or for working right up to deadlines and/or being 'a little bit late'?
> If the latter is the case, could your attitude to deadlines be a problem for your professional competency?

A habit of delivering work right on a deadline or occasionally a little after is not, in the scheme of things, what most people would call a problem. The volume of work and workplace stress may be such that it is physically impossible to complete tasks before deadlines and still have some balance in life. But if your normal, 'unstressed' approach to completing work is to

178

finalise and deliver it on the deadline, you may not be leaving sufficient margin for your own error or allowing for delay caused by others.[2] On occasion, both of these factors will cause you to overshoot and be late. If this is truly occasional, no reputation loss is likely, but otherwise, your competence will inevitably be questioned even though your other skills are not at issue.

This chapter applies a moral consciousness to several challenges to our technical competence. We begin with the underlying conflict between so-called professionalism and commercialism, where only professionalism will sustainably support your competence. Next, our obligation of competence to clients arising from the law of contract and tort is considered not just in its own right, but because it is also subject to moral constraints. And the very extensive requirements of financial competency also deserve attention, if only because they represent trouble when ignored. Staying clear of the major global risks to competence (corruption, bribery and money laundering) is of increasing importance. In fact, 'staying competent' means benefiting from applied morality at many levels, but particularly in risk management and continuing education.

Finally, we must recognise that all of us will 'fail' in our competence and be careless at some stage. Making mistakes is inevitable, and although the word 'negligence' has a frightening ring to it, our understanding and acceptance of this reality does not mean that our moral sense has abandoned us or that we ought to give up on a desire to perform to the best of our ability. Fortunately, there are safety nets – as outlined in Appendix B – that have been developed by the profession over the years to deal with negligence. The chapter concludes with an explanation of the statutory schemes that exist to compensate clients for our incompetence and, regrettably, theft. Both of these schemes came from the profession's own recognition of the claims of general morality on our competence and integrity.

8.2 Commercialism and competent legal practice

In Chapter 2 the point was made that sustainable commercialism must be ethically sound. This statement referred to the connection between lawyers' business practices – that is, their sense of commercial reality – and their everyday ethical behaviour. It was argued that business without ethics,

180   The Good Lawyer

including lawyers' businesses, has no long-term (sustainable) legitimacy. But it is also the case that even if you are an ethical lawyer, you will not be in practice very long if you cannot run a business. As a new lawyer you might protest that you plan to join a large firm where you will have no real influence on the business and no immediate need to learn about the financials of law firms or, for example, how to operate a trust account. But that is short-sighted. Supervising lawyers will be watching for your commercial sense from an early stage. They will want to know if you can see how the mounting time charged to a client's file affects how much return (and profit) the firm might make from the client. They will watch for your intuition as to what aspects of a file could lead to further work and they will be especially interested in how you manage your client contacts so that the firm's overall relationship with the client is respectful, creative and leads to prompt payment of the firm's bills.

Even if you are in a larger firm and are not the primary client contact, you will have opportunities to show business sense to those around you. You will need that awareness not just to survive, but to be successful in legal practice. So the challenge is to reconcile that commercial sense with your professional (ethical and moral) sense. Fortunately, they are not inherently opposed concepts. In fact, their relationship is intimate. In 2000, the International Bar Association (IBA) agreed on and published a resolution entitled 'Professionalism versus Commercialism', in which this statement appears:

> 4. ... [A] lawyer's independence requires his/her economic independence, which can only be guaranteed by sufficient income from his/her professional activity; [but] 5. . . . at the same time the pursuit of commercialism, meaning an excessive and inappropriate emphasis on profit without regard to professionalism, is inconsistent with the role of a lawyer and should be discouraged.[3]

The IBA is the world representative body for practising lawyers. All Australian law societies and bar associations are members. Surprisingly for an organisation that is very commercial in its outlook, the IBA has actually defined commercialism as a perversion to be avoided by lawyers. So while we need a commercial sensitivity in legal practice, commercialism is to be avoided. The IBA can be commended for its insistence on a general moral position in relation to lawyers making excessive profits. But there is a gentler understanding which allows for the need to recognise our commercial objectives and avoid the extremism which the IBA cautions against. What is required of us as modern lawyers is the wisdom to know when our commercial consciousness (considered as an extension of our competence) is taking us to the point that desire for profit is becoming excessive and is therefore inappropriate, without regard for our morality. This fine balance is pivotal. There are perhaps few more fundamental challenges to lawyers today than to understand our quest for competence as a balance between desire for financial success and for moral behaviour. Achieving that balance does not mean we must disregard commercial objectives, but it does require that we nurture a reputation for delivering value to clients. There is really no shortcut to development of the 'good' reputation, because word-of-mouth is the major way our legal practices grow over the long term.

8.3 Contract, tort and the advocates' exit clause

A lot of time is spent in law school and in post-admission education in staying up to date. Knowing the law, or knowing how and where to find it efficiently, is important, because of our contractual and tortious obligations to clients to act competently; and similarly, we have obligations to not act at all when our degree of competence is insufficient or our specialisation is inappropriate. As with all professional relationships, our contract of retainer requires that we will be competent.[4] And the law of tort will expect competence and hold us responsible for negligence according to general legal principles which echo the major duty-based systems of Kantian fairness and consequentialism.

In tort law particularly, we can discern – in the duty of care, in the responses to breach of the standard of care[5] and in the mandatory insurance cover against negligence – a concern to ensure that all recipients of our services are treated fairly when mistakes are made and that, when appropriate, the financial cost of our incompetence is spread across all lawyers through the premium structure on that insurance. All of these provisions are underpinned by the law of fiduciary obligations, reflecting virtue ethics' position within general morality. As fiduciaries (see Chapter 7), we owe loyalty to our clients that is breached by incompetence and for which we ought to be willing, with courage and even humility, to accept the consequences.

182   The Good Lawyer

You may know and agree with all of this, but you may not know that there is still an ancient and disreputable relic hiding in the law about lawyers' competence. Table 8.1 below discusses the rule of advocates' immunity, an arcane exception to the moral and otherwise general legal principle that we are responsible for our actions.

Table 8.1 Advocates' immunity – a separation of law and morality?

Traditionally, advocates (both barristers and solicitors acting as advocates) have been 'immune' from legal action by clients for professional negligence relating to their work in conducting litigation.[6] A central justification was the perceived need to allow advocates to present their cases fearlessly, without immediate concern that they might be later sued if they made incorrect statements about finely arguable issues of law. Judges relied on virtue ethics to justify the immunity. For example:

> It is impossible to expect an advocate to prune his case of irrelevancies against a client's wishes if he faces an action for negligence when he does so. Prudence will always be prompting to ask every question and produce every piece of evidence that his client wishes, in order to avoid the risk of getting involved [in an action against him/herself] . . . it is difficult and it needs courage in an advocate to disregard irrelevancies which a forceful client wishes him to pursue. This question is of great importance for two reasons. First, if by good advocacy, a case is cut down to its essentials, it is more manageable and more likely to be justly decided by judge or jury. Secondly, time (and consequently the cost) is greatly diminished.[7]

In 1988, in *Giannarelli v Wraith*,[8] Mason CJ said that the purpose of the immunity is not to benefit the advocate, but to protect the public interest in the due administration of justice. This public policy rationale is based on two considerations:

- First, without the immunity, an advocate's exercise of independent judgment may be affected, leading to lengthier, more complex and costly litigation.
- Second, unsuccessful litigants would be encouraged to bring an action to show that, but for their advocate's negligence, they would have obtained a more favourable result. This would be contrary to the public policy that there should be finality to litigation. It would allow collateral attacks to be made on judicial decisions leading to an undermining of original decisions which would damage public confidence in the administration of justice. This effect would be particularly acute in criminal cases.

The issue came to the High Court again in *D'Orta-Ekenaike v Victoria Legal Aid et al*.[9] The defendant D'Orta-Ekenaike was charged with rape. Victoria Legal Aid (VLA) and his barrister advised him that he had no defence and that he should plead guilty. He did so at his committal hearing, but then pleaded 'not guilty' at the following trial. At that trial, evidence of the earlier guilty pleas was successfully and erroneously put before the jury by the prosecution and he was convicted. He successfully appealed, and at a second trial, the committal plea of 'guilty' was not led and he was acquitted. D'Orta-Ekenaike then sought to sue his barrister and VLA for negligence in the first trial. When the matter was eventually heard by the High Court, Gleeson CJ, Gummow, Hayne and Heydon JJ delivered a joint judgment, dismissing the appeal. They held that:

- what is important is the role of the advocate in the judicial process;
- the judicial process is for the resolution of disputes; and
- this process is not assisted if disputes can be re-litigated via collateral attack on one's former advocate.

Interestingly, the judges dismissed the issues of contract, cab-rank access and any conflict between duties to court and client as justifications for the immunity; they also dismissed the 'quick decision' and prolongation of trials arguments. But their decision remains the law in Australia, despite decisions to abolish the immunity in the United Kingdom,[10] New Zealand,[11] Canada and elsewhere.[12]

Today, the Australian immunity covers the advocate's conduct and management of a case in court (including an advocate who settles an action contrary to a client's instructions, even if the view that the matter should be settled is reached out of court) and work done out of court which leads to a decision affecting the conduct of the case in court.[13]

8 The morality of competence **183**

Table 8.1 (cont.)

Virtue ethics

Although the continuing immunity for advocates has been justified with the language of virtue, a love of *justice* and *compassion* for those damaged by the immunity must also be weighed in the balance. Virtue ethics does not, however, point clearly in either direction. On the one hand, there is virtue in supporting the advocate's freedom and courage to say whatever they think is appropriate to ensure that their client is justly treated, and the virtuous advocate will pursue that opportunity in good conscience, even if mistakes are made. But a desire for justice is also challenged when a clear mistake must go unremedied because there is no other way of redressing the situation. Compassion for those hurt by an advocate's mistake will suggest that the immunity is not good.

Consequentialism

Both majority and minority judges in all the major cases have relied on differing consequentialist perspectives. In *D'Orta-Ekenaike* particularly, the majority relied heavily on consequentialism.

However, in *Giannarelli*'s case, Justices Deane and Toohey disagreed with the majority opinion that there should be immunity at common law. They thought there was no convincing justification for it, considering that the public policy considerations expounded by the majority (not to encourage collateral challenges, etc) did not outweigh the injustice (a lack of virtue) and consequent public detriment (an adverse consequence) involved in depriving a person of redress under the common law for 'in-court' negligence. The reference to virtue is real, but this view primarily represents a consequentialist reasoning process, heavily influenced by the steady widening of the law of negligence towards greater professional accountability.

In the *Hall* case (which abolished the UK immunity) Lord Steyne also used a consequentialist analysis. He said that the major issue arises in relation to criminal trials, especially in relation to defence counsel. His priority outcome was the sanctity of the trial process, so he considered it important to state that defendants convicted after a full and fair trial ought to raise any concerns they had about negligence in the appeal phase, not by suing advocates who appeared for them. He considered it an abuse to initiate a collateral civil challenge to a criminal conviction and argued that ordinarily, such proceedings should be struck out as an abuse of process. But it is not necessary to ban them. The judicial code for this approach – 'public policy' – is consequentialist and means that a defendant who seeks to challenge his conviction ought to do so directly by seeking to appeal their conviction.

Consequentialism focuses on necessity. It does not foresee a negative result if the immunity were to be abolished in Australia. Advocates' immunity is not necessary to deal with collateral attacks on criminal and civil decisions. The public interest is satisfactorily protected by independent principles and powers of the court such as *res judicata*,[14] issue estoppel[15] and abuse of process.

A final consequentialist argument for disposing of the immunity refers to the function of tort law as a process of setting external standards of behaviour for the benefit of the public. In that context, the exposure of occasional acts of incompetence by advocates will strengthen rather than weaken the legal system.

Kantian ethics

Fairness is a critical factor for those opposed to the immunity, particularly in comparison to the accountability that applies to the medical profession. If the so-called slip of the surgeon's knife is actionable and causes injury, why cannot the slip of the advocate's tongue be?

Fairness was also invoked by the House of Lords when the UK immunity was discarded. In the *Hall* case, Lord Steyne said that the 'cab-rank' principle binds barristers but not solicitor-advocates, so it cannot in fairness extend the immunity to those advocates. Furthermore, the 'cab-rank' principle is not often likely to oblige a barrister to accept a brief they would otherwise reject (see Chapter 2). The judge considered that where a vexatious (insubstantial) claim of injury results, it will usually be possible to reject that claim on the spot. And he concluded that in any event the 'cab-rank' principle cannot justify depriving all clients of a remedy for negligence which has caused them major financial loss.

Applicable law and conduct rules

Since the continued existence of the immunity as a common law principle is itself the subject matter of this illustration of competing moral viewpoints, the applicable law offers no additional insight. But the validity of the immunity is important for present purposes because the arguments that are used for and against its continuation draw on all three of the traditions that make up general morality.

184   The Good Lawyer

Table 8.1 (cont.)

Conclusion as to the immunity

Virtue ethics is equivocal, but the trend evident in both Kantian and consequentialist reasoning throughout the common law world is steadily in favour of discarding the immunity.

    Consequentialism weighs outcomes in the balance, and most judges who have considered the issue have found that the threat of collateral actions against advocates is overstated. Kant might well suggest that if there are any remaining grievances about mistakes that cannot be addressed on appeal and must be brought by collateral action against an advocate, that action is likely to be fair and therefore justified.

The immunity of advocates is perhaps important to some advocates, though less so in recent times. Many advocates recognise that there is some risk and insure against it despite the formal immunity, if only to address any liability that could arise over the financial limits of the immunity. In making a decision to insure yourself against any negligence in court, you will be showing financial competence, a lawyering quality that is ever present and ever necessary.

8.4 Financial competency

A common response by practising lawyers challenged to give their opinion about the role of legal ethics is to say that 'ethical practice is my priority, but it's important not to go broke either'. Statements like these reflect the professionalism versus commercialism debate discussed above, but they also point to the need for each of us to be financially competent. There are key obvious financial skills: tracking income versus expenses; understanding assets and liabilities; and making sure your cash flow is adequate. All businesses monitor these figures. You must also. In fact, financial competency more or less requires us to have 'whole of business' accounting skills whether we intend to be an employee indefinitely or not. And that skill set goes further, into the realm of client service. Since most clients of lawyers are in business, understanding a set of corporate accounts is now essential for us all.

It is also important to be able to account for (record) the movement of money – yours and your clients'. This familiarity leads us to the issue of trust accounting: literally, the bank accounts which we as fiduciaries are trusted to administer on behalf of our clients. As lawyers we keep money for all sorts of reasons. When your client sells or purchases real estate, or becomes an executor of a deceased estate or gets involved in any sort of legal action, there is usually a lot of money flowing between them and other parties. A simple house purchase will typically put several hundred thousand dollars into your trust account for at least a few weeks, which you must then pay to the seller on behalf of your client when the property is ready to be 'settled'.

Comparatively few lawyers actually operate a trust account, but ignorance of the lengthy set of basic rules designed to support the trust relationship would be the same as knowing how to use a tablet while being unable to write by hand. Trust accounting 'basics' do not assume our dishonesty in the absence of rules, but the framework does make it easier to remember that trust money is not ours and cannot be treated as a financial resource. Trust money is not available to 'borrow' when costs are slow to come in and our practice overdraft gets too high. In fact most of the trust account rules are there to support our honesty by creating the sort of paper trail that makes it very difficult to knock off clients' funds, and makes it easier to keep our own money and their money entirely separate. The other necessary virtues are *diligence* and *fidelity* (*loyalty*), and although the rules do support fairness to our clients, they also place a scary emphasis on the consequences if we do not exercise due care or succumb to dishonesty. The courts are very clear about this:

> [the court] has a duty to vindicate the inviolability of the trust imposed upon a practitioner to treat his client's money in all respects as their money and to use their money for their purposes and no other ... Whenever a client's money is deliberately used for a purpose other than the purpose for which the client entrusts it to the practitioner, there is an act of dishonesty ...[16]

The scope of the overall trust accounting framework (and the insurance policies that often cover its use) is related to the question of whether a lawyer's activity occurs 'in the course of or in connection with legal practice'. 'Legal practice' is not defined in the Uniform Law, but 'legal services' are circuitously defined to mean 'work done, or business transacted, in the ordinary course of legal practice'.[17] However, the concept of 'engaging in legal practice' is intended to invoke common law learning on what defines the practice of a lawyer.[18] Table 8.2 below sets out the trust accounting framework which is broadly uniform throughout the country.

Table 8.2 Trust accounting basics

The purpose of trust account regulation[19]	• To prevent wrongful use of trust money and • To facilitate detection of wrongful use – including money laundering!
The five principles of trust account regulation	1. Separation of your own and clients' money; 2. Designation of client money as 'trust money' (the 'fiduciary' distance); 3. Separate identification of each client's money and each transaction in relation to that money; 4. Precise record keeping to facilitate identification of irregularities; and 5. External auditing, with criminal and professional sanctions for breach (commonly including some time in jail).
Definition of trust money: money received by ...	• you or your firm in the course of legal practice for or on behalf of a person or body other than you or your firm; • you or your firm or approved clerk on account of legal costs in advance of legal services to be provided in the course of legal practice; and • a registered foreign lawyer.
Money is *not* trust money, if received ...	• as part of a service for which an Australian Financial Services Licence is required; • in the course of a separate business or entrepreneurial activity; • as payment for your fees and costs; or • as reimbursement of disbursements (expenses) paid by you.
Payment *into* a trust account	Subject to specified exceptions, you must pay trust money into a trust account 'as soon as practicable' after receipt. In practice, this means no later than 24 hours after receipt: a 'suspense account' trust ledger record should be created if it is unclear who or what the trust money relates to.

 BUT

Trust money *need not* be paid into trust account when you receive ...	• a written direction from a client when the money is received, to do otherwise (for example, to establish a controlled money account[20]); • a cheque payable to a third party, known as 'transit money'. Note: transit money is still trust money and must be recorded as such, even if not physically paid into a bank.
And payment *from* a trust account is possible	... only in these circumstances: • to pay the person on whose behalf the money was received, or at their direction; • to pay your legal costs; or • to pay a statutory deposit to the legal regulator.[21]

8 The morality of competence   **187**

Fraudulent misappropriation of client funds is a crime, and is also professional misconduct. And these crimes can affect any lawyer on the edges. Unlike nearly every other area of the law, each of us (as lawyers) has a positive statutory obligation to report another lawyer for suspected irregularities in their trust account.[22] So even if we have nothing actively to do with a theft ourselves, if we suspect something and stand by, doing nothing, we can be prosecuted.

Trust account irregularities which amount to misconduct will usually result in being struck off the roll of legal practitioners, if not jail,[23] but as the Table 8.3 case study shows below, neither the criminal conviction nor removal from the roll is really the point for clients who lose their money to fraud.

Table 8.3 Pinching a lot of trust money – Magarey Farlam

The following edited transcript of a 2013 interview from *The Law Report* highlights the aftermath of lawyer theft. The trust account rules are intended to keep us virtuous in the sense that they operate to support honesty and make it practically cumbersome and difficult to steal, but no set of rules can stop determined thieves. When fraud does occur, our collective obligation as a profession is to make sure that the victims of broken trust are not just left to fend for themselves.

The admission, licensing and disciplinary processes address client protection by attempting to prevent misconduct and provide remedial education and supervision after misconduct occurs. But clients need compensation. This is the role of so-called fidelity or guarantee funds, which are intended to repay clients when their money is stolen. In this interview, one client (Chris Snow) paints the picture of the inadequate fidelity compensation system in one state, South Australia.[24]

Damien Carrick (*The Law Report*):   [An] … important issue is ensuring that there is a quick, fair response when a law firm collapses and clients have their money trapped in a firm's trust accounts. It's a matter close to the heart of Chris Snow … When Chris's father died his estate and trust was handled by established Adelaide law firm Magarey Farlam. Three months after his father's death, the firm collapsed.

Chris Snow: In July 2005 they discovered the first of a series of frauds in their trust accounts. Then I think they were about $108,000, first up. But by the time the forensic accountant thing had been done, six months later, the frauds were put up to $4.5 million – that had been stolen from 42 of their 250 clients.

Damien Carrick: Were you one of them?

Chris Snow: No, I was not one of the 42, I was one of the 208 who were not stolen from.

Damien Carrick: But when the firm collapsed you were nevertheless affected.

Chris Snow: Yes, very much so, because when a fraud occurs in a law firm in South Australia it comes under the Legal Practitioners Act and it comes under the trust account and guarantee fund parts of that, which are all administered by the Law Society. And everyone was dragged through three Supreme Court cases and we had our assets frozen for 21 months. The people who were stolen from then had to go on to a fourth Supreme Court case before they were able to recover their funds.

Damien Carrick: Ultimately, those whose money was stolen were able to recover it through the courts, and clients like Chris whose assets were frozen, well, ultimately they were able to get their money back too. Chris Snow doesn't want victims of future collapses to endure what he and the other Magarey Farlam victims went through.

Currently, when money is placed in a solicitor's trust account the interest is siphoned off. About 60% is used to fund legal aid, and the rest goes towards what is known as the solicitor's guarantee fund, which is a fund to compensate victims of fraud by law firms, and also to fund the regulatory scheme. In South Australia the guarantee fund normally has about $20 million in it.

188   The Good Lawyer

Table 8.3 (cont.)

> **Chris Snow:**   Now you'd think that the victims of fraud would be able to go to that fund, given that the bulk of it is their money, and given that they've made a substantial grant to legal aid, but they can't. It is what's known as a fund of last resort, which means that they have to go off and sue everybody under the sun: the partners, the auditors, the insurers, the banks, anybody else who's potentially liable. When they have exhausted that process, if they have not been able to obtain all their funds, then they can come back to the guarantee fund and say 'Please can we have compensation.' And the Law Society which administers it will say, 'Yes, but the payments we can make are themselves capped at 5% of the balance.' So 5% of $20 million is $1 million, and that is per case; that covers all claims in one case, not each particular claim.
>
> **Damien Carrick:**   One law firm, not one claimant.
>
> **Chris Snow:**   Correct, yes. So in Magarey Farlam there were 42 victims. They would have had to share $1 million, even though they had lost $4.5 million . . . [There are proposals to improve the South Australian compensation system, but they are unlikely to remedy all of these problems. See the discussion below, in relation to client compensation funds.]
>
> **Damien Carrick:**   Chris Snow would like to scrap solicitor trust accounts run by individual law firms. He also wants to scrap the under-funded solicitors' guarantee fund that's currently in place for when those trust accounts are emptied. Rather he would like to see a single statutory industry-wide trust account that is fully insured. He says this is a system that operates well in France and is currently being brought in by the Bar Council in the UK.

> ***Questions for reflection:***
>
> 1. If you had a suspicion of a breach of trust involving the stealing of clients' funds by someone in your law firm, would you say anything?
> 2. If you had similar information about someone in another law firm, would your answer be any different?
> 3. Would your answer to either question be affected by the provisions of the Uniform Law, which imposes a civil penalty of 50 penalty units for your failure to report a trust deficiency?[25]
> 4. Is there a valid basis in general morality for reporting other lawyers to the regulators?

Understanding how trust accounting works is initially a bit intimidating, but quickly becomes second nature as you get used to more and more direct client contact. Similarly, the wider challenges to competency can also be daunting. We have to balance learning what the law is while at the same time meeting ongoing deadlines to advise on that law. In this area also there are emerging moral imperatives. They can all be traced back to commercialism, as the term was defined by the IBA in 2000.

8.5 Billing and bribery: Challenges to competency

There are many aspects of modern legal professional life that make it difficult to stay up to date with changes in the law and procedure, let alone with the technology of practice, the significant turnover in colleagues and the constantly new personalities and moralities of those we work with. All of these factors compete daily for our attention and require our understanding as to their effect on our work quality and productivity. But the major impact on our competency and resilience as lawyers comes from the way in which most legal work is valued: that is, by the dominant six-minute billing systems. These were referred to earlier (see Chapter 2). Six-minute billing is superficially attractive to law firm managers because it makes it easy to measure who is likely to be productive and who is not. Never mind if many new lawyers find it dehumanising and leave the profession. Similarly, it is theoretically easy to bill clients according to the time spent. Never mind if clients feel uncertain about whether the time is well spent. But the challenge to competency from such time-based billing is more subtle. Measuring your worth every six minutes transforms your reasonable commercial consciousness (which is desirable) into an excessive commercialism based in narrow technique, which is dangerous. Our competency ought to be understood as a capacity to efficiently and morally analyse and integrate our legal knowledge and emotional intelligence in addressing a legal problem. But commercialism expressed in six-minute intervals mutates our competency into a lesser, internally conflicted animal. In six minutes we can deliver a service with zeal, but with only as much zeal and no more than can be promptly paid for and with little or no reflection or discussion about quality or moral legitimacy.

Understanding the conflict of zeal and budgets ought to make us very wary of time-based billing and push wherever possible for more moral approaches, such as value or staged billing.[26] These minimise ongoing lawyer–client conversations about timesheets, but address and assess the broad quality of the work being done, including its moral sustainability and its fair value to both you and your client. But as long as time-based billing dominates, that sort of holistic discussion will be exceptional. And in this current climate, it is no wonder that other adverse consequences of commercialism are emerging to challenge our competence.

One of these challenges is the issue of corruption. In this book, several examples have already been given of lawyers who have engaged in, turned a blind eye to or covered up corrupt practices. Some are also linked to bribery. Bribery is a further challenge to competency because it undercuts effort and defeats quality. Where unjust enrichment is allowed or becomes endemic, who will bother too much with competence? In a very real sense, a lawyer who succumbs to just one small bribe may be more prone to the next offer of a bribe, and less and less invested in notions of professional excellence, except in terms of self-preservation. In corrupt societies, the only valuable

190   The Good Lawyer

type of competence is that required to avoid being caught. And bribery is not just a sideshow that will never affect you. On a global scale, corruption and bribery are so entrenched that there are staggering estimates as to its size. David Steel, a judge of the UK High Court, has said:

> The scale of the problem is gigantic. The World Bank estimates that 15% of all companies all over the world pay bribes to coin or retain business. The figure for Asia is 30%. In some countries of the former Soviet Union the figure is 60%. Globally this results in the payment of bribes year by year of over $1 trillion.[27]

Lawyers all over the world have been involved in hiding bribery, sometimes unwittingly, and sometimes because they are themselves players in the corruption. In the latter case, commercialism is at the heart of the problem and the preferred mechanism to hide the corruption is money laundering. Lawyers' trust accounts are well suited to money laundering because lawyers do not have to routinely disclose the identities of the beneficial owners of the various sub-accounts to banks or regulators, making them ideal to hide and 'clean' the proceeds of crime. It is easy in theory to simply reject an approach to use our trust account in this way, but reality is more complex.

As lawyers we can be unwitting participants in legitimating others' corruption and money laundering unless we are competent enough to be alert to what is really going on in a complex commercial fraud, as this UK example illustrates:[28]

The London law firm and a hidden property purchaser

A reputable London law firm (LF) was asked by a new client, a property investment company (PIC), to advise on the acquisition of a large property in London.

LF undertook appropriate due diligence checks on PIC and accepted the retainer. LF was advised by PIC that a property valuation had already been conducted. However, LF noted that the valuation had been carried out over one year before and the value of the properties had significantly dropped during that time. When LF advised PIC that it would be prudent to obtain a further valuation, PIC indicated that it was being given instructions by an undisclosed party who did not wish to obtain a further valuation.

LF wisely decided to request further information regarding the undisclosed purchaser (including details as to the source of funds, particularly in view of the refusal to conduct a further valuation) in order to comply with money laundering laws and the requirements to understand on whose behalf the transaction was being conducted.

8 The morality of competence   **191**

> Although PIC produced a huge volume of documentation, including copies of various passports, the documents did not really clarify the identity of the undisclosed purchaser. The documentation relating to the source of funds included copies of certain International Bills of Exchange, but it was not clear how these had come into the possession of PIC's client. When LF requested an explanation, it was advised that the purchase was to be put together by liquidating certain International Bills of Exchange which were assigned to an individual in Switzerland and had come into existence as a result of a libel case in the US.
>
> PIC then informed LF that the original International Bills of Exchange had been couriered to LF. Upon receipt, LF noticed that the total amount of the Bills amounted to an astounding sum – about a quarter of the US GDP. Following receipt, LF was then instructed to send the original documentation to a bank in another jurisdiction.
>
> **Indicators of money laundering**
> PIC provided a huge amount of documentation, but it did not make sense. This is a tactic employed to try to put law firms off asking more questions.
>
> PIC never confirmed who their underlying client purchaser was.
>
> When finally provided, the explanation as to how the International Bills of Exchange had come into existence was excessively complex, to the point of being unlikely.
>
> The total amount of the original Bills that had been couriered was way in excess of the purchase price and also amounted to a sum of money that was completely fanciful as the personal resource of a private purchaser.
>
> There was no reason for purported originals of the International Bills of Exchange to be sent to LF when the initial issue was only the *bona fides* of the purchaser. On reflection, LF suspected that its own reputation was being used as a way of legitimising the documentation to the final recipient, the foreign bank, and that that bank was going to be used as the unwitting money launderer.

When it succeeds, our unwitting money laundering represents a failure of our own due diligence. The overall money laundering problem inside some professions is of such concern that the UN has created a special agency to combat it: the Financial Action Task Force (FATF). FATF requires bankers, accountants and lawyers in member states to submit to regimes which track, disclose and report their financial dealings on behalf of clients. In Australia, those reports must be made to the federal government's anti-money laundering agency, AUSTRAC. Failure to report certain transactions to AUSTRAC can be both a crime and misconduct.

Will you be competent enough to recognise a money-laundering approach if it occurs? More importantly, how can any of us remain

192　The Good Lawyer

competent enough to stay up to date with both the law and the techniques of bribery and money laundering? Fortunately, there are mechanisms that assist.

8.6 Staying competent

Reading, and lots of it, is an everyday routine for lawyers. We do it all the time, but there never seems to be enough time to absorb everything. Speed reading courses are popular because they help us train ourselves to read faster and retain more of what we read. But staying competent is not just about coping with the daily inflow of digested new case reports, or reading up on new money-laundering techniques, or working out how to store client information securely or knowing how to use the latest voice recognition software or tablet.

Competence may be a function of your diligence and an obligation of consequentialism, but it needs to be approached strategically, with judgment and wisdom. Competence is also therefore about: being systematic in re-educating ourselves (continuing professional development); understanding paradigm shifts in the way information is organised (for example, through artificial intelligence); understanding how we can better resolve arguments (for example, alternative dispute resolution); concentrating our practice in certain types of law (specialisation) so that we do not try to cover everything; and finally by being alert to the experience of others as they manage their own similar practices (risk management). Diagram 8.1 shows how the dimensions of competence intersect and strengthen each other and relate closely to different aspects of our general morality.

Each of these elements of competence deserves some further discussion in relation to general morality.

8.6.1 Continuing Professional Development (CPD)

Australian lawyers know very well that the degree of change is accelerating, but only in the last few years have all jurisdictions implemented continuing professional development (CPD) schemes to try to keep up to date. Their common feature is an insistence that as lawyers we spend at least 10 hours (and thus gain a required 10 points) per annum on updating ourselves through short courses and other designated means of knowledge transfer.[29]

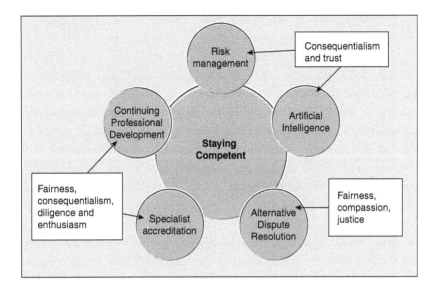

Diagram 8.1 Competence and morality

You must keep a log book and make it available for random audit by local law society auditors. If the 10 hours are not completed and recorded annually, you cannot renew your practising certificate.

A typical required range of CPD knowledge areas[30] is:

- Ethics and Professional Responsibility
- Professional Skills (for example, speed reading, new research techniques, advocacy, mediation, drafting submissions)
- Substantive Law (at least one hour; most points will be obtained under this heading)
- Practice Management and Business Skills (for example, accounting, budget planning, human relations policy, occupational health and safety).

CPD has attracted occasional criticism as a concept which patronises us as professionals, but the principle of CPD is still worthwhile because it represents a form of general morality in action. CPD helps us to maintain competency and therefore show fairness to our clients, and achieves an outcome that benefits the greatest number possible. Our diligent attitude to

CPD reinvigorates our motivation and demonstrates the legitimacy and value of ongoing learning to our peers.

CPD programs can, however, be of poor quality and be ineffective. Where CPD is self-regulatory – as is the case in Australia – programs are diminished to some extent because of their structure. Physical attendance at CPD courses is not recorded by seminar providers, so you self-report your attendance history when applying to renew your practising certificate. Audits of these records are sporadic. There is also no assessment. And providers of CPD are not monitored, so it is possible for a second or third-rate provider to offer CPD training. The length and content of CPD is also questionable. The overall total of 10 hours per annum is a minimal expectation. Could you describe yourself as diligent if you took part in only 10 hours of CPD per annum? And only one hour per annum must cover legal ethics, with no breakdown as to what that single hour should contain. Private study can be enough to meet up to five hours per annum of required CPD hours.[31]

These criticisms have merit, but CPD is also fairly defended as a cost-realistic program that is likely to encourage improved competency. If you see CPD as one of Aristotle's appropriate habits, then you may be encouraged to go beyond what the CPD schemes require. CPD will then improve your risk management and professional standards schemes, as discussed below. In this sense CPD relies on the virtues of *honesty* and *enthusiasm* for its depth and impact.

General outcomes from CPD could be better with minimal improvements, such as the recording of attendances at CPD presentations and the assessment of what is learned.

8.6.2 Artificial Intelligence

Artificial intelligence (AI) might appear an exotic ingredient in a discussion about competence. Is it not just a way of staying up to date with the law? But the significance of AI – with Google as the current best general purpose example – is in its capacity not just to increase the speed of our access to current law and procedure, but to decide on the way that recovered information is organised, presented to us (or in fact withheld from us). Software that helps to retrieve, identify and even discard potentially relevant documents for purposes of the discovery process in litigation is a case in point (see Chapter 6). As a highly competent lawyer, you will still be able to set the parameters or filters of your search engines and retrieval programs to reduce or disable exclusionary sub-routines and determine the way in which information is presented, but the speed with which new AI engines emerge may progressively limit your user interventions at one level or another. And this is where your morality and emotional intelligence are important.

We are already required to trust that the developers of retrieval programs, especially those that access cloud storage of client information, are in fact identifying all that information and presenting it to us. As the technology advances, that trust will be harder for us to verify and AI competence will have to be subcontracted to specialists within the firm, just as ordinary information technology already is. Trust in our colleagues' diligence and our judgment as to their strengths and weaknesses as technicians becomes even more important than our own understanding of the AI capabilities. Our competence will then sit even more obviously at the intersection of a consequentialist need to be certain about what the law is and what our 'facts' are, and the virtues of old-fashioned trust and judgment in other humans. And we will need those qualities for other reasons as well.

8.6.3 Specialist accreditation

If you have read all of the preceding chapters, you will have some idea of what type of legal practice attracts you. General practice suits some people and rural general practice has huge lifestyle advantages which can be positive for long-term competence, but general practitioners face a significant and lonely challenge in staying up to date across many fields of law. Enter the concept of specialist accreditation, which will help you maintain both competency and your attraction to law. Just as CPD has a primary role in maintaining expertise, accreditation as a specialist lawyer takes that process considerably further and, for considerably more effort, publicly recognises you as a lawyer who is prepared to focus on and become expert in a particular area of legal practice. Critics sometimes discount the accreditation process and claim that is is merely about better marketing and creating an opportunity to charge higher fees. These advantages are there for you, but specialist accreditation is fundamentally concerned to make legal practice more satisfying for you and provide better value for your clients. It is also very demanding of your time and concentration, requiring the virtues of *dedication, perseverance* and the pursuit of *excellence.*

Many Australian jurisdictions offer accreditation programs. An example is that of the Law Institute of Victoria, whose schemes over the last 20 years have attracted over 900 lawyers across 15 fields of specialisation.[32] Specialisation is attractive if you value your reputation for competence and you want to be acknowledged by others as up to date. You may be slightly less adaptable and have less capacity to function as lawyers outside your specialisation,[33] but your commitment to competence will not be questioned. Similar considerations apply to schemes which seek to limit the potential for mistakes by managing your risk in a structural sense.

8.6.4 Risk management

Risk management is the last of the mechanisms which have been established to ensure reasonable competence and limit the chances of large claims against you for incompetence. Risk management is a collective term covering a number of negligence prevention strategies developed by insurers over the years. For example, in the field of real estate conveyancing, it is not uncommon for lawyers acting for a purchaser to insufficiently scrutinise a certificate of the title to the property and fail to notice restrictions on the uses to which the purchaser may put the property. Best practice in risk management would require a lawyer who is new (or returning) to the field of conveyancing to undertake a short course in the law before they commence seeing clients. Apart from short courses, there are also all kinds of 'risk alert' bulletins, practice audits, practice management courses, trust account courses and claims history reviews. All are designed to identify where particular categories of mistake are likely to emerge in different types of law firm and alert the lawyers concerned to their risk.[34]

Risk management initiatives are commonly sponsored by professional indemnity (PI) insurers (see below) who must pick up the pieces when negligence becomes an issue. If you adopt every reasonable mechanism designed to reduce your risk of mistake and the need to claim on your PI insurance, you will not only help to control your costs of practice but maintain your reputation for competence. Risk management is actually the overarching strategy to ensure competence, since it encourages not only the above initiatives, but all of the behaviours and attitudes that value CPD, AI competence and specialist accreditation.

8.7 Conclusion: Moral competency and competent morality

Lawyering offers many opportunities to do 'good' and it is not hard to see that technical skill and moral consciousness have to go together if that goodness is to be seen in each lawyer. This chapter has taken this point a bit further, suggesting that the competent lawyer is in fact someone who is moral in their outlook and behaviour. And in each case, that morality is represented in their consideration of each of the claims of Kantianism, consequentialism and virtue ethics.

In the concluding chapter, the whole of the exploration of our underlying general morality is summarised with an additional purpose – professional strengthening. The profession as a whole has an opportunity to adopt a cultural or regulatory pact, designed to make it possible for all future lawyers to be good and capable of flourishing. That task is worthwhile for several reasons: because it is only fair to you as a new lawyer to support your growth and development; because sustaining you as a moral lawyer means sustaining society; and particularly because the goodness inherent in most of us – and in many lawyers – is worth nurturing in and for itself.

Notes

1. Dal Pont points out that the term 'competency' is defined according to the stance of the observer. See Dal Pont, *Lawyers' Professional Responsibility* (5th edn), para 4.20.
2. Delays caused by others may be a growing phenomenon of our social complexity. If your colleagues and professional opponents must deliver work to you before you can deliver work to your client, delay is something that must be factored into your own schedule of outcomes.
3. Adopted September 2000. See www.ibanet.org/PPID/constituent/professional_ ethics_committee/default.aspx. (The document can be found under 'Resolutions'.)
4. See Dal Pont, n 1, para 5.05.
5. Ibid., paras 5.25–5.140.
6. There are a number of exceptions to the immunity. It does not cover a breach of fiduciary duty, contempt of court or disciplinary proceedings – *Clyne v NSW Bar Association* (1960) 104 CLR 186. The immunity covers solicitor–advocates, [except

198 The Good Lawyer

to the extent of the work they do as solicitors: *Feldman v A Practitioner* (1978) 18 SASR 238] on the basis that it is the function of advocacy that is protected rather than the occupant of the role; the immunity does not cover negligent failure to advise on the existence of a cause of action, because it has no relevant connection with the in-court conduct of counsel: *Saif Ali v Sydney Mitchell & Co*[1980] AC 198.

7. See *Rondel v Worsley* [1969] 1 AC 191, per Lord Reid at 273.
8. (1988) 165 CLR 54, at 557.
9. [2005] HCA 12.
10. *Arthur J.S. Hall & Co. v Simons* [2002] 1 AC 615.
11. *Chamberlains v Lai* [2006] NZSC 70.
12. In European Union countries advocates have no immunity. In the US prosecutors have immunity and in a few states this is extended to public defenders but otherwise lawyers have no immunity. Academic opinion in Australia is divided but may be turning against the immunity. See G. Hampel and J. Clough 'Abolishing the advocate's immunity from suit: Reconsidering *Giannarelli v Wraith*' [2000] 24 *Melbourne University Law Review* 1016–27; P. Gerber, 'Burning down the house to roast the pig: The High Court retains advocates' immunity' (2005) 28 *UNSW L J* 646; but to the contrary M. Groves and M. Derham, 'Should advocates' immunity continue?' (2004) 28 *Melbourne University Law Review* 80.
13. Preliminary work such as drawing pleadings is generally covered by the immunity. See *Feldman v A Practitioner* (1978) 18 SASR 238 at 238–39 per Bray CJ; *Keefe v Marks* (1989) 16 NSWLR 713 at 719 per Gleeson CJ.
14. *Res judicata* – the rule that if a dispute is judged by a court of competent jurisdiction, the judgment is final and conclusive for the parties involved and an absolute bar to further action. See *Butterworths Concise Australian Legal Dictionary*, Butterworths, Sydney, 1997, 345.
15. Issue estoppel – a judicial decision which completely decides an issue of fact or law, so that it cannot be raised again by the same parties. See *Butterworths Concise Australian Legal Dictionary*, Butterworths, Sydney, 1997, 220.
16. *In Re a Practitioner* (1982) 30 SASR 27 per King CJ.
17. *Legal Profession Uniform Law Application Act* 2014 (Vic), Sch 1, s 6.
18. See *Solicitors' Liability Committee v Gray & Winter* (1997) 147 ALR 154.
19. The legislative regulation of trust accounts is contained in state legislation. The examples given here are from the *Uniform Law*. See *Legal Profession Uniform Law Application Act 2014* (Vic), Sch 1, Part 4.2.
20. Controlled money is effectively a deposit of your client's money in your trust account which earns interest for your client, rather than for government purposes. See Appendix B3.
21. A statutory deposit is a periodical, refundable payment you make to the government, which represents a proportion of the balance of your trust account. See Appendix B3.
22. *Legal Profession Uniform Law Application Act* 2014 (Vic), Sch 1, s 154(2).
23. Fortunately, merely 'technical' breaches of trust account requirements involving no dishonesty may be classed only as unsatisfactory conduct. See *Re Mayes* (1974) 1 NSWLR 19; *Law Society of NSW v Foreman* (1991) 24 NSWLR 238.

24. See full transcript, *The Law Report*, ABC Radio National, 16 April 2013, at www.abc. net.au/radionational/programs/lawreport/sa-legal-profession-laws/4629776.

25. *Legal Profession Uniform Law Application Act 2014* (Vic), Sch 1, s 154(2). In Victoria, one penalty unit equals $144.36 at the time of writing. See Office of the Chief Parliamentary Counsel at www.ocpc.vic.gov.au/CA2572B3001B894B/pages/faqs-penalty-and-fee-units.

26. See Parker and Evans, *Inside Lawyers' Ethics*, Ch. 9.

27. David Steel, Judge of the High Court (Queen's Bench Division), 6 March 2012, extract from p. 1 of 'International and National Legal Regulation Counteracting Corruption, Money Laundering and the Financing of Terrorism', interview for the St Petersburg International Legal Forum, May 2012.

28. I thank Stephen Revell, Partner, Freshfields, Bruckhaus Derringer, Singapore, for this example. It is based on a UK case which has been altered to protect the identities of those involved.

29. See Dal Pont, n 1, para 4.30.

30. This list is the Victorian requirement. See www.liv.asn.au/For-Lawyers/Regulation/The-CPD-Scheme.

31. For example, see the Law Institute of Victoria, *Law Institute Continuing Professional Development Rules* 2008, Rule 4.4, at www.liv.asn.au/PDF/Practising/Professional-Standards/Acts/2008CPDRulesLIV.aspx.

32. This scheme is intended to recognise 'an enhanced skill level, as well as substantial involvement in established legal specialty areas. The LIV requires such specialists to demonstrate superior knowledge, experience and proficiency in a particular area of law'. See www.liv.asn.au/Professional-Development/Accredited-Specialisation.

33. In WA, Victoria, New South Wales and Queensland, general purpose *Lawyers Practice Manuals* have gradually developed via the clinical legal education and community legal centre networks. These manuals provide current 'how to' practice information to lawyers who are not general practitioners. See, for example, the *Lawyers Practice Manual* (Vic), which has in excess of 50 chapters and is published by Thomson Reuters, at www.thomsonreuters.com.au/lawyers-practice-manual-victoria-online/productdetail/59464.

34. See, for example, the programs offered by a major insurer, the *Legal Practitioners' Liability Committee* (LPLC) at www.lplc.com.au/about-us/.

Chapter 9

PRACTICAL WISDOM FOR LAWYERS

9.1 Introduction: A far greater authority

Whether you are a secondary student of legal studies, a tertiary student of law or practical legal training or a newly admitted lawyer, your moral sense will still be in development. And if you allow your humanity to dominate, that development will go on indefinitely, enriching your understanding of what it means to be a morally active lawyer. The nature of our humanity has been at the centre of this book's enquiry into ethical choice. Our humanity as law students and then lawyers is the quality that will make us stand out in the legal profession. And our sense of general morality is the way into that humanity. We do not need to be aggressive or verbally violent in our day-to-day legal lives to be financially successful, but we do need knowledge of our moral convictions and the courage to apply them if we want any sort of success to last beyond a few years. The many examples of lawyers who continue to grow and make positive contributions to the community over decades show that this growth is possible.

The approach to learning and applying general morality in this book revisits David Luban's vision for a vital, creative and socially justified legal profession. His injunction to lead a moral life as a lawyer takes us beyond the easier and conventional role morality (though that will always have a place) and into a dimension of far greater authority. The idea that a general moral sense ought to guide us through difficult ethical challenges places us at the centre of all major social movements – those that address equality

9 Practical wisdom for lawyers   **201**

and sustainability of human access to health, food and education. If we can grasp our wider social role we are not just sustaining our clients' interests (for they also depend on stable social systems) but we are doing justice in the most profound way.

Our sense of general morality is self-evidently not just a matter of nature *per se*, but something we create for ourselves.[1] Looking back over the last 70 years, the postwar reactions to Nazism and the whole of the Holocaust experience have been hopeful. The UN Charter and all that has flowed from it in global human rights awareness points to a gradual but definite continuing evolution of morality in our consciousness. The fact that there are still constant smaller wars does not mean that aggression and immorality are norms, but that the effort to entrench greater morality is a never-ending effort, one in which lawyers can be highly influential.

As agents for justice, our functions go much further and will need to go much further. Access to justice is disappearing, or has disappeared, unless you are rich or very poor. The equality – or inequality – of the financial resources of the parties to a dispute has never been more important, as it is now perhaps the only real factor in the fairness of the contest. This is why the possibility of mandatory *pro bono* work raises its head repeatedly, even though the effects of such compulsion are likely to be morally adverse.[2] And the hand of corruption, bribery and money laundering is becoming more prominent, seducing even relatively small law firms as underlying morality becomes more problematic – and even contributes to global poverty.[3] A global survey by the International Bar Association in 2010 found that half of all lawyers who responded felt that lawyers' corruption was an issue in their jurisdiction.[4]

There are also technical challenges for lawyers that will impact on ethics. Some predict, though are not yet taken seriously, that so-called singularity technologies will progressively merge human and machine intelligences.[5] And these may be evident first in knowledge processing and will therefore affect litigation, with potential for such merged intelligences to minimise moral accountability. How much of this comes to pass is unknown, but there is unlikely to be any lessening in the need for a moral sense from professional leaders and practitioners as our societies progress and degrade in varying degree.

Arguably, as lawyers our sense of general morality ought to increasingly compel us to the conclusion that we cannot afford to retreat into role morality as our default position. Our final social utility (and the reason for any privileges we retain) lies in our willingness to help the whole of the community access justice: that is, to ensure equality of access to health, food and education. This may be a more urgent conclusion than 30 years ago, when Luban and his co-authors made their stand. The challenges are far clearer in this century than they were in 1983. The global survival stakes are rising. Likely 3–4°C global average temperature increases in the next 80 years, far more people, less food, more displaced persons and fewer jobs for our children and fewer still for any grandchildren, are all predictable. Already, we face social pressure to evade our anxiety and emotionally insulate ourselves from these trends, making a general moral sense less accessible. Such pressure will rise steadily in broadcast media that are invested in an economic growth model, as opposed to a sustainable society model. Some still hope that technological developments – for example, through computing, solar cells, genetic engineering and emissions trading – will provide enough of an answer. But these 'fixes' look increasingly less adequate to offset the many other far deeper indicators of global stress.

So what role is there for general morality? While we cannot be certain, we can predict that social decline is more likely, not less likely, if we reduce our efforts to develop general morality: in particular, our virtues of *benevolence*, *justice* and *compassion*. These are the virtues that strengthen the rule of law and reduce poverty, increasing the willingness of peoples everywhere to make an effort to pull together, even in the smallest of ways. Similar energy and *diligence* is needed to maintain our sense of *integrity* and *honesty*, rather than tolerate fraud, corruption and tax evasion disguised as avoidance. All of these lapses in virtue reduce the state revenue needed to provide the health, food and education that may just be enough to help us come through the next 80 years. Faced with what we know is ahead, general morality, and particularly the goodness of virtue ethics, is not an abstract or academic luxury for us as lawyers, but a crucial resource if there is to be any chance of succeeding in these major struggles for our species and for all the other species upon which we closely depend.

The concluding challenge is to assess the potential of the statutory regulatory environment to encourage a general moral consciousness in lawyers and to raise the possibility of a whole-of-sector consensus that might confine role morality to its proper context, while broadening the appeal of truly contextual ethical thinking.

9.2 Strengthening the general morality of legal profession discipline structures

There is a reasonable expectation that Australian parliaments and the organised profession will provide some leadership in relation to the values and behaviours we display in legal practice. If such leadership could be identified, the capacity of the profession as a whole to review its ethical approach could be considerable. Certainly, that leadership has been offered elsewhere and confidently asserts general moral priorities over dominant role morality. For example, 'the "Preface" to the Canadian Bar Association's Code of Professional Conduct provides that its "primary concern" is "the protection of the public interest"'.[6] Farrow observes that according to:

> The New York Lawyer's Code of Professional Responsibility of the New York State Bar Association (NYSBA), a lawyer 'should be temperate and dignified, and refrain from all illegal and morally reprehensible conduct'. As well, the Basic Rules on the Duties of Practicing Attorneys (Basic Rules) of the Japan Federation of Bar Associations (JFBA) provide that the 'mission of an attorney is to protect fundamental human rights and realize social justice'.[7]

And:

> [i]n the United States, the ABA acknowledges that its Model Rules 'do not . . . exhaust the moral and ethical considerations that should inform a lawyer, for no worthwhile human activity can be completely defined by legal rules'. Similarly, in Japan, even when a lawyer 'endeavor[s] to realize his or her client's legitimate interest,' that lawyer 'shall follow the dictates of his or her conscience'.[8]

In Australia, however, there is very little direct reference to general morality in either legislation, conduct rules or in the pronouncements of the Law Council of Australia. The Uniform Law suggests only what *may* be included in conduct rules and refers to the duty to uphold the duty to the courts and the administration of justice.[9] To that end, independence, confidentiality and conflicts of interest are mentioned, but there is virtually nothing of the general moral awareness that foreign lawyers see as important in their own codes.

This categorical, formulaic approach is replicated in the *Australian Solicitors' Conduct Rules* (ASCR), which echoes the Uniform Law pronouncement that the fundamental duty of a lawyer is to the court and to the administration of justice.[10] Similar sentiments appear in the Australian Bar Association's *Barristers' Conduct Rules*.[11] Competence, dignity, honesty and integrity are cited as other 'duties',[12] but there are no references to the dictates of conscience or the claims of wider public interest. It is not surprising, therefore, that it is only in the language used by courts to describe their obligation to supervise lawyers that we see a wider and deeper social consciousness.

In earlier chapters there has been some discussion of how regulation can encourage ethical infrastructure, and how appropriate cultures in law firms and in-house legal practice could develop according to general morality. These encouragements parallel the long-standing and inherent jurisdiction of the courts to control the behaviour of lawyers according to general morality, commonly expressed as 'what a fair-minded, reasonably informed member of the public would conclude'.[13] These supervisory mechanisms are important, but have not had the same day-to-day impact as the formal processes for licensing and discipline exercised by legal profession regulators.

In all jurisdictions[14] there are bodies which license lawyers on an annual basis (typically, legal services boards), investigate and prosecute lawyers for misconduct or unsatisfactory conduct (increasingly, legal services commissioners) and state and territory professional associations (law societies and one law institute[15]) which, in addition to representing their members in a quasi-trade association capacity, either prosecute those same members for misconduct or operate as the delegates of either board or commissioner for purposes of complaint investigation and related regulation. These so-called dual roles have long been questioned on general moral grounds. The most recent example of what can be described as a structural conflict of interest came from South Australia in the aftermath of the *McGee* case.[16] It is likely that an inter-jurisdictional uniform legal services commissioner and legal services council will be operating and covering only New South Wales and Victoria in the near future. But the general structure of the Australian regulatory environment is still fairly consistent across the states and territories (see Diagram 9.1).

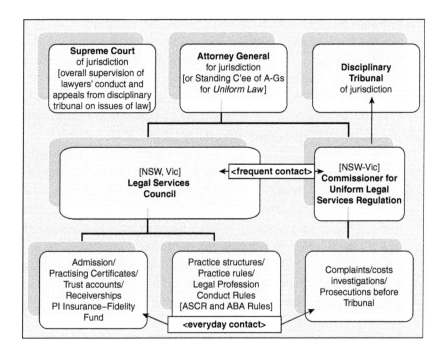

Diagram 9.1 Framework of Australian lawyers' regulation

In each jurisdiction, there has been some discussion of the bodies that govern all aspects of the profession. Although the so-called uniform model for legal regulation applies initially to the two jurisdictions mentioned above, the governance framework that has been established for them is likely, over time, to influence – if not be used in – other jurisdictions as well. The provisions of the 'national model' are therefore deserving of brief comment. Importantly, the Supreme Court in each jurisdiction maintains overall supervisory authority over lawyers' conduct, and that authority continues under the uniform model.[17] In this respect, each court's powerful insistence of the virtues that underlie the 'fit and proper person' test for admission[18] will continue to be evident in their judgments.

Membership of the Uniform Law Legal Services Council has been intensely debated for several years. The outcome is that of the five members, the effective majority will consist of lawyers.[19] At least one and perhaps more of the positions (which must be chosen from among people with backgrounds in legal practice, consumer protection, regulation of the profession and financial affairs) will undoubtedly be filled by a person with a legal background, even if that person is not currently practising as a lawyer. The chair of the Council (who is one of the five) is appointed by the Attorney General of the host jurisdiction, and that appointment must be with the concurrence of the presidents of the Law Council of Australia and the Australian Bar Association. Accordingly, there is no possibility that non-lawyers will be able to have any significant impact on the governance of the profession, though there is an opportunity for client and consumer interests to be heard through the single member who may, but not must, be appointed as one of the general representatives on the Council. The structure of Council membership is therefore an exercise in consequentialism, with the various law societies, and in particular the Law Council of Australia, calculating that they can cope with a nominal non-lawyer presence on the Council, including a person with consumer credentials, because the person in that position can be managed and if necessary limited by the overall lawyer majority.

If a Uniform Law Legal Services Council will therefore be politicised, the key to strengthening the general morality of the profession will depend on the role and character of the Commissioner for Uniform Legal Services Regulation. The key function of the Commissioner – who is appointed by the NSW Attorney General – is to investigate client complaints and lawyers' conduct. They will be responsible for ensuring, as far as possible, consistency in all prosecutions before disciplinary tribunals. This Commissioner is to be 'independent' of the Council,[20] but subject to the authority of the Council to 'monitor and review the exercise of the functions of the Commissioner'.[21] The vital moral function and *loyalty* of the Commissioner is, however, not to the profession, but to the administration of justice and the *integrity* of the profession in the eyes of the public. These higher virtues will occasionally call upon the Commissioner's courage and determination, to ensure that prosecutions or administrative action proceed against powerful lawyers.[22] This function will only rarely be needed, but it will be the litmus test of their actual independence. And the role may be more difficult than in the past because a national Commissioner will ordinarily delegate prosecution authority to a local Commissioner in the relevant jurisdiction. Ideally, the national Commissioner will be effective in leading other Commissioners on such decisions rather than directing them, while publicly defending their position and rejecting any verbal suggestions from Council members that they reconsider or retreat. But will a national Commissioner have the necessary courage, given the statutory right of the Council to 'monitor and review' their functions?

In the above structure, consequentialism limits the Commissioner's exercise of their virtues. In practice, the extent of the Commissioner's independence will depend on the quality of their personal relationships with all other Commissioners and Council members, particularly the chair. If the Commissioner is personable, knowledgeable, diligent and displays backbone when needed, these virtues will play the most significant role in any overall strengthening of general morality in the profession.

9.3 Practical wisdom in regulation

If there is a social case for general morality dominating role morality, then it will need to begin early, in law school, and be carried on through all phases of a lawyer's professional development. Collectively, an achievable set of strategies is needed to 'make' you a good lawyer and then help you show practical wisdom. If good lawyers are to develop and retain 'goodness', they need not only a wider understanding of goodness through law school ethics curricula, law-in-context discourse and clinical methodology; they also need practical processes that directly confront the debilitating issues faced by too many new lawyers – narrowing networks, strained personal relationships, anxiety caused by long hours and overbearing billing budgets, fewer 'raw' experiences of others' suffering and a lesser incentive to be morally accountable. These processes must include the opportunity, if not the obligation, during law school to provide *pro bono* services, practical legal training (PLT) that does not reduce morality to rules, continuing professional development (CPD) that explores the depth of general morality by identifying and assessing lawyers' individual ethical preferences and some sort of law society-moderated ethical networking mechanism.

These mechanisms can only be educationally founded, but in a sense they must also be sustained by what amounts to a regulatory 'pact' between the legal educators, non-government organisations, courts and legal services boards of each jurisdiction. There is not much doubt that we do need to find a way to effectively 'vaccinate' law students and lawyers against depression and apathy, and to develop the antibodies of better ethical awareness. By revisiting general morality as Luban's framework of choice, our own capacity for a better life is enriched. Our clients' lives likewise.

The consensus for such a pact is not yet present, but its principles are implied in several stakeholder pronouncements, particularly from the courts, depression foundations and the occasional law society president, even if others, such as the Law Council's Large Law Firms Group, will be more sceptical. If it is accepted by law schools and the profession that new lawyers' accumulating emotional and moral decline is leading to early and numerous departures from practice, then a political consensus is possible. Leadership from a national Legal Services Commissioner and Legal Services Council chair might be enough to forge the necessary consensus. They might bring together a whole-of-sector continuum: those with responsibility for secondary legal studies courses, career guidance, law schools' curricula, pre-admission character assessment, law society membership, CPD renewal, *pro bono* programs, annual licensing and mental health, as well as prosecution and post-disciplinary remediation.

The question is: what reason or inducement would any of the law schools, PLT providers or the profession have to collaborate so closely? Since the major drivers of all three are now market position and competition, why would an appeal to general morality – and especially virtue ethics – mean much to them? Because the NGOs, courts and any uniform legal regulatory structure have non-market drivers, and their influence is continuing to grow as more and more lawyers suffer and leave. These stakeholders may see more clearly the links between strengthening general morality and better reputational strengthening, better long-term sustainability and hence profitability, better life–work balance and better support for the priority of the rule of law over the market. In law's post-religious public culture, renewed general morality, and particularly virtue, may be the strongest framework to fill the gap and provide meaningful work for those new lawyers whose commercial existence exposes them to too much regret, too little life and not enough justice. General morality may be the 'social capital' which will ensure that lawyering and the legal profession retains social and economic value and does not disappear in favour of a host of other legal service providers like accountants and artificial intelligence software.

The supportive task of the book in this very wide agenda has therefore first been to offer a method for you as a law student or lawyer to understand general morality and differentiate the duty-based approaches from virtue ethics, recognising that in this differentiation, the contribution of each to sharper thinking about ethics is more accessible. Other taxonomies, such as positive psychology and Parker's four legal ethical types, play their role here also. Similarly, in each of the main chapters, a coherent – and attractive, I hope – explanation is proposed for seeing all ethics topics in terms of general morality and not just role morality. This wider framework goes back to the fundamentals of the human condition and empowers a primary motivation to be a good lawyer: a lawyer who stays engaged with practice, seeks justice and does not slowly retreat in exhaustion or disillusion.

9.4 Conclusion: Maintaining physical and moral resilience inside legal workplaces

There are many challenging work practices inside legal practice and most of them have been alluded to earlier. The long hours of work and the pressure to meet monthly budgets are the obvious stressors, even when your own time management is effective. More subtle are the ethical challenges that have prompted this book, particularly the psychological processes that can dull ethical sensitivity and encourage a wrongful obedience to supervisors' authority. These phenomena can be quite strong inside large law firms and in-house legal practice, where external agencies do not know what is happening and clients prefer to resolve disagreements in private. Lawyers who are unhappy generally think they only have one route: a complete exit from the profession. But the other more hopeful options canvassed above are not fanciful, and if it is impractical for you to assist change in one workplace, then there are others.

There is no need to leave legal practice entirely. If you have developed a sense of self-care, you will be OK about changing employers and preferring those with better workplace practices and better ethics. You will be part of a wider movement among young and new lawyers that is slowly shifting the goal posts. You may in fact be among those who will lead the future profession in reclaiming and strengthening its core functions – not just in the rule of law, but also in the morality of justice. In moving to a better firm – be it a mid-tier, a regional or rural practice or a small niche practice,

210 The Good Lawyer

or even one of the (fewer) good, large practices – your actions will contribute to a strengthened professionalism.

There are many second and mid-tier managing partners who want to build personal and organisational resilience through mindfulness programs for employee lawyers and partners, who want to develop their ethical infrastructure at the organisational level and who are prepared to critically examine the processes of unethical rationalisation. Choose these firms, using the questions in Chapter 2. These firms are not just doing what they are doing to prepare for new regulatory scrutiny; they are doing it because they want to deal creatively with growing consumer demands on their firms, especially for costs' disclosure and accountability, and they want to retain well-balanced, emotionally sensitive lawyers who know their ethical priorities and will build up desirable clientele.

Some partners will particularly value women lawyers. One former managing partner of a large firm puts it this way:

> For more than 20 years, a majority of Australian law graduates have been women. Although there is not a shortage of lawyers in Australia, there is and always will be a shortage of good lawyers with high-level skills and common sense who can work efficiently to meet the ever-increasing demands of clients. Again, a majority of these high-quality lawyers are women ... To retain them, firms must provide flexible working hours, maximise the use of work-at-home technology, and provide real partnership opportunities, not just the window dressing of 'possible partnership'.[23]

The majority of law students today are women, but at the moment many do not stay for long in legal practice. This testifies to the overall distance yet to be travelled in many areas, but particularly work–life balance, for both women and men. However, supportive workplaces such as those specified above do exist already.

As is clear from this book, our economy does not need more lawyers, but better lawyers. Better lawyers will find better legal employers by persistently saying what it is they need in order to stay. This is not primarily an enormous salary, which will disappear entirely in our periodic economic downturns in any case. It is primarily an exciting, compassionate and justice-focused workplace, where your character development, judgment and resilience are prioritised and ethical awareness is valued as a business strategy.

9 Practical wisdom for lawyers 211

To assist that purpose, Appendix A contains an ethics awareness scale that allows you (if you are reading this book as a practising lawyer) to assess your personal ethical preferences according to Parker's four-part typology, referred to earlier.[24] This scale has been empirically developed for the Australian legal practice environment[25] and will help you position yourself in relation to many of the concepts discussed in this book.

Notes

1. Henrietta Moore reviews the sources in 'How wisdom is learned', *Australian Financial Review, Review*, 9 April 2010, 2. Very little is hardwired into the brain when it comes to social interaction: far more is due to our intensive socialising experiences – our social constructs – than we assume.
2. See John Corker and Michael Legg, 'Take care in pushing student pro bono', *The Australian*, 26 April 2013, 26.
3. See Adrian Evans, 'Connections between the ethics of combating money laundering and reduction in global poverty', in *Poverty, Justice and the Rule of Law: The Report of the IBA Presidential Task Force on the Global Financial Crisis*, International Bar Association, London, 2013.
4. See Anti-Corruption Strategy for the Legal Profession, 'Survey: Risks and threats of corruption and the legal profession', International Bar Association, OECD, UN Office on Drugs and Crime, 6, at www.anticorruptionstrategy.org.
5. See, generally, Amnon Eden, James Moor, Johnny Søraker and Eric Steinhart (eds), *Singularity Hypotheses: A scientific and philosophical assessment*, Springer, Berlin, 2012.
6. Farrow, 'Sustainable professionalism', 74, referring to the CBA *Code of Professional Conduct, Preface*, ix, at www.cba.org/CBA/activities/pdf/codeofconduct.pdf.
7. Ibid., 74.
8. Ibid., 76.
9. *Legal Profession Uniform Law Application Act 2014* (Vic), Sch 1, s 423.
10. ASCR 3.1.
11. See www.nswbar.asn.au/circulars/2010/feb/rules.pdf.
12. ASCR 4.1.2–4.1.4.
13. See, for example, the comments of Hollingworth J in *Dale v Clayton Utz (No. 2)* [2013] VSC 54, para 160.
14. See Parker and Evans, *Inside Lawyers' Ethics*, and Dal Pont, *Lawyers' Professional Responsibility* (5th edn), Part 6, for the current regulatory structure in each state and territory.
15. The Law Institute of Victoria.
16. See Ch. 6.5.
17. *Legal Profession Uniform Law Application Act 2014* (Vic), Sch 1, s 264.
18. See Ch. 2.
19. *Legal Profession Uniform Law Application Act 2014* (Vic), Sch 1, s 15.

The Good Lawyer

20. *Legal Profession Uniform Law Application Act 2014* (Vic), Sch 1, s 401.
21. *Legal Profession Uniform Law Application Act 2014* (Vic), Sch 1, s 396(b).
22. Repetition of a *McGee*-like situation will damage public confidence in the profession profoundly. See Ch. 6.5.
23. Ian Robertson, 'Law firms will need to offer much more than legal advice', *The Australian, Legal Affairs*, 3 February 2012, 34. Robertson was then Managing Partner of Holding Redlich, a national law firm.
24. See Ch. 1.
25. The scale is an adaptation of that appearing in Adrian Evans and Helen Forgasz, 'Framing lawyers' choices: Factor analysis of a psychological scale to self-assess lawyers' ethical preferences' (2013) 16(1) *Legal Ethics* 134 and Parker and Evans, n 14, Appendix.

APPENDIX A[1]

Self-assessment of legal ethical preferences [Part 1]

Instructions

1. Consider each statement carefully and decide whether you agree with it, or not. The reliability of this instrument depends on your candour and willingness to be thorough in your response to each statement.
2. Please indicate your degree of support for each statement by inserting an 'x' in the appropriate column to the right of that statement.

Statement	Strongly disagree	Disagree	Slightly disagree	Slightly agree	Agree	Strongly agree
If I heard a lie uttered by my client or my witness in court, I would correct the deception as soon as possible.						
Public interest lawyering is very attractive to me.						
I prefer dialogue, mediation and a careful focus on principled negotiation in resolving disputes for my clients.						
Achieving what my client wants has to be my main priority.						
I might do more than just refuse to act if my client insisted on an illegal course of action.						
The context and circumstances of an individual's suffering are more important than universal legal principles.						

213

214 Appendix A

Statement	Strongly disagree	Disagree	Slightly disagree	Slightly agree	Agree	Strongly agree
Sometimes it's necessary to think less about your client's personal circumstances and more about what their case could do to improve justice.						
I put my client's interests first regardless of who the client is or what area of law is involved.						
I would much rather take a collaborative or restorative approach to problem solving than a combative stance.						
My aim is to do all for my client that my client would do for themselves, if they had my knowledge and experience.						
I find I can actually do a better job for my clients by helping them navigate beyond 'pure' legal advice and into the realm of policy and purpose behind legislation.						
My clients' enterprises ultimately depend upon their acceptance of the purpose and not just the letter of the law.						
I prefer to think of law reform and better access to justice as my chief interests.						
Saying 'no' to clients is sometimes necessary in order to preserve the system on which (even though they might not care either way) their own welfare ultimately depends.						
I find it hard to practise within 'the rules' when my clients demand something else.						
Clients need to know that I am not in their pocket.						
Social reform and the careful redistribution of wealth through the law are more important than my personal contentment.						

Appendix A   **215**

Statement	Strongly disagree	Disagree	Slightly disagree	Slightly agree	Agree	Strongly agree
Apology, reconciliation and the acceptance of moral responsibility are more important than the 'just' and rigorous enforcement of legal rights.						
Concerns for justice and service are all very well, but if 'push comes to shove', what my client wants has to come first.						
Totals						

Now . . .

3. Change each 'x' in each column to a number, as follows: Strongly disagree [1], Disagree [2], Slightly disagree [3], Slightly agree [4], Agree [5] and Strongly agree [6].
4. Transpose each number to the same statement on the following 'Scale to self-assess legal ethical preference' and total the scores for each ethical type.
5. The higher the score for each type, the more important that ethical preference is to you.

Scale to self-assess legal ethical preference [Part 2]

These statements are expressed in an abstract form to assist comparability. Please keep in mind that how we consider abstractions and how we actually act on them are two different things.

It is very unlikely that a single, overwhelming preference will emerge. Rather, your individual understanding of the relative strength of different preferences is useful for your future decision making.

To maximise the benefit of self-assessment, it is useful if you debrief your results and converse as to your reactions, scepticisms and learning with others who undertake the same self-assessment. This conversation is the key to any greater insights and hence awareness of preferred ethical approach.

Moral activism	*Values*
I prefer to think of law reform and better access to justice as my chief interests.	
Sometimes it's necessary to think less about your client's personal circumstances and more about what their case could do to improve justice.	
I find I can actually do a better job for my clients by helping them navigate beyond 'pure' legal advice and into the realm of policy and purpose behind legislation.	
Public interest lawyering is very attractive to me.	

216 Appendix A

Social reform and the careful redistribution of wealth through the law are more important than my personal contentment.	
Total	

Zealous advocacy

Concerns for justice and service are all very well but if 'push comes to shove', what my client wants has to come first.	
Achieving what my client wants has to be my main priority.	
I find it hard to practice within 'the rules' when my clients demand something else.	
I put my client's interests first regardless of who the client is or what area of law is involved.	
My aim is to do all for my client that my client would do for themselves if they had my knowledge and experience.	
Total	

Responsible lawyering

If I heard a lie uttered by my client or my witness in court I would correct the deception as soon as possible.	
My clients' enterprises ultimately depend upon their acceptance of the purpose and not just the letter of the law.	
I might do more than just refuse to act if my client insisted on an illegal course of action.	
Clients need to know that I am not in their pocket.	
Saying 'no' to clients is sometimes necessary in order to preserve the system on which (even though they might not care either way) their own welfare ultimately depends.	
Total	

***Relationship of care*[2]**

I prefer dialogue, mediation and a careful focus on principled negotiation in resolving disputes for my clients.	
Apology, reconciliation and the acceptance of moral responsibility are more important than the 'just' and rigorous enforcement of legal rights.	
The context and circumstances of an individual's suffering are more important than universal legal principles.	
I would much rather take a collaborative or restorative approach to problem solving than a combative stance.	
Total	

Notes

1. ©Adrian Evans, Monash University, 2012.
2. As only four items were statistically significant for the Relationship of care (instead of the usual five), please add 25% to your total score for this preference, so that the result is comparable to that recorded for the other preferences.

APPENDIX B

Safety nets for lawyers

There are two principal[1] mechanisms designed to limit your own liability when a mistake is made. One of these – mandatory professional indemnity (PI) insurance – comes close to passing the test of moral legitimacy, but the other – the so-called professional standards scheme – is less satisfactory.

B1 Professional Indemnity Insurance – the 'back-up' for practitioner negligence

All lawyers must have PI insurance with an approved PI insurer.[2] There are three major PI insurers in Australia, one for each of Victoria, New South Wales and Queensland. Each of these insurers operates a monopoly in their own state and each tries to compete with the others in attracting the business of the national firms wherever they can. The home-state monopolies are important and morally praiseworthy in both consequentialist and Kantian terms because they ensure small, higher risk legal practices can get basic indemnity cover. The greater good of all lawyers is ensured by extending cover to the few who are small and have a lesser capacity to stay up to date and a greater risk of losing focus in the pressure to take on more clients than may be wise. And all clients are treated fairly no matter who their lawyer may be. Without that mandatory cover, those lawyers could not practise at all, since fully commercial insurers might not wish to ensure them at any price.

Most claims on PI insurance deal with negligence, where the negligent work is done in the course of legal practice and does not involve fraud or dishonesty, but PI policies are fairly expensive. Typical premiums for 2012–13 are in the region of $6400 per annum for a lawyer who owns their practice and $1600 for an employee lawyer.[3] Like car insurance, there are incentives for minimising your risk (and penalties for failing to do so). Accordingly, per claim excesses (or deductibles) are several thousand dollars per law firm partner. So-called deterrent deductibles apply if you have claimed previously, and can approach six figure amounts in some cases.

PI insurers are extremely conservative by nature and use these financial inducements to reinforce their risk management, but their conservatism is underpinned by clear moral priorities. Mandatory PI insurance is virtuous, fair and consequentialist in its operation, with a refreshingly direct ownership of these qualities. One of the major PI insurers makes this statement on its website: 'The values maintained by the LPLC are Equity and fairness; Transparency; Probity; Stability; Predictability, Strength and Prudence.'[4]

218

Appendix B **219**

B2 Professional standards schemes

In contrast to PI insurance, professional standards schemes are not primarily intended to benefit the wider public. Rather, their focus is on limiting compensation that may be paid to certain types of clients who suffer as a result of lawyers' negligence. All jurisdictions now have these schemes in place. In exchange for the implementation of the risk management strategies enumerated above, a professional group can apply to government to have the civil liability of its members capped at certain levels. Lawyers have successfully applied to implement a professional standards scheme in several Australian jurisdictions.[5] Damages for civil claims against lawyers now attract caps, unless the claim relates to a personal injury, breach of trust, fraud or dishonesty. The caps operate providing there is a PI policy in place, and limit damages to the amount covered by the policy.

Professional standards schemes have not met with any opposition because they wisely stay away from limiting damages that may be payable to individuals for injury or for the most obvious types of immoral behaviour. To that extent, they exhibit justice to the most common class of victims of our negligence while preserving the possibility of justice for all victims when losses are caused by immoral (and often criminal) behaviour. However, there is a pseudo-consequentialist train of thought in their more fundamental purpose of limiting other types of liability. The caps are intended to apply when lawyers advise businesses inappropriately and the extent of the business loss is beyond the limit of the PI insurance cover. By stopping claims that would go too far beyond the limits of any PI cover, the caps mean that fewer court cases occur. It could almost be said that these schemes are designed to ensure that professional sectors and business groups do not engage in unseemly public arguments.

For example, a lawyer who is a successful corporate tax adviser may make a significant and obvious mistake in calculating a tax provision for a large mining company. When discovered, the effect of that mistake is to cause a drop in the company's share price and the suspension of a proposed public share offering. That event raises the company's cost of borrowing by a quantifiable multimillion dollar amount. But for the professional standards scheme and its associated PI cover, the amount of that loss, which could be well above the PI insurance limit, may be payable by the tax adviser personally (assuming the normal principles of tort liability could be established). The professional standards scheme means that in many of these situations it will be rare for the lawyer's negligence or the mining company's financial problems to be examined in open court. This legislated corporate privacy raises many questions of general morality. Does the greater good lie in the containment of professionals' losses, the avoidance of expensive court processes and the privacy of wealthy parties? Or is the greatest good for the greatest number more closely connected to the public interest in the transparency of corporate mistakes and the greater public accountability that comes from that, especially when ordinary shareholders' interests are affected?

The answer to these questions may be affected, in part, by the recognition that professional standards schemes are limited to negligence – a fact of life which all lawyers experience at some point and for which moral blame is unjustified and unnecessary. But the same cannot be said of the exclusions from professional standards capping: breach of trust, fraud or dishonesty. Lawyers who fail in these areas are often morally culpable, but that is of little consolation to their victims, because not only is there no conventional

220 Appendix B

insurance cover, but the lawyers themselves are often insolvent by the time any fraud is discovered. South Australian firm Magarey Farlam (Chapter 8) was in this situation. In these cases, the final safety net of fidelity (or client) compensation is supposed to come to the rescue and save clients, but the question is: which clients? And at whose cost?

B3 Fidelity compensation

Fidelity compensation schemes operate in all jurisdictions and with similar features. They are intended to compensate clients when the money they have deposited in their lawyer's trust account is stolen by their lawyer or by someone inside their lawyer's firm. Fidelity compensation is important to our collective responsibility to our clients, but the ethics of its actual operation is not always obvious. Clients are not commonly aware that fidelity schemes exist. If they were, they might question why there is a need for them; and the answer might not encourage trust. In fact, the suggestion that lawyers will steal from their clients is quite confronting. Most of us will never be tempted, but some of us succumb. The vulnerable lawyers are a fairly clearly defined group. Virtually all the claims involve sole practitioners or small firms. The typical profile is a male, aged 25–45, but some notable cases have involved women.[6] Most (if not all) thieves are caught, and when caught, the most common period of imprisonment (depending on the amount stolen and the character of the defendant) has been 4–6 years.

Client compensation funds are state-based and initially they had three sources of income – annual contributions or levies paid by solicitors, financial penalties and interest on fund investments. During the recession of the early 1960s it became obvious that more money was needed. That period saw the first post-World War II economic slump, and as the economy turned downwards, more lawyers turned to their trust accounts for 'help'. Annual levies were no longer enough to keep up with the claims. So it was decided to ask the banks which held all these trust accounts to pay the interest on trust balances to the client compensation fund in each state and territory. Until that point, that interest had simply been kept by the banks. Quite soon it became obvious that the interest earned on these trust balances was huge – far more than was necessary (in good economic years) to compensate clients for theft. From that point on, fidelity compensation became part of a much larger and more complex problem of public finance ethics. Diagram B1 shows the current structure, with several sources of income and several destinations for often large accumulated balances.

Initially, the interest earned on balances in trust accounts was simply appropriated (and described as 'statutory deposits') because it was not feasible to calculate how much money was earned on each individual client deposit in each trust account. Computers were too primitive in the 1960s. Nowadays the task of allocating individual amounts of interest to individual clients' accounts is easy – so clients can receive the interest on their own deposits if they know to ask for it through the mechanism of a controlled account[7] – but neither the Law Council of Australia nor any government is willing to change the scheme so that clients receive what is, in Kantian terms, their own property. As Diagram B1 indicates, too many other people want clients' money.

At the global level, many law societies and governments agree that client compensation schemes are essential if the overall reputations of legal professionals are to be protected. It would be completely unacceptable if clients' trust, having been shattered by

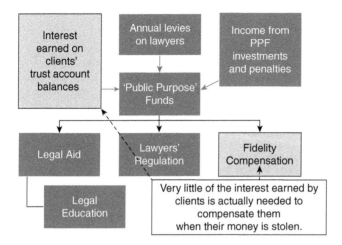

Diagram B1 Funding the fidelity compensation system

their lawyer, were then also ignored by the profession as a whole and their stolen money were gone for good. An extension of that beneficial attitude explains, in part, why it is also common for professions to acquiesce in and even promote the use of interest earned on clients' funds to contribute to legal aid.[8] But this usage still begs the Kantian question: whose interest is it? In the US and the UK it is accepted that all interest must be paid to clients when it can be identified.[9] Only South Africa and Australia use clients' interest to pay for lawyers' regulation and contribute to their continuing professional development.[10]

The conundrum of clients' trust account interest gives rise to some essential choices for lawyers, according to general morality. Table B1 examines these choices.

Table B1 The funding of legal aid when governments are uninterested – should we keep clients in the dark?

Nationally, interest income from lawyers' trust accounts can total over $100 million per annum when the economy is strong.[11] So all interested parties agree that there is a lot at stake when its uses are being considered. The basis for transferring interest to other purposes was consequentially pragmatic: that the amount of the interest in each individual case was often too small to calculate and that even if it could be calculated, the cost of the calculation and allocation process (prior to digital computing) was too high compared to the amount of that interest in each case.

However, the impact of digital computing has been profound. Trust interest is now allocated automatically to clients in Scotland, for example.[12] Modern computing has succeeded in lowering the cost of collection and crediting interest to a client's account, where that task may not have been economical previously.

The siphoning of interest by governments from solicitors' general trust accounts continues, with the consent of the legal profession. Unfortunately, the status quo depends upon clients' ongoing ignorance that they can insist upon receiving their interest if they wish, through a controlled money account.

222 Appendix B

Table B1 (cont.)

Virtue ethics

Lawyers' fiduciary obligations to clients are grounded in the virtues of respect, fidelity and honesty. Collectively, these virtues encourage trust, upon which the lawyer–client relationship depends. The silence of the legal profession on the issue of a conduct rule requiring some disclosure may therefore indicate some lack of virtue when it comes to these funds.

Consequentialism

Consequentialists assert clearly and confidently that the use of clients' interest is completely appropriate. They point to the use of clients' money for legal aid to impoverished clients as justified by that greater good, outweighing any smaller losses to the larger number of clients who can afford to use private lawyers.

This perspective may be compelling if it is applied only to funding legal aid and not to the use of clients' interest to pay for the cost of regulating lawyers (admitting, licensing and disciplining) and contributing to the cost of their continuing professional development (CPD). These administrative expenses are necessary, but their transfer to clients on consequentialist grounds depends on a more tenuous calculation that lawyers' silence about the source of the interest is justified by the need of those same clients to benefit from better admission, licensing and disciplinary processes: that is, from better ethics. These greater goods are self-serving and stretch the proper use of consequentialism too far.

Kantian ethics

The use of the interest on clients' accounts is a good illustration of the difference between 'ethics' and 'rules'. Supporters of clients' right to the interest assert the Kantian perspective that if clients are going to contribute to things like legal aid and lawyers' ongoing professional development and even the investigation of complaints against lawyers, then they ought first to be consulted. As mentioned earlier, trust money can be held separately for an individual client, and when that occurs it is called 'controlled money', because it earns interest for that client.

Kantianism encourages us to raise the issue of a controlled account with all clients and even to install software that automatically creates such accounts for all our clients. However, there is no professional conduct rule requiring us to advise a new client that they can earn interest on their 'controlled' funds if they wish. Such a rule is justified by Kantian ethics.

Applicable law and conduct rules

The law of fiduciary obligations (see Chapter 7) requires lawyers, as fiduciaries, to account to their clients for the use of their money. Such an accounting must include, in each case, an enquiry by each lawyer as to whether their client can earn interest on their trust balance, having regard to current technology and global best practice. Failure to take this step would, in an appropriate case, support an application to the court by a client for a declaration as to whether their fiduciary interests have been so prejudiced.

The Uniform Law framework appropriates interest on lawyers' general trust accounts to the purposes identified above. There is no question about the legality of those appropriations even if the underlying moral legitimacy is questionable. However, the Uniform Law endorses the concept of controlled money and in no way interferes with the right of a lawyer to ensure that any or all of their clients receive interest on their trust balances.

Conclusion as to appropriation of clients' interest

Government support for adequate legal aid is now so tenuous that at least one aspect of the consequentialist view is powerful. Compared to many private clients, legally aided clients are close to impoverishment and their interests ought to be uppermost in the minds of lawyers.

The adoption of software that creates controlled accounts for all clients would reduce the funds available for legal aid. However, lawyers' denial of their fiduciary accountability to their own clients is also fundamentally unfair. A virtuous lawyer may decide that they will raise the possibility of creating a controlled account with all their clients but in each case, also determine whether to encourage that client to forego their interest, to the general benefit of legal aid. A virtuous lawyer is unlikely to support the appropriation of clients' interest for any purposes other than fidelity compensation and legal aid.

Appendix B   **223**

Notes

1. A law firm which incorporates itself under the federal *Corporations Act 2001* and becomes an incorporated legal practice (ILP) protects its shareholder lawyer members' personal assets in the event of a negligence claim. See Dal Pont, *Lawyers' Professional Responsibility* (5th edn), para 5.315.
2. *Legal Profession Uniform Law Application Act* 2014 (Vic), Sch 1, s 45.
3. These are the premiums payable to the *Legal Practitioners' Liability Committee* for the year 2012–13. See www.lplc.com.au/policies_and_premium/premiums.
4. Ibid.
5. See Dal Pont, n 1, para 5.315.
6. See Evans, 'A concise history of the Solicitors Guarantee Fund (Vic): A marriage of principle and pragmatism'. For the Queensland history see Adrian Evans, 'Queensland fidelity compensation 1990–2004: The end of the money tree' (2004) 23(2) *University of Queensland Law Journal* 397–410.
7. Statutory authority for these arrangements is contained in the *Legal Profession Uniform Law Application Act 2014* (Vic), Sch 1, s 139.
8. Interest is collected and accumulated in so-called IOLTA funds (Interest on Lawyer Trust Accounts) and then distributed to legal aid organisations.
9. The decision in *Brown v Inland Revenue Commissioner* [1965] AC 244 forced the introduction of rules prescribing the manner in which interest was to be accounted to clients. See also *Phillips v Washington Legal Foundation*. [The US Supreme Court in *Brown v Legal Foundation of Washington* 538 US 216 (2003) has reaffirmed in a 5–4 decision the right of US IOLTA funds to take interest from trust accounts without 'just compensation', with the proviso that the taking must only occur if there was no possibility of earning net interest.]
10. Adrian Evans, 'Professional ethics north and south: Interest on client trust funds and lawyer fraud – an opportunity to redeem professionalism' (1996) 3 *International Journal of the Legal Profession* 281–300. See also Evans, 'The development and control of the Solicitors Guarantee Fund (Victoria) and its ethical implications for the legal profession'.
11. See, generally, Reid Mortensen, 'Interest on lawyers' trust accounts' (2005) 27 *Sydney Law Review* 289.
12. See Evans, n 10.

INDEX

academic integrity of law students, 24
active and passive deceit, 117–19
  and 'acceptable silence', 119
  applicable law and conduct rules, 119
  consequentialist perspective, 118
  Kantian ethics perspective, 118
  virtue ethics perspective, 118
administration of justice, 151, 166, 206
admission to legal practice, 22–7, 175
  character test, 22–3, 72, 80
  disclosure of criminal history, 23
  disclosure requirements, 25, 26
adversarial advocacy, 66, 92
advocates' immunity, 182–4
  applicable law and conduct rules, 183
  consequentialist perspective, 183
  Kantian ethics perspective, 183
  virtue ethics perspective, 183
agency, 66
Allens Arthur Robinson, 170–1
Aristotle, 4, 86, 98
articles of clerkship, 22
artificial intelligence, 194–5
AUSTRAC, 191
Australian Bar Association, 206
  Barristers' Conduct Rules, 204
Australian Education Network, 11
Australian Qualifications Framework, 3
Australian Solicitors' Conduct Rules, 8, 53,
  100, 116, 151, 204
  adoption of in Australian
    jurisdictions, 53
  composite nature of, 54
  and conflicts of interest, 55, 158, 175
  and ethical principles, 54

exceptions to confidentiality, 140
and role morality, 91
Rule 9, confidentiality, 139–42
Rule 10, successive conflict, 172
Rule 11, concurrent client conflict,
  167–8, 169
rules of discovery as guidance for
  action, 101
autonomy, 93
AWB Ltd, 93–4, 146–8

Baker and McKenzie (law firm), 50
barristers, 32, 90
  ethical opportunities and challenges, 44
  obligations of, 90
Bathurst, Chief Justice Tom, 47
Beaton Research and Consulting, 87
benevolence, 202
Big Pharma, 170–1
bribery, 35, 146–8, 189
  see also corruption
British American Tobacco Australia
  Services, 34–5

Canadian Bar Association Code of
  Professional Conduct, 203
Canadian legal profession, 72
Carrick, Damien, 187–8
character, 11–13, 85–113
  and reputation, 86
  strengthening of, 86
  and virtues, 97
charges for services, 161, 163–4
  applicable law and conduct rules,
    164

224

Index **225**

approaches to, 161, 189
consequentialist perspective, 163
Kantian ethics perspective, 164
six-minute billing, 5, 41, 189
virtue ethics perspective, 163
civil litigation, ethical opportunities and
challenges, 40–2
Clayton Utz (law firm), 34, 136, 173
client–client conflicts of interest,
instability of, 170–1
client privilege, 9, 63, 138–43, 148
and confidentiality, 139
and corruption, 146–8
restrictions disallowing, 143
uses to which it is put, 143
clients' funds, stealing, 52
clinical legal education, 12, 15
Best Practices for CLE, 12
cloud storage of documents, 137–8
Clyne v NSW Bar Association, 124
Cocking, Dean, 102
collaborative law
and conflicts of interest, 158
ethical opportunities and challenges, 39
commercial fraud, 190–1
commercial law, 16
and conflicts of interest, 157, 164
ethical opportunities and challenges,
40–2, 100
commercialism
and competence, 179–81
sustainable, 179
Commissioner of Stamp Duties v Byrnes, 129
community law, ethical opportunities and
challenges, 43
compassion, 202
competence, 9
and artificial intelligence, 194–5
and billing and bribery, 188–92
commercial, 180
components of, 178
and continuing professional
development, 192–4
in contract and tort law, 181–4
financial, 10, 179, 184–8
and goodness, 3–5

maintaining, 192–7
and morality, 10, 178–9, 193, 197
morality of, 178–99
obligation of, 179, 181
risk management, 196–7
specialist accreditation, 195–6
competition among lawyers, 2, 208
concurrent conflicts of interest
applicable law and conduct rules, 171
and ASCR 11, 167–8
'commercial' and prohibited conflicts,
165
consequentialist perspective, 171
court intervention in, 166
informed consent, 168
Kantian ethics perspective, 171
virtue ethics perspective, 170
confidentiality, 9, 63, 134, 138–43, 166
and ASCR 9, 139–42
and client privilege, 139
and decisions about care for disabled
clients, 140
and trust, 151
conflicts of interest, 2, 9, 155–77
and the ASCR, 55
client–client, 162–71
'commercial' and prohibited
conflicts, 165
concurrent conflicted, 162–71
definition, 155–60
and general morality, 175
information barriers, 167, 169
judgment on the meanings of terms,
168, 173
lawyer–client conflicts, 160–4
preventative purpose of the rule, 159
and role morality, 156
successive conflicts, 169–74
consequentialism, 7, 70, 71–2, 95, 192, 207
as guidance for action, 101
contempt of court, 130
continuing professional development, 10,
192–4, 207
length and content of, 193, 194
outcomes from, 194
quality and effectiveness of programs, 194

226 Index

contract law, 181–4
Corbin, Lillian, 35
corporate in-house counsel, 204
  and confidentiality, 141
  ethical opportunities and challenges, 42
corporate/transactional law
  and confidentiality, 141
  and conflicts of interest, 157, 164
  culture of firms, 106
  and ethical dispute resolution, 50
  ethical opportunities and challenges,
    40–2
  and general morality, 93
  and role morality, 92, 93, 94
corruption, 146–8
  applicable law and conduct rules, 147
  consequentialist perspective, 147
  Kantian ethics perspective, 147
  and money laundering, 190–1
  virtue ethics perspective, 147
  see also bribery
Council of Australian Law Deans, 12
courage, 88
creative tax law, 33–4
crime, and law, 69
criminal law
  conduct rules on silence, 117
  and conflicts of interest, 157, 164
  ethical opportunities and
    challenges, 38
  lawyers who know too much, 125–7
  murder, 144–6
  and role morality, 8, 92, 125
criminal law and knowledge, 125–7
  applicable law and conduct rules, 127
  consequentialist perspective, 127
  Kantian ethics perspective, 127
  virtue ethics perspective, 126
Cummins, Philip, 159

Daicoff, Susan, 87
Dale, Christopher, 173–4
Daugerdas, Paul, 33–4
deontological ethics, 70
depression, 17, 20, 89
detachment, 92

discovery, 100
  use of AI in, 194
  procedural rules of, 148
dispute resolution, ethical, 50, 122
documents
  back-dated, 105
  changing nature of record-keeping, 136
  cloud storage of, 137–8
  destruction of, 93, 120–2
  as evidence, 120
  hiding or disposing of, 120–2
  production of, 34–5, 120–2
  retention of corporate documents, 122
*D'Orta-Ekenaike v Victoria Legal Aid
  et al.*, 182
due diligence, 191, 192
duties of lawyers, 115
duty not to abuse process, 122–5
  applicable law and conduct rules, 124
  consequentialist perspective, 124
  difficulties in identifying abuse, 123
  Kantian ethics perspective, 124
  virtue ethics perspective, 124

Eames, Justice Geoffrey, 34
emotion, 18–21
Enron Corporation, 48, 94, 137
entitlements, clients', 67–7
ethical awareness, 104, 106
ethical decision making, 69, 73, 87
  role of emotions in, 19
ethical opportunities and challenges, 37
ethics, 6, 62–84
  consequentialist, 7, 70, 71–2, 95, 192, 207
  guidance from different frameworks,
    101
  Kantian, 7, 70, 92, 95
  and law, 68
  virtue ethics, 4, 7, 72, 96, 208, 209
  see also general morality, morality, role
    morality
ethics assessment scale, 10, 213–17
ethics of duty, 95, 209
  deontic character of, 74–5
  duty as absolute, 77
  duty based on general principles, 77

Index **227**

duty justified by reason, 78
emphasis on what action to take, 74–6
goodness as rightness, 76
impartiality of duty, 78–9
importance of rules, 78
moral theory of, 73
practical necessity as obligation and
obedience, 77
universality of, 79
and virtue ethics, 74–9
expertise, and goodness, 3–5

family law
and conflicts of interest, 157,
158, 164
ethical opportunities and
challenges, 38–9
and role morality, 91, 92
Farrow, Trevor, 67, 203
fidelity compensation, 220–2
fiduciary responsibility, 156, 160, 166, 181
Financial Action Task Force, 191
financial competency, 9, 179, 184–8
consequences of dishonesty, 185,
187–8
'fit and proper person' test, 22–3, 72, 80

Garrow, Robert, 144–6
general morality, 7, 70, 86–7, 150, 151,
200, 202
and conflicts of interest, 175
and legal ethics, 85, 208
as social capital, 208
strengthening of, 203–7
general practice law, ethical opportunities
and challenges, 39
Giannareli v Wraith, 182
global financial crisis, 48, 94
global warming, 50
goodness, 72, 207
choosing to be a good lawyer, 32–61
definition, 3
and expertise, 3–5
practice of, 62
teaching of, 5
and virtue, 100

Google, 135–6, 194
government lawyers, ethical opportunities
and challenges, 42

hiding embarrassing documents, 120–2
applicable law and conduct rules, 122
consequentialist perspective, 121
Kantian ethics perspective, 122
virtue ethics perspective, 121
hiding the true purpose of a legal action,
122–5
Hippocratic oath, 63
honesty, 118
Hood, Brian, 35
humanity, 200

independence, 48, 161
informed consent, 168
integrity, 24, 206
International Bar Association, 201
definition of commercialism, 180
resolution on professionalism and
commercialism, 180

James Hardie Industries Limited, 93,
117, 136
Jenkins and Gilchrist (law firm),
33–4, 128
judgment, 6, 178, 192
guidance on, 54
Juris Doctor degree, 3, 16, 20
justice, 66, 67, 69–73, 88, 98, 118, 161, 202
dedication to, 13, 201
the objective of the legal system, 96
promotion of through ethical dispute
resolution, 50

Kantian ethics, 7, 70, 92, 95
categorical imperative, 71
duty-based nature of, 71
as guidance for action, 101
Keddies Lawyers, 163–4
Kessler, Judge Gladys, 94–5, 120
Kierkegaard, Soren, 86
Kirby, Judge Michael, 12
Kronman, Anthony, 36

228 Index

Lake Pleasant bodies case, 144–6
Larcombe, Wendy, 20
Large Law Firm Group, 55, 158, 208
large law firms, 8
  autonomy in, 93
  conflict clearing centres, 105, 169
  and conflicts of interest, 9, 55, 156, 157,
    172, 173
  culture of, 106
  domination of industry sectors, 55
  employment in, 17
  ethical audits of, 106
  ethics of, 105
  information barriers, 173
  and loyalty, 159
  misconduct, 106
  and morality, 104–6
  regulation of, 36
  reputation, 55
Latilla v Inland Revenue Commissioner, 129
law
  and authority, 66, 200–2
  and character, 85
  and crime, 69
  and ethics, 68
  mystique and power of, 18
  positivist and normative
    understandings of, 15
  reasons for studying, 1–2
Law Council of Australia, 53, 203, 206
  Large Law Firm Group, 55, 158, 208
law firms
  actual practice and ethical policies, 46
  approaches to charges for services,
    161, 189
  approaches to questioning, 45
  choice of, 32–61
  culture of, 33–5, 87, 204
  ethical culture of, 45, 47, 51
  life–work balance, 42, 46, 208, 210
  looking after clients, 46
  policy on handling ethical issues, 46
  pro bono work, 46
  questions to ask of, 45–7
  reputation, 46
  time sheets, 47

  working environment, 47–51, 209–11
Law Institute of Victoria, 196
law schools, 1
  choice of, 1, 5
  culture of, 19
  identification of good schools, 11–14
  questions to ask of, 14–15
  reactions to questioning, 15
lawyer–client conflicts, 160–4
  over costs, 161
  types of, 160
lawyers
  approaches to charges for services, 161,
    189
  character and, 85–113
  choice of clients, 48
  communication about costs, 162
  contribution to social functioning,
    11–13
  cost of, 91
  cultural leadership, 88
  and depression, 17
  disciplinary prosecutions, 36, 65
  duties of, 62–4, 115
  examination of their own virtue, 96
  examples of poor lawyering, 33–5
  expectations of success, 17
  good lawyers, 32–61
  humanity of, 200
  integration of personal and
    professional selves, 99
  integration of rational and emotional
    lives, 99, 125, 190
  integrity of, 94, 206
  leaving the profession, 45, 209
  licensing of, 204
  mental health of, 52
  moral activists, 103
  number and distribution of, 2
  obeying and applying the law, 62
  popular perceptions of, 8, 89
  pro bono work, 201
  relationship of care, 103
  responsible lawyers, 103
  role of, 32
  safety nets for, 218–23

self-care, 209
substance abuse, 52, 53
typology of, 7, 102, 209
virtues of, 98
women, 210
zealous advocates, 103, 114
leadership, cultural, 88
leaving the scene of an accident, 149–50
    applicable law and conduct rules, 150
    consequentialist perspective, 149
    Kantian ethics perspective, 149–50
    virtue ethics perspective, 149
legal aid, funding for, 221
    applicable law and conduct rules, 222
    consequentialist perspective, 222
    Kantian ethics perspective, 222
    virtue ethics perspective, 222
legal communities, 32–3
legal education, 1–31, 207
    admission to legal practice, 22–7
    attributes of, 11–14
    balance of socio-legal and commercial
        emphases, 15, 16
    commercialism and competence,
        179–81
    elective subjects, 5, 15–16
    emotional intelligence, 12, 15
    emotional resilience and wellbeing, 20
    ethical sensitivity, 12
    experiential learning, 19
    identification of good schools, 11–14
    and interest in law, 12
    keeping up to date, 188, 192, 194
    legal ethics, 13, 15
    orientation of, 13
    positivist and normative
        understandings of law, 15
    practical legal training, 21–2, 207
    pre-admission stage, 21
    pro bono work, 15
    process of, 16–17
    research capacity, 13
    and student health, 18–21
    subjects covered, 1
    theoretical knowledge, 11
    Threshold Learning Outcomes, 21

traineeships, 22
types of degrees, 3
legal ethics
    and general morality, 85
    self-assessment of preferences, 213–17
    virtue and character as foundation,
        95–7
legal practice
    admission to, 22–7
    character and attitudes in, 102–4
    choosing a law firm, 32–61
    discipline structures, 203–7
    economic and structural challenges, 6
    ethical challenges of, 2, 68–9
    identification of good environments, 33
    moral realities of, 5
    moral sensitivity, 69
    and role morality, 89–91, 102–4
    sole practitioners, 157
    technological and cultural challenges,
        10, 201
    and virtue ethics, 80
    women in, 210
    and zealous advocacy, 114
legal process outsourcing, 6
legal process, subjectivity of, 99
legal rules, 6
Legal Services Commissioner, 130, 208
Legal Services Commissioner v Mullins, 117
*Legal Services Commissioner v Stirling
    (Legal Practice)*, 118
Legal Services Council, 208
life–work balance, 42, 46, 208, 210
Lincoln, Abraham, 6, 68
LLB degree, 3, 16, 20
Logan, Alton, 63–4, 66, 144
loyalty, 155–77
    definition, 156
    indivisibility of, 157, 172
Luban, David, 3–4, 7, 54, 67, 94, 200

Machiavelli, Nicolo, 102
Magarey Farlam, 187–8, 220
Markovits, Daniel, 102, 106
Mayne (drug manufacturer), 170–1
McCabe, Rolah, 34–5, 120–2

230 Index

McCabe v British American Tobacco
   Australia Services, 120–2, 136, 143
  successive conflict connected to,
   173, 174
McGee case, 149–50, 151, 204
mediators, 39, 123
Meek v Fleming, 117
mega-corporate 'enablers', 40–2
mental health, management of, 17–18,
  52, 105
misconduct, 52–3, 65, 130
money laundering, 190
  indicators of, 191
Moorhead, Richard, 72
moral activists, 103, 115
moral regeneration, 37
moral sensitivity, 69
morality
  and behaviour, 64–5
  centrality to lawyering, 67
  and competence, 178–9, 197
  evolution of, 201
  general morality, 7, 70, 85, 86–7
  and individuality, 65
  and lawyering, 65–8
  and neurology, 64–5
  role morality, 7, 66, 89–91
murder, 144–6
Myers, Alan QC, 174

negligence, 179, 196
neuroscience, 64
NGO lawyers, ethical opportunities and
  challenges, 43–4
Note Printing Australia, 35

Oakley, Justin, 73, 90, 102
oral evidence, 120

Parker, Christine, 7, 209
parliamentary counsel, ethical
  opportunities and challenges, 42
personality, 87
  see also character
Petersen, Christopher, 88
Poole, Melanie, 18–19

positive psychology, 8, 87–9, 97, 209
positivism, 66
practical legal training, 21–2, 207
  commercial providers, 21
  inside a law firm, 21
practical wisdom, 10, 200–12
practising certificates, renewal of, 193
privacy, 99, 151
  and client privilege, 142
  and cloud storage, 137–8
  computer passwords and, 136–7
  unravelling of, 135–6, 141
pro bono work, 15, 46, 201, 207
professional competence, 9
  see also competence
professional development, 10
  see also continuing professional
   development
professional indemnity, 196, 218
professional life and private life, 24
  see also life–work balance
professional secrecy, 134–54
  corruption, 146–8
  leaving the scene of an accident, 148–50
  murder, 144–6
  see also secrecy
professional standards schemes, 219–20
professionalism, 13, 72, 99, 141
  character, context and capacity, 73
  commercialised culture, 35
  and commercialism, 48, 179, 184
prosecutors, ethical opportunities and
  challenges, 42

Rakoff, Judge Jed, 48, 69, 94
rationality, 18–21
Re OG case, 24
regulation, 10, 52–3, 202, 205
  coercive investigation, 36, 37
  and ethical infrastructure, 204
  failures of, 36–7
  need for a formal complaint, 36
  parties involved in, 207
  practical wisdom in, 207–9
  regulatory tribunals, 130
  uniform model for, 205

Index **231**

relationship of care, 103, 115, 151
reputation, 32, 46
  and character, 86
  ethical, 105
  and virtues, 102
Reserve Bank of Australia, 35, 48
resilience, 18, 88
  moral, 209–11
  organisational, 210
responsibility, professional, 37
responsible lawyers, 103, 115, 151
Richardson's case, 24
risk management, 196–7
  mechanisms of, 196
role morality, 7, 8, 66, 89–91, 118, 201
  and conflicts of interest, 156
  criticisms of, 90, 91–5
  and detachment, 91
  function of, 92
  and legal practice, 102–4
  limits of, 151
  psychological toll of, 91
rule of law, 13, 15, 37, 202
  'thin' concept of, 95

Scruton, Roger, 64–5
secrecy, 2, 9, 134–8, 146–8
  leaving the scene of an accident, 148–50
  and murder, 144–6
secrecy about murder, 144–6
  applicable law and conduct rules, 145
  consequentialist perspective, 145
  Kantian ethics perspective, 145
  virtue ethics perspective, 145
Securency, 35
self-respect, 80, 141
Seligman, Martin, 88
Snow, Chris, 187–8
solicitors, ethical opportunities and
    challenges, 42
specialist accreditation, 195–6
  programs available, 196
Steel, Judge David, 190
stress, 17, 50
  see also mental health, depression
striking off, 130, 187

studying law, reasons for, 1–2
supervised workplace training, 21
Survive Law website, 46

tax avoidance, 94, 128–9
  applicable law and conduct
    rules, 129
  consequentialist perspective, 129
  Kantian ethics perspective, 129
  and tax evasion, 128
  virtue ethics perspective, 129
tax evasion, and tax avoidance, 128
taxation law, 33–4, 128
teleological ethics, 70
Tertiary Education Quality Standards
    Agency, 11
Threshold Learning Outcomes, 21
Tomain, Joseph, 4, 96
tort law, 181–4
  duty of care, 181
traineeships, 22
transactional law, 164
  and confidentiality, 141
  and conflicts of interest, 157
  and general morality, 93
  and role morality, 92, 94
transparency, 161
tribunals, and role morality, 92
trust, 142, 195
  and confidentiality, 151
trust accounts, 52, 184
  consequences of dishonesty, 188
  misappropriation of funds in, 187
  and money laundering, 190
  regulations on, 185, 186
truth and deception, 2, 8, 114–33
  active and passive deceit, 119–19
  case studies, 116
  consequences of being caught, 130
  criminal lawyers who know too much,
    125–7
  duty not to abuse process, 122–5
  hiding embarrassing documents,
    120–2
  hiding the true purpose of a legal
    action, 122–5

232 Index

truth and deception (cont.)
  tax avoidance, 128–9
  tools for analysis of, 114–16
Tuckiar v The King, 126–7

Uniform Conduct Rules, 53–6
Uniform Law, 185, 203, 204
Uniform Law Legal Services Council
  function of the Commissioner, 206
  independence of the Commissioner,
    207
  membership of, 205
unjust enrichment, 189
unsatisfactory conduct, 52
utilitarianism, 71–2

values, 6, 62–84
Van Hooft, Stan, 73, 97
virtue ethics, 4, 7, 70, 72, 96, 208, 209
  aretaic character of, 74–5
  caring perspective, 78
  criticisms of, 98–101
  culture-relativity of, 79
  emphasis on character, 74–6, 100
  and ethics of duty, 74–9
  extension beyond legal duties, 79–4
  goodness as excellence, 76
  as guidance for action, 99, 101
  and legal practice, 80
  need for judgment, 77
  and paternalism, 99

practical necessity as expression of
  character and response to values,
  77
responsiveness to circumstances, 77
virtue influenced by emotions, 78
virtue is partial, 78–9
virtues, 6, 62–84, 88
  benevolence, 202
  and character, 97
  compassion, 202
  courage, 88
  honesty, 118
  identification of, 97–8
  instruments for evaluation of, 89
  justice, 88, 118, 161, 202
  self-respect, 80, 141
  transparency, 161
  wisdom, 88, 161, 181, 192

Wendel, Brad, 66, 67
Westraders case, 129
White Industries v Flower and Hart,
  123–5, 136
Why Good Lawyers Matter, 72
wisdom, 88, 161, 181, 192
  practical wisdom, 10, 200–12
women lawyers, 210

zealous advocacy, 7, 66, 80, 89–91, 103,
  114
  limits of, 114

For EU product safety concerns, contact us at Calle de José Abascal, 56–1°, 28003 Madrid, Spain or eugpsr@cambridge.org.

www.ingramcontent.com/pod-product-compliance
Ingram Content Group UK Ltd.
Pitfield, Milton Keynes, MK11 3LW, UK
UKHW020153060825
461487UK00017B/1379